THE PEASANT
OF THE GARONNE

JACQUES
MARITAIN

TRANSLATED BY MICHAEL CUDDIHY

AND ELIZABETH HUGHES

Never take foolishness too seriously
—Chinese Proverb

THE PEASANT
OF THE GARONNE

*An Old Layman Questions Himself
about the Present Time*

Holt, Rinehart and Winston

New York   Chicago   San Francisco

ACKNOWLEDGEMENTS

Grateful acknowledgment is made to the following publishers who have so generously granted permission to reprint from their publications:

P. J. Kenedy & Sons, New York, for passages from *Liturgy and Contemplation*, by Jacques and Raïssa Maritain, copyright © 1960 by P. J. Kenedy & Sons.

Charles Scribner's Sons, New York, for passages from *On the Philosophy of History*, by Jacques Maritain (1957), and for passages from *The Range of Reason*, by Jacques Maritain (1952).

English translation copyright © 1968 by Holt, Rinehart and Winston, Inc.

Published in French under the title *Le Paysan de la Garonne: Un vieux laïc s'interroge à propos du temps présent*, copyright © 1966 by Desclée De Brouwer.

Published simultaneously in Canada by Holt, Rinehart and Winston of Canada, Limited.

Library of Congress Catalog Card Number: 68–10182

First Edition

Designer: Ernst Reichl
8657454
Printed in the United States of America

CONTENTS

Preface, p. ix

1 A. D. 1966, p. 1

Thanksgiving, p. 1
Three contradictory descriptions, p. 4

2 Our Cockeyed Times, p. 12

Itching Ears, p. 12
Epistemological time-worship, p. 12
Logophobia, p. 14
Contemporary Trends, Especially the Trends of
"Left" and "Right," p. 21
At the time of the "Letter on Independence," p. 21
Today, p. 24

3 The World and Its Contrasting Aspects, p. 28

The Religious or "Mystical" Truth Concerning the World In Its
Relation With the Kingdom of God, p. 28
God so loved the world, p. 29
The world hates me, p. 32
Some conclusions, p. 35
The "Ontosophic" Truth, p. 38
Concerning the world in its natural structures, p. 38
The natural end of the world, p. 40
On the temporal mission of the Christian, p. 41
A Long Misunderstanding With Bitter Fruit, p. 44
Speculative vocabulary and practical vocabulary, p. 44
The "contempt of the world" and its perilous vicissitudes, p. 46
Schema XIII, p. 50
The Teaching Church Has Put An End to the Long
Misunderstanding, p. 50

v

Kneeling Before the World, p. 53
Factual behavior and thought more or less confused, p. 53
The Saints and the world, p. 58
The insane mistake, p. 60

4   The True New Fire—Christians and Non-Christians, p. 64

The announcement of a new age, p. 64
Practical cooperation in a divided world, p. 65
Brotherly love among men who are all (at least potentially)
    members of Christ, p. 70
Two short anecdotes, p. 78
The law of the cross, p. 79

5   The True New Fire—The Liberation of the
    Intelligence, p. 84

Preliminary notice, p. 84
The Truth, p. 87
A few words on the capacity of human reason, p. 94
Philosophy and ideosophy, p. 98
The liberation of philosophic eros, p. 104
Contemporary phenomenology, p. 107
The need for fables or intellectual false currency, p. 112
Teilhard de Chardin and Teilhardism, p. 116

6   The True New Fire—The Requests and Renewals
    of Genuine Knowledge, p. 127

A great wise man, p. 127
The intuition of Being and the contemplation of Being itself
    subsisting by itself, p. 132
The philosophy of St. Thomas, p. 135
Philosophy and theology, p. 141
Truth and freedom, p. 166
Vitaï lampada tradunt, p. 170

7   The True New Fire—The Affairs of God's Kingdom, p. 174

The One and Holy, p. 174
The personality of the Church, p. 175
The Church, Bride and mystical Body, p. 176

The Church, kingdom of God begun here on earth, p. 183
The Church, Holy and Penitent, p. 185
The Church, People of God, p. 189
Contemplation in the World, p. 194
By way of introduction, p. 194
A digression (on the temporal mission of the Christian), p. 198
Another digression (on the condition of the layman) and
    the end of the introduction, p. 205
The two necessary aids on the never-ending road, p. 213
Liturgy, p. 214
Contemplation, p. 220
The diversity of the Gifts of the Holy Spirit, p. 229
Contemplation on the roads, p. 232
The Disciples—James and John, p. 254
The True Face of God, or Love and the Law
(text by Raissa), p. 257

Appendices, p. 261

1   On a text of Saint Paul, p. 261
2   On two studies concerning the theology of
    Pere Teilhard, p. 264
3   A short epistemological digression, p. 270
4   On the unity and visibility of the Church, p. 274

PREFACE

The subtitle of this book needs no explanation. I will merely note that in the expression "an old layman" the word "old" has a twofold meaning: it says that the author is an octogenarian, and that he is an inveterate layman.

As for the title, it is explained by the fact that there is no Danube in France, and that the Little Brothers of Jesus, with whom I stay, live at Toulouse on the Garonne River. Consequently, given my purpose, I considered the Garonne a suitable equivalent for the Danube. A peasant of the Danube—or of the Garonne—is, as anyone who has read La Fontaine knows, a man who puts his foot in his mouth, or who calls a spade a spade. This is what, in all modesty, and not without fearing to be unequal to the task (less easy, to be sure, than one might believe), I would like to attempt.

December 31, 1965   Jacques Maritain

1 A. D. 1966

I turn first to the holy visible Church (she is, I realize, invisible as well), the Roman Catholic Church, which on December 8, 1965, brought to a close her second Vatican Council. Where does this holy Church find herself visibly manifested in her universality? In the ecumenical assembly which is the Council, and in the individual person who is the Pope, the first taking its existence and full authority from the second; both assisted by the spirit of God, clothed in the whiteness of truth, and crowned with charisms that bring on this poor earth some reflections of Eternal Light. And in beholding the Church, I kneel (that's a vanishing custom, but so much the worse) in profound thanksgiving.

For everything the Council has decreed and accomplished, I give thanks. For still other things I would doubtless have liked to give thanks if the Council had also done them. But it was obviously not called to do those things: from the beginning, and by the will of John XXIII himself, it was pastoral rather than doctrinal (although it devoted two of its Constitutions to important points of doctrine). And it is clear that this was in response to a providential design; for the historic task, the immense renewal that it had to bring about, had to do with progress in evangelical awareness and attitudes of the heart rather than with defining dogmas.

Good heavens, weren't these dogmas defined, once and for all? (For the new dogmatic definitions that come with time simply make explicit and complete the old ones; they don't change them in any way.) Wasn't the Church's doctrine established with certitude, and on bases solid enough to permit endless progress, by all the preceding Councils and by a centuries-old labor? What man, having received theological faith, could be foolish enough to imagine that eternal

1

certitudes would begin to waver, to grow hollow with doubts and question marks, to dissolve themselves in the stream of time?

No one, however, has to look very far to marvel at the resources of human foolishness, and to understand that foolishness and theological faith can certainly keep house in the same brain, and hold a dialogue there—as everybody is doing now with everybody else—even though such contact is likely to prove unhealthy for the latter.

I will have to come back to this, although it scarcely amuses me, in order to say something about the neo-modernism that flourishes today.

For the moment, I would like to continue my thanksgiving in peace.

☆

It is a joy to think that the true idea of freedom—of that freedom to which man aspires in his profoundest self, and which is one of the privileges of the spirit—is henceforth recognized and given a place of honor among the great germinal ideas of Christian wisdom; and likewise the true idea of the human person, and of his dignity and his rights.

It is a joy to think that religious freedom has now been proclaimed, —this is not any freedom to believe or not to believe according to my momentary disposition, and to fashion an idol at my pleasure, as if I did not have a fundamental obligation to Truth; it is the freedom that each human person has, in the face of the State or any temporal power whatever, to watch over his eternal destiny while seeking truth with all his soul and complying with it as he knows it, and to obey what his conscience holds as true in matters of religion (my conscience is not infallible but I never have the right to act against it). And at the same time it was proclaiming religious freedom, the Council placed in a new light, which our time particularly needs, the sacred treasures of Catholic doctrine concerning the Church and Revelation.

It is a joy to think that the Church, with increasing vigor and a new accent, enjoins us to treat really as brothers—as brothers whose friendship is for us an invaluable gift, and for whom our zeal to save their souls does not require that we convert them into ashes if they are heretics, but in each of whom we should honor the human race, and see Christ's gaze on them and on ourselves—yes, treat as brothers all those whom we know more or less distant from the Truth, whether they are Christians who do not accept the Catholic Creed, or the faithful of a non-Christian religion, or atheists. The Council especially noted that such fraternal sentiments are due the Jewish people; anti-Semitism is an anti-Christian aberration.

It is a joy to think that the Church recognizes and declares more explicitly than ever the value, beauty, and dignity of this world which, nevertheless, she sees "in the power of the evil one" (1 John 5:19), insofar as it refuses to be redeemed—this world with all those goods of nature which bear the mark of their Creator's generosity, and of which many, however, are at one time or another torn from us by the holy Cross, in view of other goods that invisibly bring heaven to earth.

It is a joy to think that the Church, which as such is occupied solely with the spiritual domain, or with things *quae sunt Dei*, affirms and blesses the temporal mission of the Christian.

It is a joy to think that the Church has now emphatically highlighted the status of her lay members. Of course, it has always been known that laymen belonged to the mystical Body of Christ, but they have long been believed tied to the follies of the age, and to a state, if I may say so, normally recognized as Christian *imperfection*. It is now clear to all that insofar as they are members of the mystical Body, they too are called to the perfection of charity and the wisdom of the Holy Spirit, and to the labors through which the kingdom of God is expanded. Besides, as members of the earthly city, who work directly on their own responsibility and initiative for the well-being and progress of the temporal order, it is normally up to them to instill into such a work what can be transmitted of the spirit of the Gospel, and of the intelligence and wisdom that reason and faith together sustain.

It is a joy to think that the Pope "neither wants to nor ought to exercise henceforth any power other than that of his spiritual keys," [1] and that at the summit of the Church's towers he watches, in union with the efforts of bishops of the entire world, to maintain intact the immense treasure of truth with which Christ's Church is entrusted, while fully carrying out in its integrity the immeasurably significant renewal launched by the Council.

☆

[1] Paul VI, *Discourse to the Roman Nobility*, January 14, 1964.

In truth, every vestige of the Holy Empire is today liquidated; we have definitely emerged from the sacral age and the baroque age. After sixteen centuries [2] which it would be shameful to slander or claim to repudiate, but which have completed their death agony and whose grave defects were incontestable, a new age begins; the Church invites us to understand better *the goodness and the humanity* [3] of God our Father, and calls us to recognize at the same time all the dimensions of that *hominem integrum* whom the Pope spoke of in his discourse of December 7, 1965, at the last meeting of the Council.

Here is accomplished the great reversal of virtue of which it is no longer the human which takes charge of defending the divine, but the divine which offers itself to defend the human (if the latter does not refuse the aid offered).

The Church has broken the ties which pretended to protect her, and has rid herself of burdens which people used to think equipped her better for the work of salvation. Free henceforth from these burdens and these ties, she mirrors better the true face of God, which is Love, and for herself asks only liberty. [4] She spreads her wings of light.

Will they shelter our cities and our fields if the world, for its part, decides to leave her truly free? Or will they serve her to flee to the desert, if the world sets itself against her in order to enslave her and bind her in chains? These things are not predetermined in human history, they depend on our unforeseeable choices.

THREE CONTRADICTORY DESCRIPTIONS

One of the fundamental axioms of a sane philosophy of history, I have often noted, is that the history of the world progresses *at the same time* in the line of evil and in the line of good. In certain periods —our own, for example—one sees the effects of this simultaneous double progress erupting in a kind of explosion. This does not make it easy to describe these moments in man's history. It then becomes necessary to propose several contradictory descriptions, all of which will be true. Moreover, the three descriptions I would like to propose

[2] My reckoning begins with the century of Constantine (the Edict of Milan, 313). It is a simplification which I believe permissible.

[3] *Benignitas et humanitas* (φιλανθρωπία) *Salvatoris nostri Dei* (*Tit.* 3:4).

[4] Paul VI, *Message to the Heads of Government*, December 8, 1965.

touch only on certain aspects of our time, those of spiritual order. Let us turn no longer to the holy Church visibly manifested in her universality, let us turn to the Western world (I speak of it because I know it a little less badly than I do the others), and let us think of the workings which are taking place in its depths. It appears to be a great age. The rationalist and positivist visions of the universe seem completely out-of-date, people are sick of them (let us forget for a moment that there are worse visions). An immense spiritual ferment, immense religious aspirations are at work. Souls are hungry for authenticity, frankness, devotion to a common task; they discover with a kind of intoxication the mystery of the human being, the possibilities and the demands of fraternal love. It is like a nostalgia for the Gospel and for Jesus.

And there, where a nearer and more urgent call is heard—be it in relatively limited sectors, though more populous than one thinks, be it sometimes in very tiny flocks, but whose initiatives count more than anything (poor contemporaries of the atomic bomb, what is facing us is the power of micro-actions) [5]—we find a burning and purified faith, a passion for the absolute, a fervent presentiment of the liberty, the breadth and variety of the ways of God, a whole-hearted longing for the perfection of charity, all of which are seeking and finding for us new means of giving our lives to bear witness to the love of Jesus for all men and to the generosity of God's spirit.

☆

So much for the first description. The second says completely the opposite. When one considers the neo-modernist [6] fever (I was bound to mention this sooner or later), very contagious, at least in circles described as "intellectual," compared to which the modernism of Piux X's time was only a modest hayfever, and which finds expression above all in the most advanced thinkers among our Protestant

[5] The saints have always known this—they had read the Gospel.
[6] The word modernism has aged, but nevertheless I do not know a better; and to have aged makes it especially good: for nothing ages so quickly as fashion, and those theories which make truth or its conceptual formulations a function of time. The "perspectivism" pretends not to be modernist because it holds that a similar unalterable truth can be expressed by conceptual formulas incompatible with each other which come successively to the surface in the course of time. Let us leave it to its illusions.

brothers,[7] but is also active in equally advanced Catholic thinkers, this second description gives us the picture [8] of a kind of "immanent" apostasy (that is, which intends to remain Christian at all costs). In preparation for many years, hastened by certain veiled hopes of the repressed regions of the soul which were stirred up here and there on the occasion of the Council, the manifold manifestation of this apostasy is sometimes falsely ascribed to the "spirit of the Council," or even to the "spirit of John XXIII." We know well to whom it is proper to trace the paternity of such lies (and so much the better if in this way man finds himself a little exonerated). But the point is, people no longer believe in the devil and in the bad angels, nor the good ones, naturally. They are only ethereal survivors of some Babylonian imagery.

In such a nice perspective, the objective content to which the faith of our forefathers clung, all *that* is myth, like original sin for example, (isn't our big job today to get rid of the horrendous guilt complex?), and like the Gospel of the Infancy of Christ, the resurrection of the body, and the creation. And the Christ of history, of course. The phenomenological method and form criticism have changed everything. The distinction between human nature and grace is a scholastic invention like transubstantiation. As for hell, why take the trouble to deny it, it is simpler to forget it, and that's probably what we had also better do with the Incarnation and the Trinity. Frankly, do the mass of our Christians ever *think* of these things, or of the immortal soul and the future life? As for the Cross and the Redemption, ultimate sublimation of ancient myths and sacrificial rites, we should consider them as the great and stirring symbols, forever inscribed in our imagination, of the labor and collective sacrifices needed to bring nature and humanity to the degree of unification and spiritualization—and of power over matter—where they will be delivered at last from all the old servitudes and will enter into a kind of glory. Will death then be

---

[7] The divergences and conflicts of ideas are as vast among Protestants as Catholics, and it could be that Taizé, for example, can give the latter some useful lessons.

[8] What I have brought together in this picture are not the views of honest seekers, but of extremists whose names are well known to experts on these matters, along with the opinions which prevail in the milieux influenced by them—for example, among some priests who boast of no longer genuflecting before the tabernacle.

vanquished? Perhaps science will discover how to make us immortal. (Why not? Descartes was already dreaming of it.) However, that is not what matters; what matters is the everlastingness of the cosmos, and the immortality of humanity glorified in it and with it.

Our faith, having been thus duly emptied of every specific object, finally can become what it really was, a simple sublimating aspiration; we can be lifted up to a state of complete euphoria by a powerful intake of air, recite with an enlightened fervor the Symbol (Creed) of the Apostles (symbol, what a predestined name!) and love, serve and adore Jesus with all our hearts, the Jesus of faith and of an *interior,* truly visceral Christianity.

For with all this one is more Christian than ever. All these people have simply ceased to believe in Truth, and believe only in verisimilitudes pinned to *some* truths (that is, statements or verifications of observable detail) which moreover grow obsolete overnight. Truth with a capital T, what does that mean? *Quid est Veritas?* We should recognize that Pilate got the picture, and that this procurator was a good "progressist." One must use lower case letters everywhere. "Everything is relative, that is the only absolute principle"—as our Father Auguste Comte has already put it. We are done with classical positivism, true enough. But the fact remains that we live in Comte's world: Science (the side of reason) completed by Myth (the side of sentiment). He has been a prophet of the first order.

I might add that he was more honest than you, studious expurgators of revealed truths. He at least fabricated the myths of his "subjective synthesis" fairly and squarely out of whole cloth, not, like you, by reinterpreting a whole religious heritage to which you believe yourself more faithful than anyone, nor by trying to deceive the thirst, and the heart, of those whose faith you imagine you share.

☆

This second description gives a more complete idea of our era. With it, however, we are still far from exhausting the subject. We must make a third, which in its turn will reveal other aspects. We know well that we cannot restrict ourselves to the words men utter in the universe of logic, to what they *are* and *do* as evidenced by the conceptual terms they use; we must take into consideration what occupies the depths of their psyche, what they *are* and *do* in the wholly singular domain of the irreducibly subjective and irrational, even that which at times escapes their own awareness.

From this viewpoint, one can immediately observe that among all those who speak like Pilate, there are surely many who have not deliberately refused that desire for Truth without which one is not a man. Among all the men of science whose sole concern seems to be inventing new approaches or hypotheses, there are surely many who in reality, whatever they may say, do not prefer seeking to finding. Would they put so much care and toil into seeking verifications of a passing day if, in the unconscious or supra-conscious regions of their minds, they were not seeking and loving the Truth without realizing it themselves?

But what is most important to notice, on the other hand, is that the frenzied modernism of today is incurably ambivalent. Its natural bent, although it would deny it, is to ruin the Christian faith. Yes, it busies itself as best it can to empty the faith of any content. But along with that, among a good number of its adherents, there is something like an effort to render to this faith a kind of desperate witness. It is certainly with sincerity, and sometimes in the fever and anguish of a fundamentally religious soul, that the leaders of our neo-modernism declare themselves Christians. Let us not forget that they are victims of a certain pre-accepted philosophy, a Grand Sophistry (*we know Being, on condition that it is put in parenthesis and abstracted out of sight*). I will have a word to say about this in another chapter.[9] This permits people to speak intelligently, while playing on our heartstrings, about a whole armload of things which positivism had placed under interdict, and is far more successful than positivism in preventing us from finding the least extramental reality in them, the least *that exists independently of our mind.* There is nothing left for the intellect to do but discourse on verisimilitudes, the cost of which is borne by what takes place in human subjectivity. To affirm the existence of a transcendent God becomes from this moment a non-sense. Divine transcendence is only the mythical projection of a certain collective fear experienced by man at a given moment in his history. In general, according to the pre-accepted philosophy to which I am alluding, everything that tastes of a world other than the world of man

9 Cf. Ch. 5, p. 106.

can only fall under the head of the out-of-date if it is a question of the "background world" of poor philosophic realists, or, of the Myth if it is a question of the supernatural world of religions.

This is the intelligible heaven, the *Denkmittel* accepted as self-evident (that is to say, as demanded by the age), and the taboos to which our most liberal (that is to say the most conformist) theologians and exegetes have submitted their thought. Poor "sophisticated" Christians, it is Socrates they would need.

One has to be quite naive to enlist in the service of such a philosophy if one has the Christian faith (which is nothing without the Word—infinitely independent of human subjectivity—of a revealing God who is infinitely independent of our mind). This is especially so if one belongs to the Catholic religion, which of all religions (along with the religion of Israel—*benedicite, omnia opera Domini, Domino*) is most steadfast in recognizing and affirming the reality—irreducibly, splendidly, generously *in itself*—of the beings whom the Creator has made, and the transcendence of this Other, who is the Truth in person and Being itself subsisting by itself, in whom we live and move and have our being,[10] the living God by whose strength we live,[11] and who loves us and whom we love. For to love is to give what one is, his very being, in the most absolute, the most brazenly metaphysical, the least phenomenalizable sense of this word. But we must put all this in parentheses, too, mustn't we, if we are to follow the new golden rule? And once someone has been taken in hand, and surrounded on all sides by the so-called philosophy in which he has put his trust, what can become of him if he does not side with those who flatly deny Christ? With a soul split between doubt and a nostalgic tenacity—and a pity full of fright for the modern world, in which a total reshaping of religion seems the last bulwark against atheism—it will become necessary to set out in search of heroic remedies to enable faith in Jesus Christ to survive in a mental climate essentially incompatible with it. Why be astonished that so many modernists believe they have a mission to save a dying Christianity—*their* dying Christianity for the modern world? It is for this goal that, as good soldiers of Christ, they devote themselves to such an exhausting work

10 *Acts* 17:28.
11 *Cor.* 13:4.

of hermeneutic evacuation. Even their fideism, contrary as it is to Christian faith, is nevertheless a sincere and tortured witness to this faith.

Clothed in the panoply of God, shod with zeal, armed with the breastplate of justice, the helmet of salvation, the shield of the faith, and the sword of the spirit? This armor of Saint Paul [12] is certainly not for them, it is only a museum piece. I see them, rather, hanging by one hand from Jacob's ladder, kicking wildly all the while, and, with their free hand, tossing one another telescripts of the most recent hypotheses. You can't deny it's daring, but look out for cramps.

The author of *Honest to God* [13] is an Anglican bishop, so totally disheartened by the religious indifference of his contemporaries that in his struggle to help them he accommodates divine things in a way that will become acceptable to them and will at last awaken their appetite. He, too, is a fighter for the faith. If he offers us a dog-tired Christianity which goes along with the stream (his famous "Christianity without religion"), it is because he is a worried and helpless good Samaritan who wants so much to save addicts that he opens a shop where he can give them all free drugs in capsules and packets labeled "to the Divine Lamb." And man is such a bizarre animal—it could happen, after all, that one of these addicts, at the hour of his death, might take comfort in thinking that someone loved him, and remember the name of Jesus.

From quite another point of view, we may note finally that if temporal activity and the necessary transformations called for by the present state of the world seem to fascinate a good many young Christians, both clergy and laymen, to such an extent that this *alone* counts in their eyes, and that they passionately undertake to secularize their Christianity completely—from now on, everything for the earth! —yet their fundamental motive, to which they blindly give complete priority, is actually a burning desire to make the witness of the Gospel enter history. Again the oddness of human nature: it is with a worried

[12] *Eph.* 6:13–17.
[13] It is known that this work was published in France through the efforts of a review, a little Machiavellian in its orthodoxy, with the idea of turning people away from modernism by making them see the final aberration to which it was leading them, from surrender to surrender. To the surprise and chagrin of the publishers, the book revealed itself an extraordinary best-seller, everybody threw themselves on it enthusiastically.

faith, quite insufficiently enlightened, and yet profoundly sincere in Jesus Christ, that they betray the Gospel by dint of serving it—after their fashion.

☆

The three descriptions I have proposed are mutually contradictory yet equally true, because all three, while including, in a certain sense, the mass of our contemporaries, do not aim at the same polarities in men's souls. Frankly, I'm fed up with such descriptions, and I have no intention of making a sociological or clinical portrait of my times. I question myself, not as to the value of our times, but as to the values which have an impact on them. It is not our era that worries me, but the ideas one runs into at every street corner, some of which could certainly stand a good scrubbing. Before starting to discuss ideas and problems, however, I would like to make two more remarks [14] regarding the collective behavior we observe today.

[14] Each will constitute a section of the next chapter.

2 OUR COCKEYED TIMES

Itching Ears

EPISTEMOLOGICAL TIME-WORSHIP

This is the sickness announced by Saint Paul for a time to come (*erit enim tempus* . . .), but from which no time, it seems, has been completely immune. As a matter of fact, our own time seems to have broken all records handsomely.

It should be noted that Saint Paul makes professors play a central role in the spread of the sickness. A time will come, he tells us,[1] when men will be taken in tow by a crowd of *didaskaloi* because their ears will itch. In other words, this sickness—which is very contagious, to judge from appearances—will have its breeding ground among the experts or the professors. And the itching in the ears will become so general that no one will be able to hear the truth any longer, and men will turn to fables—*epi tous muthous*, writes Saint Paul, to myths. But hold on, aren't these the precious myths on which we're gorging ourselves? Of course they are, but they are not the great venerable myths of the youth of mankind. Our craving is for the myths of decay, a sterile and synthetic lot (the work of professors)—in particular the myths of demythizing. (I shall make use of this word, which is now current in French jargon.)

Was it to cure these morbid cravings that Père Ubu (the funny ogre invented by a famous French humorist) threatened to "box our ears"? A sorry remedy, since it is from malnutrition and a serious vitamin deficiency that our illness comes in the first place.

Here, it seems to me, is the moment to call attention briefly to two major symptoms. The first symptom, and the one that concerns me here, is an obsessive fixation on the passing of time, epistemologi-

---

[1] "Erit enim tempus, cum sanam doctrinam non sustinebunt, sed ad sua desideria coacervabunt sibi magistros, prurientes auribus. Et a veritate quidem auditum avertent, ad fabulas autem convertentur." (2 *Tim.* 4:3–4.)

cal time-worship. To be *passé* is to be banished to Sheol. Could an author who is passé have said something true? After all, it's not inconceivable. But anyway, it's irrelevant because, since he is passé, what he said no longer exists.

This chronolatry entails vast human sacrifices—in other terms it carries with it a component of masochism. To think of the admirable abnegation (not modesty, probably, but a wish to be drowned in time) of a contemporary biblical scholar is enough to make one's head spin. He kills himself with work, he gives his life's blood, only to find himself passé in two years. And this will continue all his life. And when he dies, he will be passé for good. His work will merely enable others to pass him by and then be passed by in their turn. But of his own thought, not a trace will remain.

We do not find such masochistic abnegation among philosophers, because fashion, in their case, lasts somewhat longer (twenty years, perhaps, thirty in the most favourable instances). They have time to spin themselves some illusions, they can hope that at least during their own lifetime they will not become passé. What is surprising is the form that epistemological time-worship takes with them. Each takes his turn calling into question, in order to innovate, what his immediate predecessors (incurably passé from that moment) have said, but for nothing in the world would he dream of calling into question the work achieved prior to them by Time—at least in the line of descent leading to him. As to the philosophical lines of descent prior to his own, he doesn't give a hoot for them (they are passé); but as he sees it, the line leading to him is there (at least in the sense that it continues to engender), and that is all he needs; he has no need to know whether at the start it was or was not lacking in truth.[2] The point which the curve has reached just before him is the only base from which he can begin; it is sacred and unquestionable.

In one form or another, it is always the adoration of the ephemeral, whether to be devoured by it, or to accept, with eyes closed, what it

2 Of course, it is always in discovering new horizons that a great philosopher loses his head. In other words, if a shortcoming which will cause everything to deviate occurred at the start of his line of descent, there were, at the same time, potential gains that demanded (in vain) to be actualized in a true perspective. And the wise men who could have integrated them with their treasures were perhaps sleeping on the latter; or possibly they were busy giving courses to distracted students, or disputing one another. But all that is another story. . . .

has engendered (in the line of descent leading to him) up to the time he enters the list himself.

By being concerned for truth, and by grasping it, the spirit transcends time. To make the things of the spirit pass under the law of the ephemeral—which is the law of matter and the purely biological —to act as if the spirit were subject to the lord of the flies, is the first sign, the first major symptom of the sickness denounced by Saint Paul.

LOGOPHOBIA

The other symptom which I would like to point out is the degradation that takes place in the nature of the *rational animal* when he begins to lose confidence not only in philosophic knowledge but in the spontaneous *pre-philosophy* which is for man like a gift of nature included in that indispensable equipment we call common sense, and which is concealed as much as it is expressed by everyday language. Let us beware when we hear denigrated, on the pretext that they are "linguistic categories," those primary notions which men would be quite embarrassed to justify precisely because they are the result of primitive intuitions, born in the preconscious of the spirit, but which are at the roots of human life (when it is truly human). When everyone starts scorning these things, obscurely perceived by the instinct of the spirit, such as good and evil, moral obligation, justice, law, or even extra-mental reality, truth, the distinction between substance and accident, the principle of identity—it means that everyone is beginning to lose his head.

Let them invoke the slogan of linguistic categories as much as they like. It is not language that makes concepts, but concepts that make language. And the language that expresses them always more or less betrays them. There are primitive languages that have no word for the idea of being, but that is a far cry from saying that those who speak them do not have this idea in their mind.

And there are never words for what it would be most important for us to say. Isn't it because of that that we need poets and musicians?

Language fouls and cheapens all the primary notions and intuitions I have just mentioned: if they are theoretical, by the practical use it makes of them in the routines of daily life; if they are of the moral order, by the social use it makes of them in the rites of the tribe, superadding to them extrinsic meanings which have no value for the mind in quest of truth.

The first duty of philosophers would be to scour carefully all these notions in order to uncover the purity of their authentic meaning— a diamond hidden under rubbish—which is dependent on being, not on human usage. But as a rule,[3] philosophers take good care not to wear themselves out with such cleansing; and our children of Descartes prefer to carry on with their easier and more profitable task of destroying reason with their Grand Sophistry, their parenthesizing of reality and their Phenomenalizing of philosophic knowledge itself, for which they would like so much to find a place in the amusement park, the night clubs and the dream factories of the world of technocracy. In the final count, because people read philosophers, the philosophers foster in their minds a corrosive doubt about the value of that pre-philosophy which people are constantly obliged to use, but in which they are believing less and less.

Furthermore, while the idea of authentic philosophic knowledge is disappearing from our cultural universe, and the regime of *truth* to be earnestly beheld is undergoing eclipse, we are confronted with the dazzling advent of modern science with its symbolic language—and of that approach to the real which has in common with magic the trait of handling and mastering, through signs, what remains unknown in itself—and of that mathematization of the observable (especially in physics) which has made possible prodigious successes but (in spite of the genuine intellectual concerns of many scientists) submits the mind to the rule of *verification to be performed*. All of this leads everyone, learned and ignorant (and even the unfortunate philosophers), to believe that science—the science of phenomena—is alone capable of bringing us the certainty of rational knowledge. And all this also causes people to doubt the value of the spontaneous pre-philosophy expressed by the language of common sense.

Result: this pre-philosophy is disintegrating; and in terms of the primordial conditions laid down by his nature in the exercise of his reason, man becomes similar to an animal that has lost its instincts, to a bee that no longer has the instinct to make its honey, to penguins

3 Except for some rare Thomists. . . .

and albatrosses that no longer have the instinct to build their nests.
Nevertheless, as disoriented as we are, we must go on thinking anyway. Quickly then, and whatever it costs, let's have anything whatever to replace the effort we can no longer muster; bring on the
fables! There you have the second major symptom I wanted to point
out, and the form, malignant to be sure, of that ear-itching which particularly afflicts our times.

☆

I know very well that more or less comparable forms of the same
sickness have appeared before, particularly at the time of the Sophists
and Socrates. In that era, it was not faith that this sickness threatened, but reason—not our blasé reason of today, but reason in the
springtime of its great self-discovery, of its great cultural victory in the
history of mankind. Wasn't it required that some hundreds of years
before the Incarnation of the Word, the necessary preparations be
completed in Greece [4] on the side of Reason, as in Israel [5] on the
side of Prophecy?

Here is a useful place to pause for a moment and consider that
astonishing period of human history from the beginning of the sixth
century until the close of the fifth century B.C. One would say that
in the major cultural areas of the world the human spirit was then
going through its crisis of adolescence, and made choices that were to
be decisive for the future.

With the Buddha,[6] the Orient decisively confirmed the choice it
had made long since for the great "bound" wisdoms in which reason,
a captive of sacred traditions, remained united to the nocturnal or twilight world of myths (and of magic). At this price, it entered into
certain secrets hidden in the recesses of the universe and of the human
being, it went deeply into the ways of natural mystique, and attained
a lofty peace of purely human self-possession (at least among those

[4] Heraclitus, 576–480; Socrates, 470–399. He was dead when the fourth century
began; Plato, 427–348; Aristotle, 384–322.

[5] Jeremiah, toward the beginning of the sixth century; the second Isaiah and
the Canticle of Canticles, end of the sixth century; Job, Ecclesiastes, fifth century;
building of the second Temple, 520–515 B.C.

[6] Buddha, 563–483; Lao-tse, toward the beginning of the sixth century; Con-
fucius, 551–479. (If I speak here of "the Orient" in general, it is because of the
fact that Buddhism, born in India, passed over into China.)

who had the good fortune to complete the way of initiation). But these great wisdoms received so many riches from the world of dreams that reason was unwilling to emerge completely from the night. The proper domain of metaphysics, that of religion and its rites, that of the spiritual life (even the realm of "powers," even when one claimed not to seek them) remained undifferentiated; God and the world were mingled with each other because in such kinds of wisdom God was transcendent only on condition that the world was illusory, and by the same token God was no longer transcendent. The human mind lived under the sway of the indefinite.[7] Its relation to extra-mental being remained ambiguous, since the latter was ultimately illusory when it was a case of things, and inseparable from the human Self when it was a case of the divine Self. The possibility of a wisdom which should at the same time be a purely rational knowledge remained totally unrecognized.

At about the same period, Greece, by contrast, opted for a *free* wisdom, in which reason, passing to the "solar"[8] state, decided to risk everything by breaking once and for all with its centuries-old subjection to the twilight world of myths. (These latter would doubtlessly continue to haunt the temples and the mystery cults, but adult thought would no longer believe in them.)

At the beginning, things had almost gone askew, with the intellectual intoxication of the sophists, and their reason dedicated solely to Verisimilitude. But Socrates saved at once reason, the future of culture and the rights of Truth. He died for it, not on the cross, as the Word who became man in Israel did, but by taking hemlock, and repaying his debt to Aesculapius, like a good Athenian pagan.

A supreme Wisdom of reason, a Wisdom which was also *Scientia* or Knowledge, Metaphysics was founded; and Physics, a science of the observable world—which, confusing the philosophy of nature with the science of phenomena, believed itself in respect to phenomena (to its unhappiness as well as ours) in continuity with metaphysics. The distinction between theoretical knowledge and practical knowledge was recognized, like that between metaphysics and religion.

[7] Cf. Louis Gardet, "*L'affrontement des humanismes*," Nova et Vetera, October–December 1954, pp. 242–243.

[8] Cf. our study "*Signe et Symbole*" in *Quatre Essais sur l'esprit dans sa condition charnelle*, Paris, Desclée De Brouwer, 1939; 2nd ed., Paris, Alsatia, 1956, pp. 80–106.

Reason also came to recognize the existence of a God distinct from the world, but whose transcendence was ignored and who was only the First among the gods. The great error of Greek reason (for which the supernatural Wisdom of Israel, with its infinite and infinitely perfect God, providentially compensated) was to confuse Finitude and Perfection, and to pretend to make the spirit live under the rule of the finite.[9]

On the other hand, and here especially Socrates, saved the future of culture, Greek reason was able to become aware of that glory of the mind which is Knowing, and of the authentic relation between the mind and the extra-mental being of things. In an impulse arrested too soon, and for a fleeting, unforgettable moment, it had the sense of being; it was able to see that the human intellect, in identifying itself immaterially, *intentionaliter*, with the being of things, truly reaches that which exists outside our minds, beginning with the world of matter to which, through our senses, we are naturally adapted.

☆

The great adventure into which the choice made by Greece launched the world marked a decisive step forward. From the beginning, doubtlessly, it also entailed losses: in Hellenic and Hellenistic thought itself it was accompanied by grave shortcomings, which the Christian centuries have remedied in the light of the revelation received in Israel. No doubt Western culture, which has its point of departure in this adventure, has experienced in the last four centuries more and more grave crises in the intellectual order—with Descartes, Kant, Hegel, and finally with those who today propose to place us under the sway of Phenomena. The fact remains that in the commonplace assertions (irritating like all commonplaces) of the *Greek miracle*, there is a fundamental truth which we have a duty to recognize.

At the same time, to return to the pre-philosophy of common sense discussed previously, we must equally recognize that even if, as I have said, it is a gift of nature, it depends not only on nature, but on culture as well. In other words (and nothing is more in keeping with our nature, which itself demands the developments of culture), this pre-philosophy is a gift of nature received through the instrumentality of

9 Cf. Louis Gardet, *op. cit.*

culture, and in harmony with the characteristics of the great stages of culture. This means that the pre-philosophy which is (or was—I have noted that it is in the process of disintegration) a gift of nature for the man of our Western culture, is the result of a two-fold privilege which this culture has enjoyed (and more or less squandered). On the one hand, it has been animated and exalted by the Judeo-Christian tradition (a privilege supernatural in its origin: the divine revelation), while on the other (and it is this privilege which I am now discussing), it was born of the "Greek miracle," which was no miracle at all, but a normal awakening of the *natura rationalis* to itself, the great awakening due to the passage, fully and decidedly consented to, of the human mind under the "solar" regime of the Logos.[10]

However annoying it may be for the egalitarian vocabulary which a certain diplomatic courtesy (quite fatiguing in the long run) would have us use, there is no way of ignoring that the development of humanity and of culture implies, as a matter of course, a scale of values. Each age, yes, even the most primitive, has its worth, to which it is imperative to render justice. And if the age which follows is a superior one, in reaching it man sustains certain losses. But the gains are greater. That there is a scale of values is implied by the very notion of progress. There are ages more or less fortunate, more or less privileged. There are civilizations, human groups, and individual men, who for a given work in a given connection, are the object of a certain election—I am speaking of a natural election (or of the chosen ones of History, as one would say today). Christians who are nurtured on the idea of an election of grace (the chosen people, Abraham, Moses, John the Baptist, the Virgin Mary, and all the saints of heaven) would be misguided indeed if, because of their own good nature and their desire to be kind to everyone, they were scandalized by the idea of such a natural election or vocation, for God is the God of nature, too, and every artist chooses to his liking in order to create and perfect his work.

I apologize for using so many words. I was only wanting to justify my assertion that, just as Western culture really is (or was) a privileged culture, so the *pre-philosophy of common sense* proper to the man of that culture is (or was) a privileged pre-philosophy, in which the notions of common sense (actually common to all men) have

[10] Cf. *Quatre essais sur l'esprit, op. cit.*

(or had) reached a point of remarkably superior elaboration. This is what is disappearing before our eyes.

I will note in closing that in taking their place in that "modern civilization" to which the entire world, whether we like it or not, is today invited, the peoples whose civilizations were developed under the great initiatory wisdoms of the East, maintain, deep in their hearts, a tenderness and veneration for these great wisdoms (and may they preserve and transmit to us many truths which deserve immortality),[11] but do not seem to endeavor to rejuvenate and reinvigorate them; they know that such wisdoms belong to a past which they are leaving behind.

They are passing into the technocratic age and into Western culture at the very instant, alas, when the latter seems to be degenerating; they bring their tribute to the Greek achievement of liberating adult reason at the very moment when this achievement is in jeopardy. And so we see them exposed to incalculable losses out of necessity but for a questionable gain. In entering modern civilization they leave the cultural regime of their own former wisdoms, but the world they are entering is itself turning away from the lofty rational (and suprarational) wisdom to which it was called. It can no longer offer them either theological rationally elaborated wisdom (which its culture claims it can do without), or metaphysical rational wisdom, or philosophy worthy of the name (its philosophers, to distract it from its labors, make it hear the plaintive ballade of a being which is not being and a knowledge which is not knowledge). What such a world can offer is the magnificent ersatz of the science of Phenomena, and along with it, power over matter; a dream of complete domination of all visible things (even of the invisible) and also the abdication of the human mind, renouncing Truth for Verification, Reality for Sign.

One would hope that the new arrivals who flock from the ends of the earth to take their part in the progress of modern civilization would bring us—but nothing is more doubtful, except perhaps for some of them who might turn to the Christian faith and the rational wisdoms it has nourished—help and assistance against the powerful Disgust with Reason, the joyous (no, it is not joyous) logophobia which is festering before our eyes.

11 Cf. Louis Gardet, *"Interpénetration des cultures,"* Nova et Vetera, October–December, 1956, p. 282.

Contemporary Trends,
Especially the Trends of "Left" and "Right"

AT THE TIME OF THE "LETTER ON INDEPENDENCE"

Ecumenism, it appears, asks us not only to be "open" to our fellow men, to their anguish, their problems, their need for recognition, but also to all *contemporary trends*. That is more difficult, for there is a little of everything in these trends, sometimes euphemistically referred to as "currents of thought." For example, the neo-modernism which I have already spoken about is one of our most active contemporary currents. Besides, these trends are sometimes—what a pity!—directly opposed to one another (nature and history want it that way), like the so-called "left" and "right" trends which I particularly wish to consider in this second note.

Long ago, I wrote a short book [12] in which I spoke of the mysterious cleavage indicated by these terms, which refer not only to parliamentary benches, but to all the citizens. I drew there a distinction between two senses of the words "right" and "left," a physiological sense and a political sense. In the first sense one is of the "right" or of the "left" by a disposition of temperament, just as the human being is born bilious or sanguine. It is useless, in that meaning of the term, to pretend to be neither right nor left. All one can do is to correct one's temperament and bring it to an equilibrium which more or less approaches the point where the two tendencies converge. For at the extreme lower limit of these tendencies, a kind of monstrosity unfolds before the mind—on the right a pure cynicism, on the left a pure unrealism (or idealism, in the metaphysical sense of this word). The pure man of the left detests being, always preferring, in principle, in the words of Rousseau,[13] *what is not* to *what is*. The pure man of the right detests justice and charity, always preferring, in principle, in the words of Goethe (himself an enigma who masked his right with

[12] *Lettre sur l'Indépendance* (Paris: Desclée De Brouwer, 1935). Cf. Henry Bars, *La Politique selon Jacques Maritain* (Paris: Editions Ouvrières, 1961).
[13] "What is not is the only thing that is beautiful," said Jean-Jacques Rousseau. And Jean-Paul Sartre: "The real is never beautiful."

his left), *injustice to disorder*. Nietzsche is a noble and a beautiful example of the man of the right, and Tolstoy, of the man of the left.

In the second sense, the political sense, left and right designate ideals, energies, and historic formations into which the men of these two opposing temperaments are normally drawn to group themselves. Here again, considering the circumstances in which a given country finds itself at a given moment, it is impossible for anyone who takes political realities seriously not to orient himself either to the right or to the left. Yet things get so confused in this matter that men of the right sometimes practice a politics of the left, and vice versa. I think Lenin is a good example of the first case. There are no more dreadful revolutions than revolutions of the left carried out by men of rightist temperament. There are no weaker governments than governments of the right run by leftist temperaments (Louis XVI).

But things look completely spoiled when, at certain moments of deep trouble, the political formations of right and left, instead of being each a more or less high-spirited team held in check by a more or less firm political reason, have become nothing more than exasperated affective complexes carried away by their myth-ideal; from that point on, political intelligence can do nothing but practice ruses in the service of passion. Under those conditions, to be neither right nor left means simply that one intends to keep his sanity.[14]

This is what I tried my best to do, at a time when things were already quite spoiled ("I am neither left nor right," [15] even though by temperament I am what people call a man of the left). By keeping one's sanity I did not mean taking refuge in some kind of neutrality, but preparing the way for a political activity that would be "authentically and vitally Christian." In other words I had in mind a politics which, while drawing its inspiration from the Christian spirit and Christian principles, would involve only the initiative and responsibility of the citizens who conduct it, without being in the slightest degree a politics dictated by the Church or committing her to responsibility. May I add that until today—and despite (or because of) the entry on the scene, in different countries, of political parties labeled "Christian" (most of which are primarily combinations of electoral interests)—the hope for the advent of a *Christian politics* (corres-

[14] *Lettre sur l'Indépendance*, pp. 42–43, 43–44.
[15] *Ibid.*, p. 9.

ponding in the practical order to what a *Christian philosophy* is in the speculative order) has been completely frustrated. I know only one example of an authentic "Christian revolution," and that is what President Eduardo Frei is attempting at this very moment in Chile, and it is not sure that he will succeed. (It is also true that among those of my contemporaries still living as I write these lines, I see in the Western world no more than three revolutionaries worthy of the name—Eduardo Frei in Chile, Saul Alinsky [16] in America, . . . and myself in France, who am not worth beans, since my call as a philosopher has obliterated my possibilities as an agitator. . . .)

But let us leave this digression. Possibly it will be of some use to repeat here what I said in that distant epoch:

"The whole question here comes down to knowing if one believes that an authentically and vitally Christian politics can arise in history and is now invisibly being prepared. It comes down to knowing if Christianity should incarnate itself to that extent, if the temporal mission of the Christian should go that far, if the witness of love should descend that far; or whether we must abandon the world to the devil in that which is most natural to it—civic or political life. If we believe in the possibility of an authentically and vitally Christian politics, then our most urgent temporal duty is to work for its establishment.

". . . A healthy Christian politics (that is a politics of Christian inspiration, but one which calls to itself all non-Christians who find it just and humane) would undoubtedly seem to go pretty far to the left as regards certain technical solutions, in its appreciation of the concrete movement of history, and in its demands for the transformation of the present economic regime. In reality, however, it would have absolutely original positions, proceeding, in the spiritual and moral order, from very different principles than the conceptions of the world, life, the family, and the city, which prevail in the various parties of the left.

". . . Just as, in the spiritual order, which is supra-political, the liberty of the Christian requires that he be all things to all men, and

---

[16] Saul Alinsky, who is a great friend of mine, is a courageous and admirably staunch organizer of "people's communities" and an anti-racist leader whose methods are as effective as they are unorthodox. Cf. "The Professional Radical, Conversations with Saul Alinsky," *Harper's Magazine*, June, July, 1965.

carry his testimony to all corners, fostering everywhere those bonds of friendship, fraternal kindness, natural virtues of fidelity, devotion, and gentleness, without which we cannot really help each other, and without which supernatural charity, or what we take for it, is in danger of freezing, or of turning into clannish proselytism—to that same extent, in the political order itself, our chief concern in the absence of an appropriate vehicle for a vitally Christian politics, should be to protect the inner germ of such a politics against everything that would risk altering it.

"The more this germ remains fragile, hidden, and contested, the more intransigence and firmness are required to keep it pure. . . . From now on, in the most barren conditions, and with the awkwardness of first beginnings, the signal has been given. Even though the invisible flame of the temporal mission of the Christian, of that Christian politics which the world has not yet known, should burn in some few hearts only, because the wood outside is too green, still the witness borne in this way would at least be maintained, the flame handed on. And amid the increasing horror of a world where justice, force, liberty, order, revolution, war, peace, work, and poverty have all been dishonored, where politics does its job only by corrupting the souls of the multitude with lies and by making them accomplices in the crimes of history, where the dignity of the human person is endlessly flouted, the defense of this dignity and of justice, and the political primacy of those human and moral values which make up the core of our earthly common good, would continue to be affirmed, and a small ray of hope would continue to glimmer for mankind in a rehabilitation of love in the temporal order. The principle of the lesser evil is often, and rightly, invoked in politics. There is no greater evil in this field than to leave justice and charity without witness within the temporal order itself, and in regard to the temporal good." [17]

TODAY

It has been thirty years since this *Lettre sur l'Indépendance* was written. Since then our confusion of mind, when it comes to "right"

[17] *Op. cit.,* pp. 45–53.

and "left," has only increased. In France, rightist extremism has been invaded by cruel frustrations and bitter resentments, owing as much to a nostalgic memory of the old Marshal as to the disappointments of the Algerian War, not to mention the unhealthy feeling of belonging to the vanquished who are seeking some kind of revenge. Leftist extremism has been invaded by a fever of demagogic excess and aggressive conformism, which protect themselves poorly against the great amount of illusion and the bit of meanness that gregarian Idealism carries inevitably with it—not to mention the unhealthy feeling that one belongs to the victors and everyone should be made to know it.

None of this is very encouraging or enlightening. But the most serious thing is that the words "right" and "left" no longer have merely a political and social meaning; they have taken on above all— at least in the Christian world—a religious sense, resulting in the worst kind of jumble. How do we even find names for sociological formations which catch our attention first of all because of a certain religious attitude, but whose staunch background is a certain politico-social attitude, as if, by declaring a given religious position, one was necessarily announcing in the same breath a particular political position, and vice versa? Words such as "integralist" and "modernist" could not be employed, for they refer to religious behavior only. Nor could "conservative" and "progressive," since they refer only to politico-social behavior. We can get out of such a fix, if we try to designate these two vast trends, whose intelligibility is so feebly established and includes such a confusion of aspects, only be constructing a kind of Archtype to which we will give an allegorical or *mythical* name (here is a good case for this word). This will have the advantage of offending nobody: consequently, as the prudent authors of certain mystery stories warn us, any resemblance to any person living or dead should be considered purely coincidental, and no one should feel he has been alluded to. To designate the Archtype of leftist extremism, then I will speak of the Sheep of Panurge; and for the Archtype of rightist extremism, I will say the Ruminators of the Holy Alliance.[18]

Of course when it comes to real persons who seem to enter in any degree (there are an infinite number of degrees) into more or less close participation with either of these Archtypes, I hope I have for

---

[18] Sheep also ruminate, I know, but over dreams of the future.

them the feelings that are appropriate between Christians (and even between simple human persons) and not merely the kind of charity one would have for a criminal or a dunce. I am quite ready to evince my esteem and brotherly respect for them, and I would be sincerely happy to unite my prayers to theirs, and to go with them to receive the Body of the Lord. All the same, if I happen to find myself in agreement on some point, either philosophical-theological, or politico-social, with either the Sheep of Panurge or the Ruminators of the Holy Alliance, I feel a serious uneasiness. And I don't know which I detest more: to see a truth that is dear to me disregarded and abused by one party or the other, or to see it invoked and betrayed, by the one or the other.

Such accidents are nevertheless inevitable. And we should note here the unhappy interlacing of values which causes the Sheep to cut such a wretched figure in philosophical or theological matters (in order to be "with it" they are fideists, modernists, or anything you please), while in political and social questions their instinct prompts them to sound doctrine which they will more or less mess up.[19] The opposite is true of the big Ruminators. I keep myself as far as I can from both camps, but it is quite natural (if hardly pleasing) that I feel myself less distant from the first when it is a question of things that are Caesar's, and less distant from the second (alas!) when it is a question of the things that are God's.

We should recognize, moreover, that in its zeal neither camp gives first place to the service of pure truth. It is, above all, the alarms of Prudence that stir the Ruminators of the Holy Alliance: to bar the way to threatening dangers, to lock the doors, to build dikes. What stirs the Sheep of Panurge more than anything else is Deference to public opinion: to do as everyone does, at least as all those who are not fossils.

By and large, the two extremisms whose Archtypes have just furnished me an excuse for some bad jokes, characterize but two minorities, although for the moment the Sheep are clearly more numerous than the big Ruminators, and can boast of a much vaster influence, especially among clerical professors. The great bulk of the

---

[19] "The Christian left in France has evangelical entrails, but the brain is weak in theology." Claude Tresmontant, "*Tâches de la pensée chrétienne*," *Esprit*, July–August 1965, p. 120.

Christian people seem indifferent to the efforts of both these minorities. The people are troubled and unhappy because they feel that something great is in the offing and they do not know how to participate. They are groping, and submissively lend themselves to attempts of groupings which are often disappointing. They conform willingly (not without nostalgia among some elderly lovers of beauty in the Church) to the use of the vernacular in religious ceremonies, but complain of the miserable translations which they are forced to recite, as well as of the disorder (temporary, no doubt) which accompanies liturgical innovations. They ask themselves at times whether their religion has been changed, and they will not easily be satisfied for long with vigil services, recordings, and cheap songs with which the initiatives of certain curates have adorned the "community celebrations." Above all, they suffer from a great and genuine thirst to which no one seems to pay any heed, and their good will in accepting the substitutes makes one foresee serious disillusionment.

It is the truth they are seeking (indeed, yes), and the living sources. There is no shortage of guides, judging from the noise they make, and surely all of them have the best intentions. No doubt a few of them know the way. Let us hope that those who do can give us some inkling of what it is "to accept *as a child* the kingdom of God," without which, Jesus said, no one can enter it [20]—and it is certainly not a question of closing our eyes, for a child *looks*. We must at all costs know a little what it means to look at divine things with the eyes of a child, and in what school this is taught—and that God alone can teach us this.

January 18, 1966

---

[20] "*Quicumque non acceperit regnum Dei sicut puer, non intrabit in illud.*" (*Luke* 18:17)

3 THE WORLD AND ITS CONTRASTING ASPECTS

The religious or "mystical" truth
concerning the world
in its relation with the kingdom of God

I have often insisted (a long time ago in *Freedom in the Modern World*,[1] and *True Humanism*,[2] more recently in *On the Philosophy of History*[3]) on the fundamental *ambivalence* of the world when considered in its relation to the kingdom of God. I will begin this chapter by looking at this ambivalence again.

To do this, it is enough to refer to the assertions of the Gospel. These are essential assertions; if we forgot them, we would be mere shadows of Christians; because they give us not only what Jesus knew, but what he *lived*, in the very depths of his experience—what he lived in his life, what he lived in his death.

All my readers are in the habit of reading the Gospel, I am sure. But it is not a bad idea to bring together all the texts which have to do with the world.

If we wish to try to understand these texts, let us not forget that Jesus and the apostles, when they speak to us of the world, consider it always in its relation—its simultaneous twofold relation—to the kingdom of God. On the one hand, insofar as the world accepts its final destiny to be taken up and transfigured into *another world*, a divine world, the kingdom of God which has already begun and will endure eternally; on the other hand, insofar as the world rejects the

---

[1] (New York: Charles Scribner's Sons, 1936); *Du Régime temporel et de la liberté* (Paris: Desclée De Brouwer, 1933).

[2] (New York: Charles Scribner's Sons, 1938); *Humanisme Intégral* (Paris: Aubier, 1936).

[3] (New York: Charles Scribner's Sons, 1957); *Pour une Philosophie de l'Histoire* (Paris: ed. du Seuil, 1959).

kingdom and falls back upon itself. What is then at stake (for it has to do with the mystery of salvation) is the religious or "mystical" truth concerning the world.

I regret having to speak in a magisterial tone, which is not my manner, but it is a question of the Gospel.

GOD SO LOVED THE WORLD

"God *so loved the world* that he gave it his only Son." [4]

How could God not love the world which he himself made? He made it out of love. And see how it ruins itself, this world, with all its beauty, by reason of the freedom of the creature who is the image of God and who prefers himself to God and chooses nothingness. "That is why, when Christ came into the world, he said: 'You have not wanted either sacrifice or oblation, but you have prepared a body for me. . . .' Then I said: 'I am coming to do your will, O God.' " [5]

"For I did not come to condemn the world, but to save the world." [6]

"God did not send his Son into the world to judge the world, but for the world to be saved by him." [7]

"Here is the Lamb of God who takes away the sin of the world." [8]

He who never knew sin, he consented *to be made sin* [9] and to die on the cross, in order to deliver the world from sin.

And at the very moment when this world, insofar as it refuses the kingdom, is judged—"now is the judgment of the world," [10] (it itself judges itself)—at the moment when Jesus is going to be lifted up on the cross and to draw all things to him; [11] on the very eve of his condemnation by the world and of his going to his Father, [12] and leaving his own who were in the world and whom he loved until the

---

4 John 3:16.
5 *Hebr.* 10:5–7.
6 John 12:47.
7 John 3:17.
8 John 1:29.
9 2 *Cor.* 5:21.
10 John 12:31.
11 John 12:32.
12 John 14:28.

end,[13] at the Last Supper, at that moment when—whereas he does
not pray for the world (it is for the Church that he prays, "for those
whom you have given me" [14] and "for those who will believe in me
through their word" [15]) he asks "that they may all be one, even as
you, Father, in me and I in you, that they also may be one in us" [16]—
he adds, "so that the world will believe that you sent me." [17] How
extraordinarily important the world is! Surely, since he came to save
it.

That world which did not know the Father,[18] what I do, Christ
said, is in order that "it know that I love the Father and that I do as
the Father has commanded me"; [19] it is necessary "that the world
know that you have sent me and that you have loved them [20] as you
have loved me." [21]

The world must know this, so that the world itself, or at least all
in it who will not refuse to be saved, may be saved and enter into the
kingdom of God and be transfigured there. And the world must also
know this for its own condemnation, or at least for the condemnation of all in it that refuses to be saved and to turn toward mercy.

"The Son of man came to seek, and to save what was perishing." [22]
But he does not save us in spite of ourselves. He does not save what
was perishing if what was perishing prefers to perish.

Behind all this there is a very long history.

The world was created good (which does not mean that it was
created divine). It was created good, its natural structures are good
in themselves: the Bible intends to get this into our heads once and
for all. "God (Elohim) saw that the light was good." [23] And in the
same way, at the succeeding stages of creation, "God saw that it was

13 John 13:1.
14 John 17:9.
15 John 17:20.
16 John 17:21.
17 Ibid.
18 John 17:25.
19 John 14:31.
20 "Those whom you have given me"; and "those who will believe in me
through their word." John 17:9; 17:20.
21 John 17:23.
22 Luke 19:10.
23 Gen. 1:4.

good" keeps returning like a refrain.[24] And on the sixth day, after man had been created, "God saw everything that he had made, and behold, it was very good." [25]

And then evil made its appearance on the earth, with the disobedience of Man and Woman, deceived by the Evil Spirit. Finished, the earthly paradise, forever, for them and for all their posterity. (There are authors today who are discovering that original sin is an invention of St. Augustine; too bad they remember Genesis so poorly. I know very well they will say it is a myth, but this "myth," whose truth is vouched for by God himself, comes at the head of the Bible, a pretty long time before St. Augustine.[26])

[24] *Gen.* 1:10; 12; 18; 21; 25.
[25] *Gen.* 1:31.
[26] It would be childish to believe that before passing under the regime of the Logos, human thought was entirely given over to the illusions of the imagination.

Under what I called the twilight regime (cf. p. 16), not only did practical thought have a hold—in a way different from but as good as our own—on the realities of daily life, the making and use of tools, etc., but in the metaphysico-religious domain the forms, still wholly immersed in the concrete and swarming with images, in which human thought then expressed itself could be *adequate to what is*, although in an essentially veiled manner.

Yes, they were myths. But in our day this term has been made dangerously equivocal, even with regard to primitive thought. (This is because of the systematic and mistaken use which our phenomenologists make of it in regard to everything which, in our own thought, does not pertain to scientific observation or psychological experience.) The myths of primitive thought were not all without value as wisdom, a more profound wisdom, I readily believe, than some of our metaphysical systems. There were myths which were not *fairy tales*, myths which were *true*, that is, myths that spoke the truth (just as under the regime of the Logos there are "false" and "true" propositions). Even in the domain of "science," one can say that the network of lines which Chinese acupuncture imagines as connecting together all parts of the human body is a practical "myth" which teaches us nothing about anatomical structures but is "true" when it comes to where it is proper to insert the needle.

I have been aware of these things for a long time—without nevertheless being in agreement, far from it, with the problematic and the generalizations (incurably equivocal whatever he can do) of an author like Jean-Marie Paupert, whose good will deserves respect and sympathy but whose views on theology, as exemplified in his recent book, *Peut-on être chrétien aujourd'hui*, seem to me to be rather confused.

From the viewpoint I have just indicated concerning the two great historical regimes of human thought, it appears that (a *unique case* in the Bible, because revelation has here used elements coming down from the earliest times and re-assumed in a prophetic light focused on the past) the history of Adam and Eve is a truth, a sacred truth *veiled in its mode of expression*, which hands over to us what is most important, *absolutely* important for us to know about our origins: the

Henceforth evil is in the world, this world whose ontological structures are and remain good—we know that *malum est in bono sicut in subjecto* [27]—and which, however wounded, continues (not without losses) its movement toward the temporal goals to which its nature tends and for whose realization we have a duty to co-operate. Evil is in the world, and ferments there everywhere, sows deception everywhere, separating man from God. And while history advances and ages of civilization succeed one another, the true God remains unknown or badly known—except for one small nation, a chosen Vine sprung from Abraham, Isaac and Jacob. And men would be lost to eternal life if all who do not flee from a grace whose name they do not know were not saved by the Blood of Christ to come. And when he comes, the spiritual Power, the Doctors and Priests of the chosen people, crying out that they have no other king but Caesar, will condemn as a blasphemer the One who is the Truth in person. And they will deliver him up to an earthly Power for which truth is only a word; and acting in concert, spiritual Power gone astray and earthly Power will put him to death. That is the other face of the world in its relation to the kingdom of God.

THE WORLD HATES ME

"The world cannot hate you (who do not believe in me); but me," Jesus said, "*it hates me* because I testify of it that its works are evil." [28] As for the disciples, the world will treat them as it treated their master: "*You will be hated by all for my name's sake.*" [29] In his last farewell, Jesus will again repeat to them: "*If the world hates you,*

Event (the fall) which, as a result of a free act, a sin of Man and Woman placed at their creation in a supernatural state of innocence or harmony with God, brought mankind to pass into a state of rupture with God—which nature of itself is incapable of retrieving—whereby each man is born deprived of grace. Here, expressed in the language appropriate to the regime of the Logos, is the truth which the Church, faithful to the revelation with which she has been entrusted, and in the prophetic light of which I have just spoken, discerns in the so-called "myth" (but true under veils) of the mysterious forbidden fruit which Man, at the instigation of Woman, has eaten.
[27] *Sum. theol.*, I, 48, 3.
[28] John 7:7.
[29] Matt. 10:22.

know that it has hated me before it hated you. If you were of the world, the world would love its own; but because you are not of the world, but I chose you out of the world, therefore the world hates you. Remember the word that I said to you, 'A servant is not greater than his master.' *If they persecuted me, they will persecute you too.*" [30]

And similarly, at the Last Supper, in his prayer for them: "The world has hated them because they are not of the world, even as I am not of the world. I do not pray that you should keep them out of the world, but that you should keep them from the Evil One. *They are not of the world,* even as I am not of the world." [31] And again, at the Last Supper, he announces that the Paraclete, "when he will come, *will bring accusation against the world* by reason of the sin and of the justice and of the judgment." By reason of the sin, because of the unbelief of the world ("because they do not believe in me"); by reason of the justice, because the world has rejected the Just One ("I go to the Father, and you will see me no more"); by reason of the judgment, "because the prince of this world is already judged." [32]

It is Jesus who calls by this name the Angel of Darkness: "I will no longer talk much with you, for the prince of this world is coming, *venit princeps hujus mundi.*" [33] On Palm Sunday, when he was foretelling his Passion, and a voice from heaven was heard, "Now," he had said, "is the judgment of this world, now *shall the prince of this world be cast out,*" [34]—in other terms, is going to be dispossessed: dispossessed prince, and that much more anxious for his revenge, he will continue to prowl about us "like a roaring lion, seeking someone to devour," [35] as the liturgy describes him to us every evening in the *lectio brevis* of Compline. He will continue to infest innocent material creatures [36] on whose behalf the Church lavishes her exorcisms—and to try to make in the heads of intellectuals the nicest possible mess—he will continue until the Passion has borne all its fruits,

[30] John 15:18–20.
[31] John 17:14–16.
[32] John 16:8–11.
[33] John 14:20.
[34] John 12:31.
[35] I Peter 5:8.
[36] "He infests innocent fountains, hills, woods, he lurks in the tempest." Raïssa Maritain, *Le Prince de ce monde* (2nd ed. Paris: Desclée De Brouwer, 1963), pp. 12–13.

until the end of the world: he will let loose the world only when the world is ended.[37] (Good lord, I know very well that to a *perspectivist* the devil is a mythical survival, but I for one believe in him.) This is why St. Paul (something of a backward thinker himself), in warning us that it is not flesh and blood that we have to contend with, but evil spirits, calls them "the world despots of this present darkness," τοὺς χοσμοχράτορας τοῦ σχοτους τούτου.[38]

Thus, the world appears as the Antagonist, from which the great refusal comes. "The world was made by him, and the world *did not know him*. He came to his own home and his own people *did not receive him*." [39]

The world lies in the power of evil: "the whole world is in the power of the Evil One." [40] "Woe to the world, because of the scandals." [41] *"The world cannot receive the Spirit of truth* . . . because it neither sees him nor knows him." [42]

And the world will be condemned. St. Paul asks the Corinthians to examine themselves "so that we may not be *condemned along with the world*." [43] And Christ has vanquished the world. "In the world you will have tribulation; but be of good cheer, *I have vanquished the world*." [44]

Like Christ, the Church is of God, not of the world. And we have to choose to be friends of the world or friends of God. Because the world is not only created nature as God made it, but this very nature insofar as crowned with the triple diadem of the evil desires of human Liberty—Pride at being supremely self-sufficient; Intoxication with knowledge, not for the sake of truth but for power and possession; Intoxication in being overcome and torn by pleasure. "Do not love the world or the things in the world." [45] "If anyone loves the world, the love (ἀγάπη) of the Father is not in him. For all that seduces

---

[37] *Sum. theol.*, I, 64, 4.
[38] *Eph.* 6:12.
[39] John 10:11.
[40] John 5:19.
[41] Matt. 18:7.
[42] John 14:17.
[43] *I Cor.* 11:32.
[44] John 16:33.
[45] "μηδὲ τὰ ἐν τῷ κόσμω." A formula too abbreviated to be translated literally. "Nor what *is* in the world" forces the sense, by centering the thought on a word which is not in the Greek text.

in the world [46]—the Lust of the flesh, the Lust of the eyes, and the Pride of life—is not of the Father but is of the world. And the world will pass away, and the lust of it." [47]

"*Adulterers, do you not know that friendship with the world is enmity with God? Therefore, whoever wishes to be a friend of the world makes himself an enemy of God.*" [48]

Adulterers, you say *we* are? Ah, that's pretty rude indeed. James and John, you poor backward apostles, what kind of a story have you got there? Calling us such a name, we who are emerging at last from all the old complexes, and who are taught by our new doctors, with sacred fervor, that there is nothing more beautiful or more urgent than to be *friends of the world*, this beloved world that is evolving so superbly toward final Deliverance, thanks to the *Christian* removal of the cross? Or could there have been a peculiar misunderstanding somewhere? What is called the "post-conciliar situation" of the Catholic faithful (better to say the situation following upon the crisis, still acute, which made the restatements of the Council necessary) is certainly a curious thing.

SOME CONCLUSIONS

For the moment, I would simply like to stick to the gist of all the New Testament texts I have been citing. As I said in *True Humanism* (well, I did meditate on the matter for a long time), the world is the domain *at once* of man, of God, and of the devil. Thus appears the essential ambiguity of the world and of its history; it is a field common to the three. The world is a closed field which belongs to God by right of creation; to the devil by right of conquest, because of sin; to Christ by right of victory over the conqueror, because of the Passion. The task of the Christian in the world is to contend with the devil his domain, to wrest it from him; he must strive to this end, he will succeed in it only in part as long as time will endure. The world is

[46] "$\pi\hat{\alpha}\nu$ $\tau\grave{o}$ $\grave{\epsilon}\nu$ $\tau\hat{\omega}$ $\kappa\acute{o}\sigma\mu\omega$." What was said in the preceding note applies equally here.
[47] I John 2:15–17.
[48] James 4:4.

saved, yes, it is delivered *in hope*, it is on the march toward the kingdom of God definitely revealed; but it is not *holy*, it is the Church
which is holy; it is on the march toward the kingdom of God, and
this is why it is a treason toward this kingdom not to seek with all
one's forces—in a manner adapted to the conditions of earthly history,
but as effective as possible, *quantum potes, tantum aude*—a realization or, more exactly, a refraction in the world of the Gospel exigencies; nevertheless this realization, even though relative, will always be
in one manner or another deficient and disputed in the world. And at
the same time that the history of the world is on the march—it is the
growth of the wheat—toward the kingdom of God, it is also on
the march—it is the growth of the tares, inextricably mingled with the
wheat—toward the kingdom of reprobation.

The Gospel texts we have called to mind amount to saying that the
world is sanctified insofar as it is not *only* the world but is assumed
into the universe of the Incarnation; and that it is reprobate insofar
as it shuts itself up in itself, insofar, in the words of Claudel, as it
shuts itself up in the essential difference, and as it remains only the
world, separated from the universe of the Incarnation.

Whereas the history of the Church, which is, as Pascal says, the history of the truth, leads as such toward the kingdom of God definitively revealed and has no other end than that kingdom—on the
contrary, divided between two opposing ultimate ends, the history of
the temporal city leads at one and the same time toward the kingdom
of perdition and toward the kingdom of God [49]—as toward the terms
that are beyond its own natural ends.

I am not forgetting that the world has a *relatively* final end, which
is its natural end. This natural end is not a goal attained once and for
all; in the language of Leibniz,[50] it is an unending path through conquests, and which has no term, and over whose entire length mankind
is laboring to overcome fatality and reveal itself to itself. Nor do I forget that in the natural order the world has an opposite "end" (in the
sense of a final occurrence)—namely the losses and waste resulting
from the growth of evil (not as great, in the last analysis, but a pretty

---

[49] From a new translation by Joseph Evans of *True Humanism*, still in manuscript (French ed., pp. 114–116).
[50] He said of beatitude, "it is a path through pleasures."

nuisance for all that) in the course of history. There we have—in a purely philosophical perspective—a sort of historical hell (a faint image of the real hell) from which the world and the history of the world can only be delivered if *this world*, regenerated from top to bottom, finds itself changed into a totally new universe: the new heaven and the new earth of Christian eschatology, according to which the *absolutely* final end of history is beyond history. In other words, there will be a discontinuity between history, which exists in time, and the final state of humanity, which will take place in a transfigured world.

But let us leave this parenthesis. As I indicated at the beginning of this chapter, the Gospel does not consider the world merely in itself, in its natural structures and its historical development, its various political, economic or social regimes, its ages of culture, or with respect to the natural end which I have just mentioned. The Gospel considers the world *in its concrete and existential connections with the kingdom of God*, already present in our midst. This kingdom is the Church, the mystical Body of Christ, at once visible in those who bear the mark of Christ and invisible in those who, without bearing the mark of Christ, share in his grace—but it will be definitively revealed only after the resurrection of the flesh. The world cannot be neutral with respect to the kingdom of God. Either it is vivified by it, or it struggles against it. If God so loved the world that he gave it his only begotten Son, it was to plant [51] and foster in it *another world* where all the desires of nature would be finally more than fulfilled. If Jesus came not to condemn the world but to save it, if the Lamb of God takes away the sins of the world, this means that the kingdom of God, which is not of the world, is itself growing in the world, and that the life of grace performs in it its mysterious work; in such a way that at the final end, when the world is manifestly and definitively saved, it will no longer be *this world*, but will, at a stroke, have been transmuted into the *other world*, the universe of the Incarnation, which shall have reached its state of complete accomplishment; the unimaginable world of glory that has existed from the beginning for the holy Angels and the souls of the blessed, and where the bodies of

[51] From the moment of Adam's repentance—in anticipation of the merits of Christ.

Jesus and Mary are already present; and where, having been brought to participate in the condition of spirit, its privileges and its freedom, matter will be gentle and more fertile in beauty, the senses more penetrating and awed than ever.

The "Ontosophic" [52] Truth

CONCERNING THE WORLD
CONSIDERED IN ITS NATURAL STRUCTURES

The Gospel has a deep respect for created things, it loves the beauty of the lilies of the field that are clothed more gloriously than King Solomon,[53] and the birds of the air that have no granaries and are fed by the Father,[54] and the little sparrows that are worth nothing, not one of which falls to the ground without God's having permitted it.[55] It understands how dearly a man values every sheep of his flock,[56] and is alive to all that charms the heart in a child's glance. In the Gospel you cannot find the slightest trace of contempt for anything created. Manicheism is an offense against the Father; the logic of gnostic sects impregnated with this spirit demands that, all things considered, God the Creator be regarded as an evil God. The Catholic faith has always had a horror of them, in its view that Catharians are the worst of blasphemers. They blaspheme God, forgetting that the work of the six days was good and very good. And they blaspheme reason, too.

The man whom St. Thomas called "the Philosopher"—that deplorable Westerner who came to us from the Near East by way of Maimonides and the Arabs—Aristotle knew that all that is, is good in the very degree in which it is, and that being and good are convertible

---

52 I would like to apologize for this neologism. I had to use it for two reasons. On the one hand, the truth it refers to is both *philosophical* and *theological*; on the other, this truth is not merely *ontological*, it is concerned with the moral domain as well, since the essential inclinations of nature and its proper ends are good not only in an ontological sense, but equally in an ethical or moral sense.

53 Matt. 6:29.

54 Matt. 6:26.

55 Luke 12:6.

56 Luke 15:6.

terms, *ens et bonum convertuntur*: nothing stronger could be said. Hence St. Thomas's statement: to exist is the act par excellence. Evil is a "privation"—the absence of a good that should be there—evil is not a being. It is true that life on earth inevitably involves suffering, as a result of our fleshly condition, and also as a price paid to proceed to loftier degrees of being (or, more precisely, of life). But as to moral evil, it originates in the free will (a most high privilege in itself) of created spirits. Catholic theology has always held firmly to these principles. Nature taken in itself is good and tends to ends that are good. The same thing applies to the world—that is, in a very general sense, to the whole of created things, and, in a more restricted sense, to the material and visible universe; and, in the even more restricted sense which concerns us here, to our *human* universe, the universe of man, of culture and history in their development here below.

The "ontosophic" truth at stake when it is a question of the world taken in itself, is that, in spite of the evil that is present in it—sometimes so great as to be intolerable not only to man's sensibility but to his very mind—the good, all things considered, is there, much greater, deeper and more fundamental. The world is good in its structures and in its natural ends. As stagnant, even as regressive as the world can seem at certain times and in certain places of the earth, its historic development, seen in its entirety, advances toward better and more elevated states. In spite of everything, we ought to have confidence in the world because, if evil grows in it along with good (and in what a way!—one would have to be one of the new Pharisees intoxicated by the three "*cosmological*," not theological, virtues not to see that) there is, nevertheless, in the world a *greater* growth of good.

The Christian has (I will come back to it in a moment) a temporal mission with respect to the world and human progress. When St. James tells us not to be friends of the world, he is by no means turning us away from this temporal mission! This mission itself implies that we are not friends of the world in the sense in which the apostle understands this expression, since the temporal mission of the Christian is to be ready to give his life to instill in the world something of this Gospel, this kingdom of God, and this Jesus whom the world hates and whose spur it so badly needs. When St. John commands us not to love either the world or the things of the world, he has no intention of forbidding us to love everything good and worthy of love in the world; it is friendship with the world insofar as it is the enemy of the Gospel and of Jesus that he has in view. If all the Gospel texts which I recalled earlier (in the section, "The World Hates Me") put us on guard against the world so urgently and severely and with such unimpeachable authority, it is by no means insofar as the world and its history pursue their natural ends, but insofar as the world, taken in its relationship (only too real!—to forget it is to deny Jesus) of enmity toward Jesus and the kingdom of God, is the great Antagonist from which the great refusal comes.

THE NATURAL END OF THE WORLD

I spoke just now of the natural end of the world. I would like to clarify this briefly. The absolutely final end, the supreme end of the world is supra-mundane and supra-temporal, it belongs to the supernatural order. But the world has also a natural end (*relatively* final, or final in a given order). This end, in my opinion, is three-fold.

In its first aspect, the natural end of the history of the world is the mastery of nature by man, and the conquest of human autonomy. One reads in Genesis,[57] "God blessed them, and God said to them: 'Be fruitful and multiply, and fill the earth and subdue it; have dominion over the fish of the sea and over the birds of the air and over every living thing that moves upon the earth.'" These words imply mastery of nature: *subdue the earth*, and they cover the loftiest ambitions of human science. Here we have something temporal and earthly, and it is a goal, a genuine destination for the world. The philosopher can express the same idea in other ways if he reflects on the nature of man in his capacity as a reasoning agent immersed in animality. He can say that this goal is the conquest which man must achieve of his own autonomy; as an earthly being who harbors within himself an immortal spirit he has a natural tendency to liberate himself progressively from the control exercised over him by the physical world. At the same time it is required of him to set the human person and the different human groups (races, classes, nations) free from

[57] *Gen.* 1:28.

servitude or subjection to other men, and from that violence by which one man imposes his power on another by treating him as a mere instrument.

A second aspect of the natural end of the world is the development of the multiple immanent (self-perfecting) or spiritual activities of the human being, especially the development of knowledge, in all its different degrees. (I am speaking, of course, of authentic knowledge, immunized against the envy which tempts us today to sacrifice wisdom to science.) This development also includes the creative activity of art. (Even in moments when beauty derives no benefit from it, this activity at least implies a progress in self-awareness.) And in the realm of moral activity, it means progress in the knowledge of the natural law, the most unchallengeable example of progress in the history of mankind.

Finally, we can point to a third aspect of the natural end of the world—the manifestation of all the potentialities of human nature. This, too, flows from the fact that man is not a pure spirit, but a spirit united to matter. It is normal for a spirit to manifest itself. One could cite here a phrase of the Gospel: "Nothing is hidden which shall not be unveiled." [58]

ON THE TEMPORAL MISSION OF THE CHRISTIAN

Since my old habits have got the better of me, and since I have begun, God forgive me, to make didactic statements, I might just as well slip in a few words about the temporal mission of the Christian to which I alluded earlier.

The need for this mission appears much clearer today than for-

[58] Matt. 10:26. Also Luke 8:17. Cf. *On the Philosophy of History*, p. 125. In this connection, we added that the very shamelessness of contemporary literature, despite its often impure motivations (but it is redeemed by some autobiographical confessions of incomparable nobility), responds in its deep sources to a secret necessity and possesses "a kind of eschatological meaning." In many other ways, moreover, history has progressively, for centuries, testified to the impulse of which I am speaking, to make manifest *what is in man*.

The reflections proposed here on the natural end of the world, and those that follow on the temporal mission of the Christian, will be completed in a section of Ch. 7 (*A digression on the temporal mission of the Christian*).

merly. Under the sacral regime of medieval Christianity, and later, under the increasingly degraded and illusory vestiges and remnants of this regime in process of dissolution, it was principally through the social structures, at least in the order of visible activities (I am speaking here only of the latter) that the impact of Christianity was felt, and, even in the period of sharpest challenge, continued (more and more powerlessly after the "age of Enlightenment") to be felt in Western civilization.

What, in those times, was asked of the faithful was to give an example of the Christian virtues in their private life (they very often did so in an admirable manner, which helped the venerable tottering structure to remain standing) and, to the degree that they were able to influence public opinion or political events, to uphold the rights and claims of the ecclesiastical hierarchy.

But today all that has changed. The temporal world has succeeded in casting out every trace of the sacral regime. At the same time, civilization, passing under the control of science and technology, has unmistakably outgrown the boundaries of the Western world, and is in the process of becoming truly universal.

Christianity, then, can no longer count on the aid and protection of social structures. On the contrary, it is up to it to aid and protect these structures by striving to impregnate them with its spirit. Man's duties towards his Creator have a social as well as a personal dimension, and demand, in particular, that every religiously divided political society should recognize the various religious traditions at work among its citizens.[59] The spiritual and the temporal are perfectly distinct, but they can and should cooperate in mutual freedom.

Not only the West, but the entire world, with its vast non-Christian cultural areas, requires, within the temporal domain and on behalf of the progress of temporal civilization, the stimulus and elevation which Christianity naturally brings to the activities of nature in their own sphere.

This means that the age we are entering obliges the Christian to become aware of the temporal mission which he has with respect to the world and which is like an expansion of his spiritual vocation in the

[59] Cf. *Man and the State* (Chicago: University of Chicago Press, 1951), pp. 160–168.

kingdom of God and with respect to it. Woe to the world if the Christian were to isolate and separate his temporal mission (then it would be wind only) from his spiritual vocation! The fact remains that this temporal mission requires him to enter as deeply as possible into the agonies, the conflicts, and the earthly problems, social or political, of his age, and not hesitate to "get his feet wet."

I have said much, in other books, about the temporal mission of the Christian. It is clear that in speaking of this mission, I am thinking, above all, of *lay* Christians. That some of the clergy should become personally involved in secular affairs is quite possible, but hardly a requirement of their function. And it happens, when they are not a Richelieu or a Mazarin, that they handle such affairs less skillfully and more naively than the laity.[60] As for the latter, they can, if they like, indulge in a sort of innocent and rather infantile Christian anticlericalism (it is always tempting to make fun of *les curés*, because at bottom one really likes them and expects a good deal from them) but they would turn out to be worse than the worst *curés* if they conducted their social and political activities like arrogant dreamers, nourished on a false philosphy that divinizes the world, and bent on sacrificing everything to *efficacy*, a passing efficacy.

To be precise, it is not enough to say that the temporal mission of the Christian is, of itself, the concern of the laity. We must also say that it is not the business of *all* lay Christians (far from it!), but only of those who, by reason of their gifts and natural inclinations, as well as due to circumstances, feel for it what we can term (the phrase is rather shopworn, but it is all I have handy) *"a calling."*

Finally, we must add that this *calling* is not enough; a solid interior preparation is also required. (If, by some misfortune, I chance to feel "a calling" to touch on this subject, it will be in another chapter.)

---

[60] Let no one see here any kind of allusion to the organizations of Catholic Action. These organizations by means of which the laity *participate in the apostolate of the Church*, have by definition a *spiritual* purpose, not a temporal one. Accordingly, they have nothing to do with what I am saying here. I think that it falls to them to bring together only a relatively minor segment of the Christian laity (which would, accordingly, be withdrawn to some degree from temporal tasks) but I am persuaded that they are quite necessary. (Cf. *Carnet de Notes*, pp. 240–41.) On the laity, its spiritual vocation and its temporal mission, see Ch. 7 (*Another digression on the condition of the layman*).

A *Long Misunderstanding with Bitter Fruit*

SPECULATIVE VOCABULARY AND PRACTICAL VOCABULARY

To introduce the third part of this chapter, I must, again taking up for a moment my old trade of professor, begin with some preliminary remarks on the difference in approach and vocabulary between speculative knowledge and practical knowledge (that of the moralists and spiritual writers). Before becoming a peasant of the Garonne I insisted on this difference at some length in *The Degrees of Knowledge*. On the one hand, what is considered is the ontological structure of things; on the other, the manner in which the acting subject should conduct himself in their midst and face to face with them.

The real does not appear in the same light in both cases. The theologian declares that grace perfects nature and does not destroy it; the saint declares that grace requires us to make nature die to itself. They are both telling the truth. But it would be a shame to reverse their languages by making use in the speculative order of formulas which are true for the practical order, and vice versa.

Let us think of the "contempt for creatures" professed by the saints. The saint has a right to despise created things (while loving them); the philosopher and the theologian (who, as such, have the duty of knowing, not loving) do not have this right; for the word contempt does not have the same meaning in both cases. For the philosopher and the theologian it would mean: creatures are worth nothing *in themselves;* for the saint: they are worth nothing *for me.* And one need not be a St. John of the Cross, it is enough to be a poet to say similarly:

> *Je suis mourant d'avoir compris*
> *Que notre terre n'est d'aucun prix.*[61]

The saint sees in practice that creatures are nothing in comparison with the One to whom he has given his heart and of the End he has chosen. This is a lover's contempt for all that is not Love itself. To

[61] Max Jacob.

him, it is nothing to give up "all the wealth of his house" [62] for God. "For his sake I have suffered the loss of all things, and count them as a dung hill, in order that I may gain Christ," St. Paul said, ". . . that I may know him and the power of his resurrection, and may share in his sufferings." [63]

And by a marvelous reflux, the more he despises creatures as rivals of God, as objects of a possible option against God, the more he cherishes them in and for *Him* whom he loves, as loved by him and made truly good and worthy of being loved by the love which creates and infuses goodness in all things.[64] For to love a being in God and for God is not to treat it simply as a means or mere occasion to love God, which would amount to dispensing oneself from loving it (and at the same time ceasing truly to love God, who is truly loved only when we love his visible images, too) : it is to love this being and consider it as an end, to desire its good because it deserves to be loved in itself and for itself, this very merit and dignity flowing from the sovereign Love and sovereign Lovableness of God. They are thus founded in God and, at the same time, placed beyond all quarrels and vicissitudes. Not to stop short at the creature—that is the guarantee that the creature will be loved unfailingly, transfixed in the root of its lovableness by the arrow which pierces it. In this way the paradox becomes comprehensible: that is the end the saint embraces in a universal love of friendship and piety—a love incomparably more free, but also more tender and happier than the love of concupiscence of the voluptuary or the miser—everything that passes in time and all the weakness and all the beauty of things, everything he has given up.[65]

We would be completely mistaken, as I noted earlier, if we were to give a speculative sense to the formulas of a John of the Cross. "There is no worse philosophy than a philosophy that despises nature. A knowledge that despises what is, is itself nothing; a cherry between the teeth holds within it more mystery than the whole of idealistic metaphysics." [66]

---

[62] *Cant.* 8:7.
[63] *Phil.* 3:8–10.
[64] "*Amor Dei est infundans et creans bonitatem in rebus.*" (St. Thomas, *Sum. theol.*, I, 20, 2.)
[65] Cf. *The Degrees of Knowledge* (New York: Charles Scribner's Sons, 1959), p. 335.
[66] *Ibid.*

THE "CONTEMPT OF THE WORLD"
AND ITS PERILOUS VICISSITUDES

Well, for most of the faithful and even for the cleric, who have no access to the modest empyrean, at once temple of wisdom and insane asylum where philosophers and theologians are closeted, it is difficult to refrain from what I would call a speculative distortion and misappropriation of the maxims of the saints (by involuntarily depriving them of their real meaning). The process has taken a great amount of time, but the fact is that at a given moment they became the innocent authors, and victims, of such a misappropriation.

To make a long story short (please excuse my oversimplification), let me say that for centuries (what pedagogy there was was a little rude: in order to discourage pupils from frequenting bad places, they were told that the whole town was a death-trap), Christian homiletic teaching was busy convincing men (who naturally love created things, but not in the way saints do) that created things are worthless. The trouble was that by dint of repeating this commonplace, the ascetic writers and the preachers wound up extending St. Paul's "dung hill" to the whole of creation, no doubt in as much as it might tempt the human being, but also, finally, and without being aware of the distortion, even when the creation was taken in itself. Simply through a phenomenon of inattention, a masked manicheism was thus superimposed on the Christian faith, though without ruining it. (If one had known what one was doing, what a beautiful contradiction—and for the delight of our present-day Hegelians, what a fine dialectic! But no, one was simple trapped by a formula which, in pitch-darkness, had slipped from one meaning to another.) Hence the creature was in itself a dung hill; the world was in itself nothing but corruption. Original sin had rotted everything in nature. A Catholic would certainly not have advanced such a proposition. But it often underlay in a more or less unconscious way his idea of fallen nature. This view was an effect of that confusion of levels that I have just been describing. (It was also, perhaps, an effect of certain infiltrations of Protestant conceptions, and certainly of Jansenist influences which were so deep in France, and of which I have not spoken in order not to take too long.)

It is worth noting that by the same stroke the formulas of the practical register itself were being progressively vitiated, all the while being infiltrated simultaneously by unconscious pelagianism and manicheism. It was up to man and the human will to make the first move, and to do nothing (through fear of hell, we may presume) forbidden by and displeasing to God. Then God would reward him. And whereas St. Paul and all saints (for whom the world in itself was not evil, but rather, if anything, too good) despised the world only by virtue of boundless love for the One who loved us first, and in comparison with him, in order to share in the sufferings and the work of Jesus—"nothing, nothing, nothing, even to giving one's skin and everything else for Christ," [67]—the adulterated Christianity I have been describing, on the contrary, left the divine *agapè* in a sacred shadow; and in any case, it was not in comparison with God that the world, in its eyes, was worth nothing: it was worth nothing *in itself*. Henceforth the practical formulas which it dispensed became mainly prohibitive, and caused the values of negation, refusal and fear to be in the forefront—as well as setting oneself to regard created things as enemies, and to stay away from them. Lower the eyes, turn away the head! Flee from dangerous contacts! The moral took precedence over the theological; the flight from sin over charity and the union of charity. This description has no bearing whatsoever on the real life of the Church as it was actually carried on in the depths of her being; it has to do with that version of Christianity that reigned in the mind and afflicted the mores of the great mass, more or less badly instructed, of the people of God.

Besides, as a matter of fact, the process which I have pointed out did not (not yet) in ancient times cause such serious havoc. One lived in Christendom. One had the cult of the saints who always came to the rescue. In spite of everything, one felt oneself warmed in the bosom of the Church, and the theological still kept many means of asserting its supremacy. On the other hand, people were in general red-blooded enough and led a healthy enough life not to capsize in psychological troubles, and to maintain their equilibrium, all the while appreciating only too well this world of which one spoke so ill. They were in the custom of endowing masses, as often as they could, in order not to remain too long in purgatory, and in the meantime, they

[67] St. John of the Cross (to Ana de Peñalosa).

busied themselves vigorously with their happiness in this world, counting, not unreasonably, on the power of a firm and problemless faith and on God's generosity to have their skin saved at the last moment. In short, the practical manicheism and pelagianism which I have mentioned remained *external* parasites, like the lice on the head of St. Benedict Labre. They were not viruses attacking the substance of the Christian faith, and by the same stroke producing in it malignant reactions; for, as I have said at the beginning, this faith is allergic to any trace of manicheism.

It was in the nineteenth century, and still more in the first half of the twentieth, that everything took a decided turn for the worse. Then the virus penetrated into the substance. At the same time, the unconscious work which had for so long been carried on in secret took visible form. Men began to suffer seriously, at times cruelly, from a sort of invasion of practical manicheism, which chiefly affected educational procedures and piety, but had a much more general bearing and significance, and imposed a completely negativist attitude toward the world—with all the more aggressiveness as the world itself was making its claims and promises heard on all sides. From that moment, for a good many interior souls, the current vocabulary, with its reprobation of nature and the world, which was hitherto accepted as a matter of course in this particular rhetoric, grew increasingly difficult to bear, even when found in books as invaluable as *The Imitation of Christ* (as a result, the field of spiritual reading would one day turn out to be strangely restricted). Other souls rebelled. The mass of people felt that a grave injustice, against which they were defenseless, was committed with respect to the world, as well as with respect to themselves, and was of a nature to lead to disaster.

The kind of invasion of practical manicheism, whose effects were felt in this way, did not present itself as a doctrinal error formulated by the intellect and pronounced externally. No, it was spread *inwardly*, in the form of purely moralistic prohibitions, injunctions to flight, habits of fear, disciplines of denial in which love had no part, and which led the soul to starvation and sickliness, and to a torturing sense of impotence.

I stress this manichean-like aberration at this point, because it is part of the subject of the present chapter (the meaning of the world and the attitude of the Christian toward it), and is the poisonous fruit of that long misunderstanding I have been discussing in this section. I should add that this aberration took place in an unfortunate context which helped sensitize minds to it and, by that very fact, made its effects more damaging.

The hostility of a civilization in which Christianity—and especially such a disfigured Christianity—was called to question on all sides, and where science was held to be the enemy of religion; the weakening of natural defenses due to modern psychasthenia which was already so well kept going by psychiatrists, and the weakening of intellectual defenses due to a teaching extremely poor in matters of doctrine; the modernist crisis, with its first epidemic of itching ears and piously intended errors; and in the indispensable struggle against these errors, the almost exclusive recourse to disciplinary measures; the spiritual impoverishment of a Christian laity, who continued in general to imagine that the call to the perfection of charity, with what it implies of life of prayer and, as much as possible, of contemplative recollection, was the exclusive concern of the monks; the confusion and coalescence, which had been accepted as natural for two centuries, between the interests of religion and those of a social class furiously attached to its privileges,[68] in some members of which one saw noble virtues and religious customs, but among others, and more often, a comfortable practical atheism—all this is the context in which the rise of masked manicheism I have been discussing took place until the first third of the present century. All this was going to build up, in the unconscious of a great many Christians, clerics and laymen, an enormous weight of frustration, disillusionment, repressed doubts, resentment, bitterness, healthy desires sacrificed, with all the anxieties and pent-up aspirations of the unhappy conscience.

Comes the *aggiornamento*. Why be astonished that at the very announcement of a Council, then in the surroundings of it, and now after it, the enormous unconscious weight which I have just mentioned burst into the open in a kind of explosion that does no honor to the human intelligence? Thus, the Council appears as an island

[68] The date of the founding of the review *Esprit* in France (1932), and of the *Catholic Worker*, at nearly the same period in the United States, can be regarded as marking, at least symbolically, the point of rupture which announced the end of this confusion.

guarded by the Spirit of God in the middle of an ocean which is over-turning everything, the true and the false, pell-mell.

As far as the attitude of the Christian to the world is concerned, the pendulum was suddenly carried to the opposite extreme from the quasi-manichean contempt for the world professed in the Christian ghetto which we are in the process of leaving behind. This time, we no longer confront an aberration projected internally in forms that were somber and tormented, but an aberration which is projected externally, with all the glamor and happy arrogance of a reason maddened by frenzy for novelty. This is the second poisonous fruit, equally dangerous, if not more so than the first (on account of its intellectual character), but which will probably not last as long as the misunderstanding I have been discussing here. For when foolishness acquires such considerable dimensions among Christians, either it must be resorbed pretty quickly, or it will ultimately detach them from the Church. What foolishness? Kneeling before the world. This will be the subject of the fifth and last section of this chapter.

Schema XIII

THE TEACHING CHURCH, FOR ITS PART, HAS PUT AN END, THROUGH THE VOICE OF THE COUNCIL, TO THE LONG MISUNDERSTANDING MENTIONED ABOVE

Schema XIII—the *Pastoral Constitution on the Human Condition in Today's World*—is a document of great wisdom and admirable loyalty, even more significant, it seems to me, in its general approach than in its particular clarifications. What is paramount in such a teaching is not so much its analyses of today's problems, as correct as they are, but the exposition and complete clarification which it offers us of the attitude of the Church herself to the world, whether one considers the unalterable truths on which this attitude is based, or on the modalities required by the degree of evolution reached by the world of today.

When he sees to what degree this Pastoral Constitution is impregnated with the spirit and the basic views of the Angelic Doctor, an old Thomist like myself is cheered.

I think, in particular, that either Christians or non-Christians, all those who care for man and the future of civilization, are deeply in its debt for having made the human person, his dignity and his rights, the central theme of its vast teaching.

In this connection, let us at once take note of an especially important fact. The Pope, putting things clearly in focus, reminded us that the *aggiornamento* is in no way an adaptation of the Church to the world, as if the latter were supposed to establish norms for the former; it is a disclosure of the Church's own essential position. Well, the emphasis of schema XIII on the human person is a remarkable illustration of this truth. For is not a striking contrast between the Church and the world to be seen there? In that community of human persons which is a society, the Church, in keeping with the demands of truth, gives primacy to the person over the community; [69] whereas today's world gives primacy to the community over the person—a highly interesting and significant disagreement. In our age of civilization the Church will increasingly become—bless Her—the refuge and support (perhaps the only one) of the person. Those unfortunate clerics who do not see that would do well to re-read the Pastoral Constitution.

Allow me a parenthetical remark at this point. Thanks especially, I believe, to Emmanuel Mounier, the expression "personalist and communitarian" has become something of a catch phrase for French Catholic thought and rhetoric. I am not without some responsibility for this myself. At a time when it mattered very much to oppose to the totalitarian slogans a new—and true—one, I had gently solicited my gray cells, and finally, in one of my books of that period, advanced the phrase in question. It is from me, I believe, that Mounier got it. The expression is right, but when I see the way it is now being used, I

---

[69] I do not mean that this primacy forms the object of a particular phrase of the pastoral Constitution, but that for anyone who reads it with care, it is present and affirmed throughout *the overall framework of the Constitution*. What the pastoral Constitution brings to light is the fundamental fact that the human community is a community of persons; and that, accordingly, the common good itself demands respect for the rights of persons and the recognition of their essential aspirations. (Let us not forget that the common good of a community of persons is "common" in an eminent sense—that is, common *to the whole* and *to the parts*—and demands, therefore, to flow back on the latter, or to be distributed for the benefit of the persons who compose it. On the other hand, the goods toward which the human person tends insofar as the spiritual in him is concerned—and which, in the natural order itself, are, like truth and the things of God, *superior* to the temporal common good—overflow nevertheless upon this common good, assisting it and elevating it from above.)

am not very proud of it. For it is clear that after paying lip-service to the "personalist," it is really the "communitarian" which those who use it cherish.

But let us leave this parenthesis and return to schema XIII.

Its perspective is the same perspective—basically "ontosophic"—as that of Genesis and the *Summa theologica*. In other words, it considers the world and nature in their essential structures and in what constitutes them in themselves. This is indeed that perspective which had been neglected and ignored in an increasingly disastrous way during the last few centuries. It is this, therefore, that it was all-important to re-establish, clearly and unmistakably. To have stressed in the same document a totally different perspective, considering the world no longer in itself but in its relation to the kingdom of God, would have risked shuffling the cards by demanding of the intelligence of readers (to distinguish is a difficult and fatiguing job) an excessive and too painful effort. (I am afraid that is perhaps what I am about to do in the present chapter, but a peasant of the Garonne, who commits only himself, is, naturally enough, not afraid to stick his neck out, and can run risks which the Fathers of a holy Council have a duty to avoid.)

Placing itself, accordingly, in the perspective of Genesis and of the *Summa*—in other words, considering human nature and the world in the very elements which constitute their being—the Pastoral Constitution flatly affirms their radical goodness and the call to progress which, however thwarted by the ambiguity of matter and the wounds of sin, is inscribed in their essence. It shows, not merely in a general way, but in a very extended analysis, and with that total generosity which springs from divine charity, how the Church, even while remaining within the sphere of her spiritual mission and of the *things which are God's*, can and wants to assist the world and the human race in their endeavor to advance toward their temporal goals.

Indeed, it is the perennial doctrine of the Church which we see thereby reaffirmed—but with new and singularly important notes: it is reaffirmed *under the sign of freedom*—no longer to claim the Church's right to intervene *ratione peccati* in worldly affairs in order to repress evil (that, I believe, she will always be obliged to do, in one form or another), but to declare her right, and her will, to quicken, prod and assist from above (*ratione boni perficiendi*, if I may put it that way) and without trespassing on the autonomy of the temporal, the developments of the world toward a greater good to be attained.

The message of the Church to the age is now formulated in a decidedly and blessedly widened manner—no longer as though addressed to a Christendom which was formerly "sacral" and is now more or less secularized, but as addressed to the entire world and to the whole of mankind, to the "profane" civilization which is that of today, and is now in the process of being extended to all peoples.

The Pastoral Constitution thus opens up immense horizons. We can say that it is the final liquidation of that masked manicheism which I spoke of at such length, which had poisoned several centuries of history, until in our day it had created an untenable psychological situation, and provoked, in reaction, the most serious crisis.

As to the present crisis itself, with all the confusions, follies and denials it carries with it, and with that *fascinatio nugacitatis* to which it exposes the Christian soul, it will only be liquidated in its turn by a great and patient work of revitalizing in the order of intelligence and the order of spirituality. All that the Pastoral Constitution could do and should do from this point of view, was to lay the foundations for such a work on a solid and well-swept terrain, by serenely establishing in their exact meaning—and by the same token, tearing away from error—the truths which error was exploiting and disfiguring. We owe it a great debt because it is the *effective beginning* of the liquidation of the present crisis. The positions of the teaching Church appear clearly henceforth. As far as she is concerned, she has, through the Council, put an end from now on to the misunderstanding from which Catholic thought has too long suffered as regards the things of the world.

But among a good many Christians the misunderstanding continues and grows worse.

Kneeling Before the World

FACTUAL BEHAVIOR AND THOUGHT MORE OR LESS CONFUSED

The present crisis has many diverse aspects. One of the most curious spectacles it offers us is a kind of *kneeling before the world*, which is revealed in a thousand ways.

As we have seen, the word "world" can be understood in a number of different ways. Before what "world," then, are people kneeling? The world considered in its natural and temporal structures? Why certainly. But considered *only* in that sense, as a good many of those who kneel seem to believe or would like to believe? I mean, the pure world of science, of astronomers and geologists, physicists and biologists, psychologists, ethnologists, sociologists, as well as the world of technicians, manufacturers, trade unionists, statesmen? Come now! Have you ever seen a scientist genuflecting to the world (unless by chance he is a Jesuit, but then he is not a pure scientist, he is an apologist in disguise)? Have you ever seen a statesman genuflect to the world (unless he is not a statesman but a megalomaniac like Adolf Hitler)? That a good many Christians today kneel before the world is a fact perfectly clear. And this is what we have to look at first of all. But of what world precisely are we dealing with here? In other words, what do these Christians have in their mind, what do they think in behaving this way? This is a good deal more obscure because for the most part they think very little and confusedly. That will give us a second question to examine.

What then do we see around us? In large sectors of both clergy and laity (but it is the clergy who set the example), hardly is the word "world" pronounced when a gleam of ecstasy lights up the face of one and all. And immediately what is talked about are the necessary *épanouissements* (blossomings of dear human nature) and the necessary *engagements* (commitments), as well as the communitarian fervors, and the *présences*, the *ouvertures* (openings to the dear world), and their joys. Anything that would risk calling to mind the idea of asceticism, mortification, or penance is automatically shelved as a matter of course. (If Lourdes remains popular, the words pronounced by the Virgin who appeared there are not.) And fasting is in such bad repute that it is better to say nothing of the one by which Jesus prepared for His public mission. A friend of mine recently heard the Litany of the Saints recited in the vernacular in his parish church. When the priest reached the invocation: *per baptismum et sanctum jejunium tuum* (through your baptism and holy fasting) he confined himself to saying "through your baptism," without further ado. (We do not fast, therefore the Lord didn't fast either.) On another occasion, in the same church, my friend actually heard the line

of St. Paul: "A thorn was given me in the flesh, an angel of Satan to
harass me" [70] become "I am having trouble with my health." As to
the repugnance felt by our Catholics for fasting, it is not without
some interest to note that it is occurring in the very time when the
disciples of Ghandi have demonstrated the virtues of fasting on the
level of natural mystique and non-violent resistance.

Sex is one of the great and tragic realities of the world. It is curious
to see how much interest, carried to the point of veneration, is manifested in this subject by a crowd of Levites vowed to continence.
Virginity and chastity have a bad press. Marriage, on the other hand,
is fervently idealized, love is its essence. Of its nature, it claims to be
nothing but mutual enchantment, the delight of seeing one's self reflected in the eyes of the other. What is more beautiful than a pair
of young lovers? That's certainly quite true, especially in the works of
the great sculptors. But it's no reason for us to kiss the ground under
their feet.

I know very well that behind the silliness to which I am referring
there is the necessary and urgent awareness of serious (increasingly
serious as time goes on) and often torturous problems. I know very
well that too many people are living in despair, that there are too
many with pent-up anxieties, that far from being a life of delightful
love and mutual gentleness, marriage too often means mutual solitude
and daily apprehension; that too many situations call not only for
pity but for a new attitude on the part of those who have to judge of
them. I think that the Church, who is at last submitting these problems as a whole to a thorough study, can never be too attentive in enlightening the human being about them, nor too merciful to him in
his distresses. The fact remains that none of this makes any less silly
the Catholic veneration of the Flesh to which so many Sheep of
Panurge's are inviting us today. Such a veneration would rather be of
a nature to make us regret the ancient pagan cults of Sex and Fertil-
ity which at least were not pieces of trickery.

The other great reality which faces us in the world is Earthly social
Life with all its conflicts, its sorrows, and its immense set of problems:
starvation, destitution, war, and social and racial injustice. We know
that we must struggle unceasingly against these evils, there is no
need for me to reconsider here what I have said of the temporal mis-

[70] St. Paul, 2 Cor. 12:7.

sion of the Christian. Nevertheless, this struggle is not our one and only duty because the earth and the earthly social life are not the one and only reality. This temporal duty, moreover, is really and truly accomplished by the Christian only if the life of grace and prayer makes natural energies more pure and upright in the very order of nature.

That is what, at the present, many generous Christians refuse to see. Accordingly, at least in practice and in their way of acting, and even—for those who are boldest and most determined to go the whole way—in doctrine and in their way of thinking (of thinking about the world and their own religion), the great concern and the only thing that matters for them is the temporal vocation of the human race, with its march, embattled but victorious, to justice, peace, and happiness. Instead of realizing that our devotion to the temporal task must be that much firmer and more ardent since we know that the human race will never succeed on this earth in delivering itself completely from evil—because of the wounds of Adam, and because our ultimate end is supernatural—they make of these earthly goals the truly supreme end for humanity.

In other words, there is henceforth only the earth. A complete *temporalization of Christianity!* I said before that for the most part those Christians who kneel before the world don't do much thinking. To those who have pushed their thinking further, occasionally with a rigorous and superb logic, this conclusion appears clearly. And so we hold it at last: the Thought which the Christians kneeling before the world have in their heads; which, as I said at the beginning of this section, formed for us the object of a second question to be examined. They all have this Thought, but those who think in a confused way manage somehow never to discern it. If by some chance it were spelled out for them, many would rush to disavow it, some with horror.

The idea of the double movement in which the Christian is engaged, the march toward *beatitude* (not simple "happiness") and toward the kingdom of God—which has already come (it is the Church), but which will reach fulfillment and be fully revealed only in glory and in eternity—and at the same time the march toward the above-mentioned triple and progressive expansion and the conquests to be achieved by man—this true notion makes way to the idea of a natural Evolution which the liberty of the human being has to activate and accelerate, and which is drawing the entire world toward some glorious parousia of the collective Man: which implies contradiction, moreover (but that matters little to the grandchildren of Hegel), for if there is a final term and parousia, evolution stops, whereas the very essence of man and of earthly life demands that it continue without end . . .

Be that as it may, the distinction between the temporal and the spiritual, between the things that are Caesar's and the things that are God's, inevitably becomes blurred for the fascinated Christians of whom I am speaking. The more determined of them are already flatly denying it. That is self-evident: since the kingdom of God has no reality beyond the world, it is only a leaven in the dough *of the world*. If Christ (after all, cannot a broad-minded enough religion consider that he probably is God—as the greatest of men, a sublime flower of the human race, in whom the Soul of the world has fully concentrated itself?), if Christ has a mystical Body, it is the world which is that mystical Body.

We asked ourselves earlier before what "world" many Christians are kneeling today. Now we have the answer. It is the world of nature, yes, the world in its natural and temporal structures, but insofar as it supposedly absorbs into itself the kingdom of God, and is itself—in a state of becoming, and, at the final end, in perfect fullness—the mystical Body of Christ.

We can understand henceforth why there are three things an intelligent preacher should never speak about, and which an up-to-date Christian should think about as seldom as possible, although one has to recite the Creed each Sunday (but there are so many myths therein; and besides, one can always repeat a formula—even in the vernacular—without stopping to think about it).

The first thing to leave in oblivion is obviously *the other world* (since there isn't any).

The second thing to leave in oblivion is *the cross* (it is only a symbol of the momentary sacrifices demanded by progress).

The third thing to leave in oblivion is *sanctity*—if it is true that sanctity has its principle, at the center of the soul (even if the saint remains plunged in the activities of the world) in a radical break with the world (in the Gospel sense of the word) and with the false god of the world, its *mythical* god, "the Emperor of this world."

THE SAINTS AND THE WORLD

I take the liberty of insisting thereon: if Christians, in effect, were to renounce keeping in their hearts the *desire for sanctity* (even if they only desire it very distantly, excessively distantly, even if they live in evil), this would be an ultimate betrayal against God and *against the world*.

The saints participate throughout the course of time in the redeeming work of Jesus on behalf of the world. Their personal relation to the world is paradoxical and mysterious. For them, it seems to me, the world is above all an occasion for *dying to themselves* in order to be entirely delivered up by love to Love.

Taking up again what I wrote in a small book already a good many years old,[71] let us try, I would say, to imagine what takes place in the soul of a saint at the crucial moment when he makes his first irrevocable decision. Let us picture to ourselves St. Francis of Assisi when he throws away his clothing and appears naked before his bishop, or St. Benedict Labre when he decides to become a lice-infested beggar vagabonding along the roads. At the root of such an act there was something so profound in the soul that one does not know how to express it—let us say that it is a simple refusal, a total, stable, supremely active refusal to accept things as they are: it is not a question here of knowing whether things and nature and the face of this world are good in their essence—yes, they are, being is good in the very measure to which it is, grace perfects nature and does not destroy it—but these truths have nothing to do with the act of interior rupture that we are considering. This act has to do with a fact, an existential fact: things as they are are intolerable. In the reality of existence the world is infected with lying, injustice, wickedness, distress, and misery; creation has been corrupted by sin to such an extent that in the very marrow of his soul, the saint refuses to accept it as it is. Evil—I mean by that

[71] *La Signification de L'Athéisme Contemporain* (Paris: Desclée De Brouwer, 1949).

the power of sin, and the universal suffering which it drags in its wake
—evil is such that the only thing he has immediately at hand to oppose it totally, and that intoxicates the saint with liberty, exultation,
and love, is to give everything, to abandon everything, the sweetness
of the world, and what is good, and what is better, and what is delect-
able and permitted, and more than anything, himself, in order to be
free to be with God. To do this is to be totally stripped and given
over in order to seize the power of the cross; it is to die for those he
loves. This is a flash of intuition and will above any order of human
morality. Once the soul of a man has been touched in flight by this
burning wing it becomes a stranger everywhere. It can fall in love
with things, never will it take repose in them. The saint is alone in
treading the wine press, and among the peoples there is no one with
him.[72]

As for the one I just called the Emperor of this world, he is the
false god of the philosophers when, knowing of the existence of the
supreme Being, they fail to recognize his glory, deny the abyss of liberty which his transcendance signifies, and chain him to the world
which he himself has made: a false god responsible for the world but
powerless to redeem it, who would only be the supreme guarantee
and justification of the fabric of the world, and would give his sanc-
tion to every evil as well as to every good at work in the world; a god
who would bless injustice and slavery and misery, and make the tears
of children and the agony of the innocent a pure and simple ingredient of the sacred necessities of the eternal cycles or of the evolution.
Such a god would be the unique supreme Being, to be sure, but
transformed into an idol, the naturalist God of nature, the Jupiter of
this world, the great God of the idolators, of the mighty on their
thrones, and the rich in their earthly glory, of success without law
and pure fact erected into law. With respect to such a god, the saint
is a complete atheist [73]. . . . Such kinds of atheists are the mysterious
pillars of heaven. They give the world that supplement of soul, as
Bergson said, which the world needs.

But if the other world is done away with, and if, by the same

[72] Isaiah, 63:3.

[73] "Were not the Jews and the early Christians often treated as atheists by the
pagans at the time of the Roman Empire? There was a hidden meaning in this
outrage." (*Ibid.*, p. 28.) Cf. St. Justin, *First Apology*, VI, 1: "That is why we are
called atheists; indeed, we admit it, we are the atheists of these pretended gods."

token, God loses his infinite transcendence, then there is no longer
any Heavenly Father, there is only the Emperor of this world, before
whom everyone should kneel. And the atheists of this false god are
finished, Christians are on their knees before the world, and the
world has lost the saints.

THE INSANE MISTAKE

At the close of our reflections on the age-old misunderstanding
from which Christian thought has suffered in regard to the world, we
are thus brought back to the curious kneeling of which the spectacle
is offered today by believers whose faith in God needs to be re-invig-
orated by the blood transfusion of a passionate faith in the world.

What do we find at the origin of this kneeling? An insane mistake
—the confusion between two completely different senses in which
the same word "world" is being understood.

There is, as we have seen, an "ontosophic truth" about the world
considered in its natural structures or in what properly constitutes it;
in this sense we must say that the world is fundamentally *good*.

And there is a "religious" or "mystical" truth about the world considered in its ambiguous relationship to the kingdom of God and the
Incarnation. Then we must say that the world, insofar as it accepts to
be assumed into the kingdom, is *saved*; while insofar as it refuses the
kingdom, and encloses itself in the lust of the flesh, the lust of the
eyes, and the pride of the spirit, it is the *adversary* of Christ and his
disciples, and *hates* them.

Well, when people muddle these two understandings of the word
"world," by imagining that the first truth concerning the world de-
stroys the second, because it signifies that *there is no kingdom of God
distinct from the world*, and that *the world absorbs into itself this
kingdom*, then it is the world itself which is the kingdom of God, in a
state of becoming (and, at the final end, in glory). And it hasn't the
slightest need to be saved from above, nor to be assumed and finally
transfigured in Another world, a divine world. God, Christ, the
Church, the sacraments, are intrinsic to the world, as constituting its
soul which fashions little by little its body and its supra-individual
personality. It is from within, and by means of its soul, itself at work

within it, that the world will be saved, or rather that it saves itself and exalts itself. Down on your knees, then, with Hegel and his followers, before this illusory world; to it our faith, our hope, our love! We are more Christian than ever since Christ is in it, and is consubstantial with it (if I may employ a word so ill-considered by the French translators of the Creed).

Reality nevertheless remains what it is, not what we would like it to be. In fact God is infinitely transcendent; in fact there is a supernatural order which is the order of grace; in fact there was an event called the Incarnation of the eternal Word; in fact there is Another world, which is the kingdom of God already begun. And thus in spite of our dreams, in kneeling before the world, it is not of a world which would absorb into itself the kingdom of God, it is of a world which refuses all that, and which wants neither Christ ("*the world hates me*") nor the kingdom of God, it is of the world withdrawn into itself, and enemy of the Gospel that we are *friends*. It is to this world and the false god who is its Emperor (and not merely, as we perhaps believe unless we take the trouble to reflect a little, before the world of nature and of science) that we are genuflecting.

Such is the mistake of the Christians who are led astray by our moment in history and the sudden displacement of the pendulum, now flung to the opposite extreme from the masked manicheism which, for a century and a half, has wrought disastrous havoc.

At this point it is suitable to say with particular insistence: *haec oportebat facere, et illa non omittere*, "These things you ought to have done, and the others not to have omitted." [74] It was necessary to struggle against the world as the adversary of the saints, but without neglecting (this is said for the past) to devote oneself to the temporal progress of a world oppressed by injustice and misery. And it is necessary to dedicate ourselves to this temporal progress, but without neglecting (this is said for today) to struggle against the world as the adversary of the saints.

Not only are the two tasks compatible, they call for one another. The temporal progress of the world requires the re-enforcement that comes from the kingdom of God elevating and enlightening souls, accordingly requires the struggle against the world insofar as it is the enemy of the kingdom. The progress of souls toward the kingdom of

74 Matt. 23:23.

God requires them to love the world with that love which is charity as a creature of God on the way to its own natural ends, and therefore to cooperate in its temporal struggle against injustice and misery.

After all, why should I not point out that for thirty or forty years, I myself, to the extent of my powers, have borne witness to the necessity of this twofold task, as well as to the two contrasting truths (according to the point of view in which one is placed) that we must at all costs maintain on the subject of the world? Summarizing all this, I wrote in On the Philosophy of History: "The fact of so many millions of men starving and living in despair, in a life unworthy of man, is an insult to Christ and to brotherly love. As a result, the temporal mission of the Christian is to strive to eradicate such evils, and to try to build up a Christian-inspired social and political order, where justice and brotherhood will be better and better served." [75] And in the same book I also wrote: "St. Paul has said: 'All who desire to live a godly life in Christ Jesus will suffer persecution.' [76] It is certainly not a very optimistic statement with respect to the world. The Christian, because he is not of the world, will always be a foreigner in the world —I mean, in the world as separating itself from the kingdom of God and shutting itself up in itself; he is incomprehensible to the world and inspires it with uneasiness and distrust. The world cannot make sense of the theological virtues. Theological faith, the world sees as a challenge, an insult, and a threat; it is by reason of their faith that it dislikes Christians, it is through their faith that they vanquish it; faith is enough to divide them from the world. Theological hope, the world does not see at all; it is simply blind to it. Theological charity, the world sees the wrong way; it misapprehends it, is mistaken about it. It confuses it with any kind of quixotic devotion to whatever human cause it may profit by. And thus does the world tolerate charity, even admire it—insofar as it is not charity, but something else. (And so charity is the secret weapon of Christianity.)" [77]

If there are any prophets of the avant-garde or of the rear guard who imagine that our duties to the world, such as they have been brought to light under the grace of the Holy Spirit by the Second

[75] On the Philosophy of History, op. cit., p. 154.
[76] 2 Tim. 3:12.
[77] On the Philosophy of History, op. cit., p. 148.

Vatican Council, erase what the Lord Jesus Himself and His apostles have said of the world—*The world hates me, The world cannot receive the Spirit of truth, If anyone loves the world the love of the Father is not in him,* and all the other texts that I recalled earlier—I know well what must be said of such prophets (a saying of questionable taste but one which used to amuse an old Dominican dear to my heart): they are poking the *finger of God* in their eye.

February 14, 1966

4   THE TRUE NEW FIRE

CHRISTIANS AND
NON-CHRISTIANS

THE ANNOUNCEMENT OF A NEW AGE

On the duration of the crisis I have just been discussing, the reactions
it will produce, the rubble it will leave in its wake, the gravity that it
can assume at certain moments or in certain countries, one would
have to be a prophet to hazard the slightest opinion. Everything depends on the unforeseeable ways of God and his secret graces, together with human liberty, comprised as it is in his eternal plan. What
is certain is that the Church will emerge from this crisis wonderfully
purified; error will not have got the better of her.

It is certain also, as so many voices rightly tell us, that the Vatican
Council was *the announcement of a new age.* As I have noted before
and have no need of repeating, the Council itself sketched the broad
outlines of this new age when it *aggiornamented* the eternal treasures
of the Church, thanks to a more profound awareness and a more complete explanation of certain great truths hitherto contained in these
treasures.

On the other hand, we can observe that by a paradox not rare in
human history, what is disfigured and distorted frequently appears
before what is straight, the counterfeit product before the authentic
thing. If I am not mistaken, there were more or less heretical
fraticelli before St. Francis of Assisi. Didn't Habacuc say that the
devil marches before the feet of God? [1] One can imagine him easily
enough as a cur yelping and snarling before the feet of the Lord and
biting whoever he can. Instead of saying the "devil," the best modern
translators say the "plague," which suits my purpose just as well, since

[1] Habac. 3:5.

what I actually have in mind is the dangerous fever of veneration for the world which is raging today among a certain number of naive but often quite generous people.

Obsolete from the instant they make their appearance, the different forms of neo-modernism with which we have been concerned in the preceding chapters are products of anticipated counterfeit which set the mind off in a false track. The true new fire, the genuine discoveries which will occur in the new age we are entering, and by means of which, in the historic perspectives opened by the Council, Christian consciousness will penetrate deeper and further into the truth by which it lives and the evangelical reality, will have nothing in common with the collection of old repressed desires and confused ambitions with which the public relations men of the Old Liar are operating. Nor will it have anything in common with their pseudo-scientific and pseudo-philosophical claptrap, nor with that holy parousia of Man in the name of which they call for a Christian kneeling before the world.

The true new fire, the essential renewal, will be an *inner* renewal. One need not be a prophet to see that; it is enough to open one's eyes. To speak with competence on the different aspects of this inner renewal, it would be necessary to have an intelligence above the average, like all those who exchange ideas on television. It is very timidly, then, that I shall try to say something about that in this chapter and those that follow, as an old man who blinks his eyes and isn't very intelligent (which is not too serious) but who, for all that, is not a child of light (which is vexing). For it has been said (what follows is a loose translation): "The children of light are far from knowing their business as astutely as the children of the age." [2] Indeed, that is rather obvious.

PRACTICAL COOPERATION IN A DIVIDED WORLD

This chapter will deal with the renewal of our thought (and consequently, our behavior) toward non-Christians.

To begin with, one can consider Christians and non-Christians simply *insofar as they are men.* This is merely an introduction or

[2] Luke 16:8.

preliminary consideration of the subject; it is useful all the same.

Holding myself then, to begin with, in this perspective, allow me to use here a few passages from a speech I delivered some twenty years ago to a conference of UNESCO. (It will give an old hand like me a chance to catch his breath and, come to think of it, it was not so badly put, although in a style which is no longer mine.) It was the problem of peace among nations that occupied our minds, and it was in terms of this problem that I took for my theme "The Possibilities of Cooperation in a Divided World." [3] I asked: In this world prostrated by post-war grief, and by the leaden mantle of rival economic, political and ideological interests, shall not those who are dedicated to the works of the mind and who feel the responsibility of such a mission give voice to the primitive instinct for preservation, to the immense longing for peace and freedom, to the repudiation of death and misfortune which, despite a strange apparent passivity more closely resembling despair than strength of soul, are stirring within the deepest recesses of men's consciousness? Yet, at first glance there is something paradoxical in UNESCO's task: it implies intellectual agreement among men whose conceptions of the world, of culture, of knowledge itself are different or even mutually opposed. They belong not merely to different civilizations, but to antagonistic spiritual families and philosophic schools. How is an agreement of thought conceivable between them?

My response was that the finality of UNESCO was a practical finality, and hence "agreement among its members can be spontaneously achieved, not on common speculative notions, but on common practical notions; not on the affirmation of the same conception of the world, man and knowledge, but on the affirmation of the same set of convictions concerning action. This is doubtless very little; it is the last refuge of intellectual agreement among men. It is, however, enough to undertake a great work."

When it is a question, not of a common *speculative* ideology, nor of common *explanatory* principles, but, on the contrary, of the basic

[3] This speech was given in Mexico on November 1, 1947, at the opening of the second International Conference of UNESCO; I was the president of the French delegation. (The complete text is in my book, *Le Philosophe dans la Cité*, Paris; Alsatia, 1960); the English translation makes up Ch. XIII of my previously published collection, *The Range of Reason* (New York: Charles Scribner's Sons, 1952), Ch. XIII, pp. 172–184.

practical ideology and the basic principles of *action* implicitly recognized today, in a vital if not a formulated manner, by the consciousness of free peoples, this happens to constitute *grosso modo* a sort of common residue, a sort of unwritten common law, at the point of practical convergence of extremely different theoretical ideologies and spiritual traditions. To understand that, it is sufficient to distinguish properly between the rational justifications, inseparable from the spiritual dynamism of a philosophical doctrine or a religious faith, and the practical conclusions which, separately justified for each, are, for all, analogically common principles of action. I am fully convinced that my way of justifying the belief in the rights of man and the ideal of liberty, equality, fraternity, is the only one which is solidly based on truth. That does not prevent me from agreeing on these practical tenets with those who are convinced that their way of justifying them, entirely different from mine, or even opposed to mine in its theoretical dynamism, is likewise the only one that is based on truth. Assuming they both believe in the democratic charter, a Christian and a rationalist will, nevertheless, give justifications that are incompatible with each other, to which their souls, their minds and their blood are committed, and about these justifications they will fight. And God keep me from saying that it is not important to know which of the two is right! That is essentially important. They remain, however, in agreement on the practical affirmation of that charter, and they can formulate together common principles of action.

Thus, in my opinion, can the paradox I pointed out earlier be solved. The ideological agreement which is necessary between those who work toward making science, culture and education contribute to the establishment of a true peace, is restricted to a certain body of practical points and of principles of action. But within these limits there is, and there must be, an ideological agreement which, for all its merely practical nature, is none the less of major importance. In the justification he offers for that body of practical principles, everyone commits himself fully, with all of his philosophical and religious convictions—how could he speak with faith, if not in the light of the speculative convictions which quicken his thought? But he is not entitled to demand that others subscribe to his own justification of the practical principles on which all agree. And the practical principles in question form a sort of charter which is indispensable for any effective common action, and the formulation of which would matter to the good itself and the success of the peace-making work to which their common endeavors are dedicated.[4]

It was on these bases that some years later the United Nations formulated the Universal Declaration of the Rights of Man—a document of great historic significance. Naturally, it is just as important to refrain from indulging in illusions. And it is clear that in the manner of applying the practical principles formulated in common, considerable differences are to appear, due to the spirit, the theoretical convictions, the religious faith or the philosophical dogmas which inspire and make larger and more exalted, or narrower and lower, the action of those who, in this case, do not merely formulate, but put existentially the practical principles in question to work. Did I not note at the beginning that an agreement of thought on common principles which are merely practical is very little indeed—*"the last refuge of agreement among minds"*—in other words, a bare minimum, so much the more necessary since without it there is nothing left but inexpiable conflict, the mortal war to which the dissensions now tearing the world asunder would, if left to themselves, lead?

The fact remains that, as I said at the close of my address in Mexico, we all know that if the work of peace is to be prepared in the thought of men and in the consciousness of nations, it is on the condition that minds come to be deeply convinced of principles like the following: Good politics is first and foremost a politics that is just—every people should strive to understand the psychology, the development and traditions, the material and moral needs, the proper dignity and historic calling of the other peoples, because every people should look out not only for its own advantages but for the common good of the assembly of nations—this awakening of mutual understanding and of the sense of the civilized community, though it supposes (given the age-old habits of human history) a sort of spiritual revolution, nevertheless answers requirements of public emergency in a world which, from now on, is one world for life or for death, while it remains disastrously divided as to political passions and interests—to place national interest above everything is a sure means of losing everything—a community of free men is only conceivable if it recognizes that truth is the expression of what *is*, and right the expression of what is *just*, and not of what is most expedient

[4] Cf. *The Range of Reason*, pp. 180–181.

at a given time for the interest of the human group—it is not permissible to take the life of an innocent man because he has become a useless and costly burden to the nation, or because he impedes the successful undertakings of any group whatsoever—the human person is endowed with a dignity which the very good of the community presupposes and must, for its own sake, respect, and is also endowed, whether as a civic, or as a social or working person, with certain fundamental rights and fundamental obligations—the common good comes before private interests—the world of labor has a right to the social transformations required by its coming of age in human history, and the masses have a right to participate in the common treasure of culture and of the spirit—the domain of consciences is inviolable—men of various beliefs and spiritual lineages must recognize each other's rights as fellow-citizens in the civilized community—it is the duty of the State, for the very sake of the common good, to respect religious freedom as well as freedom of research—the basic equality of men makes prejudices of race, class or caste, and racial discrimination, offenses against human nature and the dignity of the person as well as a deep-seated threat to peace.

If a state of peace worthy of the name, firm and enduring, is to be established one day among the peoples of the world, this will depend not only upon the economic, political and financial arrangements reached by diplomats and statesmen, nor will it depend solely upon the juridical building up of a truly supra-national co-ordinating organism endowed with efficient means of action; it will depend also upon the deep adherence of men's consciousness to practical principles like those I have recalled. And, to state things as they are, it will depend also upon that *bigger soul* which, according to Bergson, our world, become technically greater, needs, and upon a victorious outpouring of that supreme and free energy which comes to us from on high, and whose name we know—whatever may be our religious denomination or school of thought—to be brotherly love, a name which has been pronounced in such a manner by the Gospel that it has stirred the conscience of man for all time.[5]

I hope these long explanations will be excused. I had to make as clear as possible, in a particular example, this somewhat doctoral yet indeed far-reaching assertion that if men are genuinely to cooperate in view of certain objectives which have to do with the common good of

[5] *Op. cit.*, pp. 183–184.

mankind, it will be only on condition that they can establish an intellectual agreement on the basis of common practical principles in spite of their irreducible divisions on the level of speculative convictions. In other words, on condition that they are able to formulate together certain common principles of action.

We can be sure that what is true in the case of this objective—peace to be assured among nations—is similarly true when it comes to any other objective of major importance for human welfare.

We need only to add that once all this is clear, and we have firmly rejected the once haughty and queer idea that divisions and oppositions in the speculative domain, however radical and irreducible, destroy any chance of genuinely effective agreement and practical cooperation, and condemn us either to perpetual wars, or to subordinating everything to the victory (by strength of argument or force of arms) of one philosophical or religious creed over all the others, we should also beware of deviating in an opposite direction with not less, but even more, catastrophic results. For it would amount to ignoring the imprescriptible rights of the *speculative order*—in other words, of truth itself, which is superior to every human interest. It could happen that in the name of realizing an agreement on the level of practical principles and of action, we would be tempted either to ignore or to forget our speculative convictions because they clash with each other, or else to dilute, conceal, or camouflage their opposition by making the yes and no kiss one another—and betraying *what is*—for the good looks of human brotherhood. This would not only be throwing truth to the dogs, but throwing to the dogs human dignity as well, and our supreme *raison d'être*. The more we fraternize on the level of practical principles and common action, the more we should strengthen the edges of the opposite convictions which divide us in the speculative order and on the level of truth, the first to be served.

BROTHERLY LOVE AMONG MEN WHO ARE ALL (AT LEAST POTENTIALLY) MEMBERS OF CHRIST

The preceding was only a preliminary consideration. I come now to something much more significant and much more important, in which I see one of the features of the new age we are entering and of the true new fire that has been kindled in our hearts.

Here I am no longer considering Christians and non-Christians simply *as men*. I am considering them *as members of Christ*: explicitly and visibly members of Christ if they are Christians (living members if they have grace, "dead" members if they have lost it); members of Christ implicitly and invisibly if being non-Christians they have Christ's grace; [6] potentially and invisibly members of Christ if being similarly non-Christians they do not have Christ's grace.

I don't know if the vocabulary I have just used is perfectly exact: that's a question for the author of *The Church of the Word Incarnate*. But what I do know is that in one guise or another and in one way or another, *all men*, at least potentially, are members of Christ, since he came into this world and suffered death for all of them and, since, barring a refusal on their part at the final instant of their life, he has saved all of them. And didn't Christ himself say that whenever we give or do not give food or drink to any man whatever, as soon as he is in want, we are giving (or refusing to give) to Him? To Him because this poor man *is* a member, at least potentially, of Christ's body.

Nothing is superior to truth. But on the level of action there are practical truths toward which viewpoints mutually opposed on the level of speculative truth can converge. That is why, as we have seen, there can be agreement and cooperation in regard to action and purely practical principles, between men who are divided in their deepest convictions.

Now, in our present remarks, it is no longer by reason of a practical common goal and an action to be conducted in common that men must reach agreement on practical common principles; it is by reason of a reality infinitely more important, though perfectly invisible, and which is not a thing *to do*, but which *is there*, at least potentially—the fact of their belonging to the Mystical Body through grace; and it is by reason of fraternal love to which all are called, and of divine charity to which all are called, that we ought to *suppose* that each has in his heart ("suppose," because no one can judge the inmost recesses of the soul)—it is by reason of this mysterious supernatural reality that men, as divided as they might be in their most profound convictions, can and should look each other in the eyes with respect,

[6] They are members of Christ *in act* since they have grace and charity, but without the consequences which, of its nature, this "in act" demands to have, being made explicit.

and desire a true mutual comprehension, and be ready to help one another sincerely.

How can this happen? By knowing (I am speaking of Christians, and Christians know this) that they are all members of Christ, at least potentially, and all called to the life of grace and charity; and by each one presupposing (I am still speaking of Christians) that the other lives in the grace and charity of God. When it comes to non-Christians, they can do this by making *an analogous supposition,* each from his own religious or philosophical standpoint (even if, in the case of the atheist, it is only the perspective of universal human solidarity and the common vocation of mankind), on levels of thought more or less inferior in the scale when compared to the level of those to whom God's Word has been revealed.

Having said that, I will pause for a moment. After all, it is to Christians that I'm actually speaking in this book (my last, I hope). And it is first and foremost for Christians that the Council was the proclamation of a new age. It is first and foremost from Christians and among Christians that a genuine renewal is to be expected. It is first and foremost in them that the true new fire should be kindled. It is therefore natural that my reflections should turn especially to them, considered in their relations—henceforth profoundly renewed—with non-Christians.

If what I have advanced earlier is true, they have to treat with non-Christians, not, certainly, by forgetting that the latter are not Christians, but by attaching to this fact, which is visible, a secondary importance so far as their own personal attitude toward them goes. The primary importance here belongs to another fact, an invisible one: that these non-Christians *are*, at least potentially, members of Christ.

Thereby we can see to what extent the new fire, the essential renewal, is an inner renewal. For it consists of a change of attitude, or a displacement of values that takes place in the deepest recesses of the soul, and has to do, first of all and essentially, not with any way of acting or externally behaving (that will come, but as a corollary), nor with any method of approach or apostolate, any tactic or strategy, or any honest and white trickery to try out on our non-Christian brothers, but with a way of *seeing* them before God, and a way of loving them *better*, in a deeper and more genuine conformity with the spirit of the Gospel. This inner renewal consists in becoming fully aware of the dimensions and "weight" of evangelical love, and in completely liberating this love in the soul, so that no final purpose, however lofty, exterior to its own essence, can come to mark out a road for it and restrict it to a particular object.

What I mean (to speak in general and of the inner attitude of the average Christian) is that for a long time we loved non-Christians— truly and sincerely—*although they were not Christians* (it was this *visible* fact which took precedence). In other words, we loved non-Christians primarily inasmuch as, having the misfortune not to be Christians, they were called to become so; we loved them primarily not as men or for what they *were*, but as *Christians to be* or for what they are *called to become*. We loved them primarily as people sitting in the shadow of death, toward whom our first duty of charity was to strive to convert them to the true faith. But now, by virtue of the great inner reversal I am stressing, we love non-Christians above all because they are, *at least potentially, members of Christ* (the *invisible* fact has now taken precedence); we love them primarily as human persons who are members, at least potentially, of this incarnate Truth whom they do not know and whom the errors professed by them deny. In short, we love them first of all in their own unfathomable mystery, for what *they are,* and as men in regard to whom the first duty of charity is simply *love.* And so, we love them first and foremost the way they are, and in seeking their own good, toward which, in actual existence, they have to advance within a religious universe and a system of spiritual and cultural values where great errors may abound, but where truths worthy of respect and of love are likewise certainly present. Through these truths, it is possible for the One who made them, for the Truth who is Christ, to touch their hearts in secret, without themselves or anyone in the world being aware of it.

No doubt, it is always in this way and with this evangelical love fully liberated in the soul, that the great missionaries loved those to whom they were sent to announce the Gospel. It was in this manner and with such a love that St. Francis Xavier loved them and that Pére Lebbe loved them. But I would note in the first place that this holy reality which dwelt within them and animated everything in them, and which is the soul of all missionary action worthy of the Gospel, was lived by them at so deep a level that they themselves

surely were aware of it, but without feeling, I think, a need to consider it apart from their mission as apostles of the Gospel, precisely
because it was an integral part of this mission. In their time such an
aspect of the inner Christian behavior had not yet been brought out
as a special matter of attention and reflection for common consciousness, and no other kind of "mission" of the Christian with respect to
the non-Christian—like the prophetic mission of Pére de Foucauld
who went and buried himself among the Berbers for the sole purpose
of loving them and understanding them with love—had yet been explicitly recognized and brought to light.

In the second place, I note (and here I must be very careful, I am
treading on dangerous ground, I know) that we may probably doubt
that all missionaries have had their own vocation as converters rooted
in that kind of evangelical love, I mean in the love of non-Christians
not only as being called to become Christians, but first of all as men
(potentially members of Christ) in other words, *for themselves* and
for what they are. When one sees how Pére Lebbe was treated by his
missionary colleagues, and forced to leave China until the Pope saw
to it that justice was done, one has a right to doubt whether the kind
of love we are now discussing was very widespread among the colleagues in question. One could not possibly reproach them for this.
They were simply living according to the commonly received conception of their day in which charity toward non-Christians, loved primarily insofar as they were called to become what they were not, had
for its primary obligation to work to their conversion to the true faith,
and was wholly absorbed in self-devotion to this goal. It was lucky if
from disappointment to disappointment, many poor missionaries did
not feel their souls invaded by bitterness. (I hope I have not offended
anyone.)

Here I am back at my theme: the absolute primacy of *agapè*, of
brotherly love fully liberated in the soul; in such a way that the great
renewal in the attitude of Christians toward non-Christians with
which we are concerned here may be described as a kind of epiphany
of evangelical love. If it were not that first and foremost, in the innermost recesses of the soul, and if nevertheless it laid claim to make all
men embrace one another, it would be nothing but mummery.

And here I look as if preaching, which is not my role at all, and makes me feel like dropping the whole business. After all, if I can't manage to master my own style, that's too bad for me. Nevertheless, I must complete the reflections I have begun.

A word remains to be said (not just one word, alas, but several pages) to avoid all misunderstanding. I have said that the true new fire, the essential renewal, is an inner renewal. But it is clear also that what takes place in the depth of the soul involves, in addition to that, a certain external behavior and is translated into the sphere of action.

From this point of view one could, it seems to me, distinguish three different zones of behavior.

A Christian who loves non-Christians in the way I have tried to define, can bear witness to this love before God by his prayer, and before men by his life; I say uniquely by his life: in responding to a newly perceived invitation in the call of the Gospel, he goes and hides himself in the midst of those he loves, with no other purpose other than to love them and to understand them with love, in sharing their life, their poverty, their sufferings, and without having the least intention of converting them, even by what is sometimes called a work of "pre-apostolate" (a pernicious word which involves a misunderstanding, and would transform into a prudent preface for action or a secret agent's tactic the authenticity and sincerity of the pure and simple fraternal love for these non-Christians *as they are,* and not as one hopes they may become; for of itself this pure and simple fraternal love suffices—*unum est necessarium*—and at that level it is to it alone, that one must bear witness). Such a life makes no sense unless it is an exclusively contemplative life, like that of the Little Brothers and Little Sisters of Jesus. There is what I call the first zone of behavior.

The second zone of behavior is characterized, it seems to me, by the fact that a Christian who loves non-Christians in the way that I have tried to define, bears witness to this love by a work which makes it visible *in the sphere of action,* or of external activity.

I am thinking here of all the works of mercy and of brotherly assistance that we can undertake, whether by ministering to the urgent needs created by misery, sickness, famine, etc., or by cooperating in the improvement of conditions of life and in the great effort accomplished by the countries underdeveloped in the social, economic, and cultural order, in view of attaining the common level of a civilization that has become universal. Here, clearly, is an immense task which is already well under way.

I am thinking also of the work, no less vast and no less important by which, in the intellectual order, scholars and specialists strive to know better the past and present of non-Christian civilizations (without forgetting people called primitive)—the social, moral and cultural structures of these areas of civilization, their special traditions, and above all their religion itself and their spirituality. Thus we find, and it is a true joy to state this, that Christian scholars are helping non-Christians to see more clearly into their own affairs and into what is closest to their hearts, and are succeeding in this much better than the pure rationalists. The work of Louis Massignon in respect to Islam has been exemplary from this point of view. (I take the liberty of adding, for those persons, however eminent, who remain insufficiently informed of the merits of the *Summa theologica*, that these days it is Thomists like Olivier Lacombe and Louis Gardet who are doing the most enlightened work in Indian and Islamic studies, and who are on terms of the most intimate and cordial friendship with the representatives of Indian and Moslem thought.) Besides, I see no reason why non-Christian scholars and specialists could not also help us, their opposite numbers, to gain a better insight into our proper affairs. For example, I wish that one of them would study, from his own point of view and in the light of his own traditions, St. John of the Cross for example or Père Surin, just as Massignon studied Hallāj. I don't say that he would understand them better than Catholic theologians, or that we would always agree with their interpretations. But I say it would give us a chance to widen our horizons and perhaps on certain points to renew our understanding of the problems involved.

The third zone of behavior is that of the apostolate and the mission. Here again, it is through a work concerning the sphere of external activity, that the Christian who loves non-Christians in the way I have tried to define bears witness to this love. But this time we are dealing with the most exalted activity, the highest conceivable work of charity. For this activity responds to an express command of the Lord: Go teach all nations. It is the continuation of the preaching of Christ when he traveled the roads of Judea and Galilee to proclaim the kingdom of God. That the Truth should be known by men is the ardent desire of the eternal Truth descended on earth to assume our flesh. Moreover, to know the Truth, the Truth that frees, is the absolutely first need of the human being. *Non in solo pane vivit homo.* . . . No activity better serves man or testifies better to the fraternal love kindled in us by the Gospel than that by means of which Truth comes to make itself known to him, and illumines his heart.

Does this mean that apostolic activity would be something better than the love from which it derives and which it manifests? Apostolic activity is what is highest in the order of activity. But no activity is higher and better than the love of charity, higher and better than *agapé*. *"There is no work better or more necessary than love."* [7]

St. John of the Cross also said: "God makes use of nothing other than love." [8] Not only the greatest missionaries, but all who are today called to missionary work have a better understanding of this; it is here that the new fire, the essential renewal announced and willed by the Council, influences missionary activity in its living works, rejuvenating and reinvigorating it, but also raising new problems for it. Thus renewed, missionary work requires from now on that each one involved in it become aware of what was in the heart of a St. Francis Xavier or a Père Lebbe. In other words, apostolic preaching must be rooted in the love of the non-Christian, loved primarily not as a potential convert, but for himself and for what he *is*—a member of Christ, at least potentially. Such a reversal of values in the depths of the soul, and therefore in techniques and methods of approach, is already an accomplished fact. There is not very much in common between the ways the great missionary orders followed fifty years ago and those they follow today. I have no competence to discuss this matter, and it is not my subject. I would simply imagine that what brought this revolution about was the will to draw all the consequences from a truth of which no one is unaware—namely, that it is not his ministers but Jesus himself who converts souls by the hidden windings of his grace, so that preaching and teaching come to achieve rather than to start the secret motions awakened in souls by his love and the love of his servants.

[7] St. John of the Cross, *Cant.* (2nd ed.), str. 28 (19), Silv. III, p. 361.
[8] *Ibid.*, str. 27 (18), Silv. III, p. 356.

TWO SHORT ANECDOTES

There is nothing simpler, and at bottom more ordinarily Christian, than the inner renewal which has been the subject of all the preceding pages. Fifty years from now, one will doubtless be astonished to think that Christians could ever have behaved otherwise. Two short anecdotes may perhaps help us grasp to what extent there is, for those of us who were born in the nineteenth century or at the beginning of the twentieth, something really new.

I knew a very celebrated writer. He was not a Catholic and his moral life was not very edifying. One day when I went to pay him a visit, he spoke to me of another great writer, a Catholic, who had been his friend. He told me how at the time when this friendship was formed he had considered himself duty bound, in fairness, to confide in that person, even at the risk of scandalizing him, the manner in which he was living. He later received letters from his friend assuring him that he now loved him all the more deeply. The letters were so beautiful and generous that the writer who told me all this had been overwhelmed by them. I can still see him opening a drawer of his writing table and showing me that bundle of letters. Though many years had passed, he wept when he showed them to me. But the Catholic writer—as sincere and generous as a man could be—was convinced that his absolutely first duty in charity toward this sinner lay in his doing everything in his power to bring him to the true light. He therefore set out, and with heart and soul, to try and convert him. In spite of long and patient efforts, he did not succeed. Concluding at last that his colleague was definitely incapable of being converted, what could he do, alas, but pass judgment against him and abandon him to the devil? This was hardly the kind of thing to soften the heart of his ex-friend, and better dispose him to receive the grace of God if some day it should come knocking more forcefully at the door of his soul. Doubtless the Catholic writer had his reasons, for the non-Catholic, in constant evasions, used a good many tricks of his own. (I am not sure that in telling me this story, he wasn't trying to win me over to his side by playing a little too strongly on my feelings.) But the fact remains that, in acting as he did, the Catholic had simply followed the line of behavior—the pattern currently accepted at that

time in regard to relations between a believer and an unbeliever. They
are both dead, and, please God, now reconciled.

The second anecdote concerns me personally. Twenty years ago a
friend of mine who was a great French theologian—and whose friendship has never faltered—told me one day that he had a bone to pick
with me, and he didn't go any too gently about it. Just what kind of
reproach was it? He was upset because whenever I dealt with a non-
Christian, I always assumed that he was acting in good faith. But the
contrary must be assumed, he maintained. Hadn't the New Law been
promulgated? Hadn't the Word of God been proclaimed in almost
every country on earth? Was grace lacking to anyone? When we spoke
to non-Christians, it was a duty to truth to presuppose—save for
exceptions (when, for example, a certain person was excused by that
exceedingly rare thing called "invincible ignorance")—*that they were
not in good faith.*

Such an attitude completely failed to take into account the dependence of the human mind upon age-old traditions, cultural
environment, and, broadly speaking, the deadweight of history. I
don't believe there is anyone today who would accept the views of
my friend. Twenty years ago they seemed self-evident to a theologian
of high merit. They conformed to the line of behavior toward non-
Christians, to the pattern still accepted at that time (but not for very
long).

On the contrary, it is clear that if we should *presuppose* (because
all men *are* members of Christ, at least potentially) that the non-
Christian we are speaking to doubtless has grace and charity—since
we are in no position to judge the innermost heart—then we should
equally *presuppose* that he is in good faith. (It can happen, naturally,
that in certain cases one could have strong reasons for thinking that a
particular individual, Christian or non-Christian, is in bad faith. But
that will be the exception.)

THE LAW OF THE CROSS

We would be making a big mistake, as I said in a preceding section,
if we believed that men who are divided in their speculative convictions are thereby prevented from reaching a practical agreement of

thought in regard to the principles that govern action. But we would
be making a mistake at least as serious in the opposite direction if, on
the pretext of making this practical agreement more secure, we tried
to camouflage the irreducible oppositions that persist in the speculative order between the parties involved, by lying as to what is and by
adapting the true to the false in order to make the dialogue more
smoothly cordial, and more deceptively fruitful.

The remark I made concerning practical agreement between men
divided in the speculative order should be driven home even more
forcefully (with pile drivers, if need be), when it comes to fostering
brotherly love among men who subscribe to different philosophical
or religious beliefs. This is the first condition of loyalty in the dialogue.

The more a Christian—let us say also this time, the more a Catholic
(for such a dialogue can and should also take place between Christians
who are doctrinally separated)—the more a Christian, or a Catholic,
gives an absolute primacy in his heart to a fully liberated brotherly
love, and, in dealing with non-Catholics or non-Christians, sees them
as they really are, members of Christ, at least potentially, the more
firmly he must maintain his positions in the doctrinal order (I don't
say he should brandish them at every turn), and must make clear the
differences which, in the realm of what is true or false, separate him
from these men he loves wholeheartedly. In acting thus, he will be
honoring them. To do otherwise would be to betray Truth, which is
above everything.

We have to grant that this is not always easy, and can make things
rather uncomfortable for him. Such is life. We must accept that.

I said once to Jean Cocteau: *We must have a tough mind and a
tender heart*, adding with a certain melancholy that the world is full
of dried-up hearts and flabby minds. Beware of flabby minds in the
ecumenical dialogue!

Nevertheless, it is not this which I would like to insist on today, but
rather the uncomfortable (more than uncomfortable) situation I was
discussing of those poor men in whose souls love and truth should be
served with an equal fidelity. (To put it more precisely, brotherly love
and the love of the One who is the Truth.) *Misericordia et veritas
obviaverunt sibi. . .*

There is no use getting excited. The new age we are entering will put
Catholics to a hard test. Doubtless, it will be for them the occasion of

a very pure joy and exultation, because of the kind of epiphany of brotherly love which it will permit. But the price will have to be paid. There will likewise be an increase of suffering and heart rending principally because of this *misericordia* and this *veritas* which desire to meet and to embrace. Where? In heaven it is no problem. But in man's world it is something else, and we are men.

To begin with, it is at the very core of brotherly love that inevitably we suffer in our hearts, because those non-Christians whom we love like members of Christ, of the beloved Saviour, do not know Christ. There can be and certainly is much of truth in their baggage. But they do not know the Truth, the Truth that frees, and it is a great misfortune for them, and one great joy less for heaven and for Jesus. They continue to struggle with many chains, they still collide against many barriers along their road; there are for them still many traps in the shadows. Would we love them truly if we didn't suffer because of what they lack? The more fraternal love grows, the more this suffering also grows. Clearly, if anyone delights in loving them, and receiving the gift of their friendship in return, but without experiencing any of this suffering, there is something unreal about his love.

One can see here—this is only a small marginal gloss which has slipped into my ever-friendly text by way of parenthesis—what a distance there is between the very pure joy and exualtation I mentioned earlier and which have as their companion a faithful sorrow) and this natural joy, very *natural* (and to which no sorrow, certainly, comes to trouble the happy expansion), which is given us today to contemplate in quite a few of our Christian brothers, entranced to be able at last to rub their noses, all atremble with enthusiasm, with the noses of all the sons of Adam.

Furthermore, and precisely because Christians and non-Christians move on different levels with regard to truth, seeing things in different lights more or less clouded by earthly vapors, it seems almost inevitable that, to the extent that mutual friendship develops between them, we will see misunderstandings and suspicions arise. Will the Christian's non-Christian friend understand the meaning and the reason for that service to truth which his Christian friend maintains more than ever in the doctrinal order, hardening the edge, if he must, to avoid syncretism and confusion? Or will he take it for some inconceivable arrogance or return to "fanaticism"? The slightest blunder will cost dear.

The Christian respects and cherishes the distinction between the things that are Caesar's and those that are God's even when, acting on his own and without committing the Church, he gives himself most wholeheartedly to his temporal mission, and when the Church herself does everything in her power, while remaining within her own sphere (which is that of the spiritual) to help the world overcome the difficulties it faces in its own order. But will the non-Christian (or even the non-Catholic) also understand the meaning and the reason for this distinction, and not be scandalized because in certain instances, the Christian (or the Catholic) must maintain at all costs the autonomy of the spiritual in regard to the temporal, and refuse to transform Christianity into a kind of theocratic agency charged with assuring the well-being of the world, universal peace, pay raises, and free room and board for all? How many explanations will have to be given, which will surely not always be recognized as valid?

Finally, and most importantly, will it not be at the cost of a rather painful overstretching in the very soul of the Christian, and of a vigilance which can rarely permit any slackening, and a struggle against often subtle temptations, and with what renunciations, and sometimes sacrifices, that can be assured, somehow or other, the double and unique fidelity to which he is bound, on one hand, to truth in the order of intelligence and theological faith, and, on the other, to brotherly love (which understands all things, said St. Paul, and forgives all things), when it comes to our relations with our neighbor, and this neighbor himself sets at naught what we most cherish? All the assistance of grace will be needed. The love of the Cross will be needed. To sum up, what I have been attempting to suggest is nothing but the *law of the cross*, of that holy Cross which it is not in fashion to mention today from pulpits. But the fashion in question, like all fashions, is a thing of the moment. In any case, this law *is there*, whatever one does or says.

Since I'm about to put my foot in it with all the frankness I obliged myself to, and perhaps with an involuntary insolence (I certainly hope not), why should I not speak the whole truth? The task which the new age we are entering expects of Christians is so difficult that they can not possibly accomplish it unless there are multiplied, in the very heart of and throughout the world, constellations of spiritual energy composed of humble stars invisibly shining, each a contemplative soul given over to the life of prayer. In each of them (this is the classic notion of "infused contemplation") the gifts of the Holy Spirit place the theological virtues in a state where they act in a higher and more perfect way, and they elevate the whole activity, including love itself, to a "supra-human mode." Without contemplative love and infused prayer, and the participation of souls given over to them in the redeeming Cross, and without the invisible support which they bring to the work of all in the mystical Body, and to that strange traffic (not lacking in irony) which Providence carries on here below, the task demanded of Christians, of all Christians, would be too heavy, and the great hope which is rising would be in vain. This hope will not be in vain, for the humble stars I am speaking of have begun secretly to glimmer; there are already more of them than one realizes strewn across the world.

Ash Wednesday, February 23, 1966

5 THE TRUE NEW FIRE

THE LIBERATION OF THE

INTELLIGENCE

In the previous chapter, I observed that the true new fire, the essential renewal, will be an *inner* renewal. I tried to sketch as best I could (doubtless not too well) what this inward renewal implies in the order of brotherly love, especially between Christians and non-Christians. I would like to attempt a similar sketch concerning the requests (and worries) of the human intellect, and what one may call (not without some temerity on the part of an old peasant) the affairs of the kingdom of God. This chapter and the next will be devoted to the first of these attempts.

PRELIMINARY NOTICE

The requests (and worries) of the intelligence—they are real enough. Even in the mass media we find a hint of them. We are, after all, animals endowed with reason: hence heirs to quite a few worries and illusions, and a good many demands as well, both exacting and inevitable. The renewals to which we are summoned by the great chime of the Council depend above all on an inspiration and spiritual élan awakened in the heaven of the soul. But such an inspiration and such an élan necessarily entail and require a vast labor of reason, renewing its own perspectives and grasping more thoroughly the articulations of the real. Only then can they recast our ordinary regime of thought and behavior. For this, neither mystical experience, nor faith, however desirable the first, and necessary the other, can suffice; both demand to be accompanied by an indispensable renewal in the order of intelligence. And if we stop to consider the present condition of

84

the intelligence, we will see (yes, we have been chained up longer and more tightly than we like to think) that what such a renewal requires is, first and foremost, a breaking of barriers and chains, a liberation: liberation of the intelligence itself, and liberation in hearts of a love which has been terribly repressed and which cries out from the depths of the abyss—the love of Truth. I say "in hearts" because it is a question of love, and I say "love"—love of that truth which is the life of the intellect—because it is desire or the will, whose primary act is loving, which puts into operation all our powers, and hence also our intellect.

Unless one loves the truth, one is not a man. And to love the truth is to love it above everything, because we know that Truth is God Himself.

Christ said to Pilate that he came into the world to bear witness to the Truth.

It is by faith that we hold the supreme Truth. Yet faith itself calls, be it in the unconscious, for a certain fermentation, a certain inquiry, a certain stirring and inner working of reason; and it normally presupposes (I don't say in each of our individual histories, but in the normal order of things considered in themselves) rational preliminaries, such as the natural certitude of the existence of God:[1] a certitude which is "natural" in the sense of *spontaneous* (then it is due to that kind of instinct of reason which is common sense), and also in the sense of *acquired* by the firm and compelling (because properly elucidated) ways of reason when it knows unshakably. (And if the first kind of certitude is valid, it is because it can flow into the second, which is that of developed and fully adult reason.) Thus faith itself demands to be completed by a certain intellectual grasp—inevitably imperfect in regard to the term to be attained, but altogether firm in regard to the structures of human knowledge—of the unfathomable mystery of God and divine things. *Credo ut intelligam.* This is called theology. And theology cannot take shape in us without the help of that natural wisdom of which human reason is capable, whose name is philosophy. In short, faith itself entails and requires a theology and

[1] Many other truths of a purely rational order have also a necessary connection with the data of faith and are presupposed or implied by them: for example, the very axiom that man is made for truth, and also the existence of the sensible world, the existence of free will; the spirituality and immortality of the human soul. Such a list could be prolonged.

a philosophy. Oh, I realize all this is quite regrettable because it is difficult and fatiguing. It would be so much nicer to be a front-line Christian going to Mass every Sunday (no longer, of course, because he has to—which is now regarded as old-fashioned—but because he knows it is the right thing to do) and then instructing himself peacefully by radio and television, and by reading picture magazines and a few "demythizing" paperbacks.

I, too, feel regret—for meanly egotistical reasons (a philosopher's life is not exactly a bed of roses). But that is the way it is; there's nothing we can do about it. That's the way it is because man is what he is. And in man there is not merely sex with all its nasty tricks, as we might be tempted to believe (doubtless against the author's wishes) on reading what a friendly colleague [2] calls "the kind of basically sexual ontology" proposed by a much admired moralist with little but his name to seduce me—what a beautiful name! In man there is also the invisible intellect, which besets him much more despotically.

But what sense is there in all this? Philosophy and theology—aren't they but Chinese curios? Or should I say (for the sake of soft ecumenism,[3] perhaps afraid that the expression might offend the Chinese) medievalist curios—which have become unthinkable for a man of today? The word *soul*, it was recently observed, is suffering the same fate; "most of the members of the 'intelligentsia' feel that this word no longer has any meaning. . . . As for the word *spirituality*, it no longer excites anything but derision on the part of serious thinkers." [4]

And the same can be said of the word *truth*. Well, it is immaterial to me, because people who think in this way, no matter how numerous, simply do not *exist*. When Villiers de l'Isle-Adam happened to find himself in front of one of them (they were not lacking in his time either), he walked up to him and, examining his face as closely as possible and with the greatest of care, said, "I'm trying my best, I look at you—I *don't see* you."

Besides, there is in all this a strange error of fact. The need for these

[2] Dr. Marcel Eck, in an open letter to the author of *Mystère humain de la la Sexualité*. [The author in question is abbé Oraison—*Translator's addition*.]

[3] Do I need to point out that I am not speaking of true ecumenism, which is certainly not *soft*?

[4] Stanislas Fumet, in an interview published by *La Table Ronde*, March, 1966.

medieval curios, repressed as it may be, is actually enormous in today's world. The aberrant forms to which such a need resorts for its gratification (just think of the large circulation of the review, *Planète*) are themselves proof of it. And speaking seriously, those who have a genuine experience of today's youth know that, as soon as, maybe in passing, the slightest spark gives them an opportunity to release what smoulders within their mind, then a thirst for philosophical knowledge, and perhaps even more, for the theological knowledge, manifests itself in them. I am an old hermit, but I know many young people; and I am also acquainted with a number of intelligent professors, who are capable of transmitting the spark—and who have told me what subjects arouse the keenest interest among their students, and make the latter ask the most anxious questions.

But I am not forgetting that, in this book, it is mainly Christians I am talking to. It is with the Gospel, then, that we should properly begin.

THE TRUTH

What do the apostles tell us?

The Spirit is the Truth, St. John says.[5] And again:

Grace, mercy, and peace will be with us, from God the Father and from Jesus Christ the Father's Son, ἐν ἀληθεία χαὶ ἀλάπῃ, *in truth and love.*[6]

No greater joy can I have than this, to hear that my children follow the truth.[7]

So we ought to support such men, that we may be fellow workers in the Truth.[8]

We are of the Truth.[9]

And Paul: *For the wrath of God is revealed from heaven against all ungodliness and wickedness of men who by their wickedness hold truth captive of injustice.*[10]

[5] 1 John 5:6.
[6] 2 John 3.
[7] 3 John 4.
[8] *Ibid.*, 8.
[9] 1 John 3:19.
[10] *Rom.* 1:18.

Those who are to perish, because they did not receive the love of the Truth which would have saved them.[11]

All shall be condemned who did not believe in the Truth.[12]

God our Savior, who desires all men to be saved and to come to the knowledge of the Truth.[13]

Charity takes its joy in the truth.[14] (A joy in which it is in communion *with the truth,* συνχαίρει τῇ ἀληθείᾳ.)

Put on the new man, created after the likeness of God in righteousness and the holiness of Truth.[15]

And James: *Of his own will he brought us forth by the word of truth.*[16]

And what does Jesus tell us? *I am the Way, and the Truth, and the Life.*[17]

For this I was born, and for this I have come into the world, to bear witness to the Truth. Everyone who is of the Truth hears my voice.[18]

God is Spirit, and those who worship him must worship in spirit and truth.[19]

The Holy Spirit is *the Spirit of Truth.*[20]

The Spirit of Truth, who proceeds from the Father.[21]

When he comes, the Spirit of Truth will teach you all the truth.[22]

Father, sanctify them in the Truth; thy word is Truth . . . And for their sake I sanctify myself, that they also may be sanctified in the Truth.[23]

If you abide in my word, you will truly be my disciples, and you will know the Truth, and the Truth will make you free.[24]

---

[11] 2 *Thessal.* 2:10.
[12] *Ibid.,* 2:12.
[13] 1 *Tim.* 2:4.
[14] 1 *Cor.* 13:6.
[15] *Ephes.* 4:24.
[16] James 1:18.
[17] John 14:6.
[18] *Ibid.,* 18:37.
[19] *Ibid.,* 4:24.
[20] *Ibid.,* 14:17.
[21] *Ibid.,* 15:26.
[22] *Ibid.,* 16:13.
[23] *Ibid.,* 17:17, 19.
[24] *Ibid.,* 8:32. Here are a good many citations drawn from the fourth Gospel. There is no reason to be surprised at the fact, since the Synoptics have gathered together, to transmit them in writing (as Luke clearly suggests) the *logia* of Jesus

And what do we read in the infinitely venerable Prologue to the fourth Gospel? *He* [the Word] *was the True light, that enlightens every man coming into the world.*[25]

And the Word became flesh, and he dwelt among us, and we have beheld his glory, glory which comes from the Father to the only Son, full of grace and truth.[26]

For the Law was given through Moses; but Grace and Truth came through Jesus Christ.[27]

The subsistent Truth which is God, and which Christ came to reveal, and the truth which is a participation in it here below—and in which we should follow, as St. John says,[28] and which makes us true in love (*Ephes.*, 4, 5)—and in which charity rejoices,[29]—we see what a place truth holds in the Gospel.

It is impossible for a Christian to be a relativist.[30] Those who make the attempt have no chance of succeeding. Let them be pardoned, after all. There is an even better excuse than "invincible ignorance," and that is what Baudelaire called "la bêtise au front de taureau," bull-headed stupidity.

But the texts we have just been reading call for more appropriate commentary. The truth of Faith is the infinitely transcendent truth of the mystery of God. And, nevertheless, this infinitely transcendent truth, God has willed that it be expressed (and here comes the prophets of Israel, the teaching of Christ, and the definitions of the Church) in human concepts and words. This is characteristic of the Judeo-Christian revelation. Revelation is not unformulatable; it is *formed*. It is so because the Second Person of the Trinity is the Word,

---

and the other recollections engraved in the memory of the disciples and the very earliest Christian community, whereas the fourth Gospel, as emerges clearly from its tone and style, is the work of a man bringing his absolutely personal witness (there were reasons for John's having been the preferred disciple) who had seized up and retained many deeper and more precious traits on which the common attention had not been fixed. Furthermore, it is worth noting that the epistles of Paul and James sound, on the question we are dealing with here, in a manner exactly similar.

[25] John 1:9.
[26] *Ibid.*, 1:14.
[27] *Ibid.*, 1:17.
[28] Cf. above (n. 7), 3 John 4.
[29] Cf. above (n. 14), 1 *Cor.* 13:6.
[30] Unless he is a physicist. I am obviously not talking here of relativist physics or Einsteinian relativity.

and because the Word was made flesh. The concepts and words that transmit revelation to us are at once *true* (they make what is hidden in God actually *known* to us) and essentially *mysterious* (*in aenigmate*: they remain disproportionate to the Reality which they attain without either circumscribing or comprehending it).

That is what teaches a philosopher to respect human intelligence, the concepts and the other instruments it fashions in order to lay hold of things, and of which the prophets of Israel and He whom they were announcing have made use of to open doors against which philosophers bump their noses. It is in the course of meditating on this that, once upon a time, a fervent Bergsonian began to perceive the weakness of that critique of the concept upon which Bergson laid so much stress, and which, after all, he himself belied in writing his great books.

And it is in meditating on this, that the Christian blesses the obscurity of Faith, through which the absolute Truth, which is *seen* only in glory, enters already, in this poor earthly life, into companionship with him. For it is in this holy obscurity that he is able to worship in spirit and in *truth*.

So much for my first remark. The second is brought to my mind with respect to the second epistle of St. John, where the apostle calls down on us grace, mercy, and peace *in truth and charity*. Just how do truth and charity come to terms with one another? In everyday practice this problem creates quite a few difficulties for us, poor fellows that we are, and likewise, as I noted in the previous chapter, no small inner pains. Yet in principle the agreement in question is perfectly normal.[31]

Charity has to do with persons; truth, with ideas and with reality attained through them. Perfect charity toward our neighbor and complete fidelity to the truth are not only compatible; they call for one another.

In the fraternal dialogue, the deeper love is, the more each one feels bound to declare, without diminution or lenitive salve what he holds to be true (otherwise he would wrong, not only truth as he sees it, but also the spiritual dignity of his neighbor).

And the more freely I affirm what I hold as true, the more I should

---

[31] See my essays, "Qui est mon prochain?" in *Principes d'une politique humaniste*, and "Tolérance et Vérité" in *Le Philosophe dans la cité*.

love whoever denies it—I don't have toward my neighbor the tolerance demanded by brotherly love unless his right to *exist*, to seek truth, and to express it according to his lights, and never to act or speak against his conscience is recognized and respected by me at the very instant when this pig-headed neighbor—always worthy of love, as dense as he may seem—takes sides against the very truths which are dearest to me.

If I truly love my neighbor, it will of course (I have already said as much) be painful to me to see him deprived of the truth I happen to know. For, all things considered, it is truth I must love above everything, while at the same time loving my neighbor as myself. If my neighbor is in error, it is a pity for him, and for truth, too. How to escape suffering from this? That is part of the inherent delight of the fraternal dialogue. On the other hand, the latter would completely degenerate if the fear of displeasing my brother got the better of my duty to declare the truth. (To do so, moreover, will not grieve too much my dear fellow being if I am not too stupid about it, and if I really have in my heart the feelings I owe to him.)

Let us beware of those brotherly dialogues in which everyone is in raptures while listening to the heresies, blasphemies, stuff and nonsense of the other. They are not brotherly at all. It has never been recommended to confuse "loving" with "seeking to please." *Saltavit et placuit,* she gamboled and frolicked and captivated them all. Salome pleased Herod's guests; I can hardly believe she was burning with love for them. As for poor John the Baptist (who did not dialogue in his prison, except with his Master), she certainly did not envelop him in her love.

My third remark will have to do with efficacy and truth. In Chapter 3 I spoke at some length about the world and the contrasting meanings of this word. The Church knows the worth, dignity and beauty of the world which God has made; she wants its good—its temporal as well as its spiritual good. She embraces it in the divine agape she has received from on high. She strives with all her heart to help it advance in the line of its earthly progress, toward its natural ends and toward better and higher conditions for mankind; she places at its disposal the treasures of light and compassion which have been confided to her. But she is not in the service of the world. She keeps herself from conforming to its lusts, its prejudices, or its passing fancies. In this sense, old Chesterton was right in saying: "The Catholic Church is the only thing which spares man the degrading slavery of being a child of his times." And with incomparably greater authority, it was also said, "Do not be conformed to this world." [32] It has always been obvious, from the way in which the "world" St. Paul was speaking about shifts for itself, that its supreme norm is efficacy—in other words, success. The supreme norm for the Church is truth.

The supreme norm which the "world" obeys, the supreme law of efficacy, threatens to impose itself with tyranny more demanding than ever in the technocratic civilization we are entering today. That is why men will have such desperate need of the witness which the Church renders to the absolute primacy of truth.

There is much one could say on the subject of efficacy. In truth, nothing in nature, especially in the living being, and even more so in the human being, is inefficacious. Neither idleness, nor even laziness, nor rest are inefficacious, except when they take place at the wrong moment. Ancient Chinese wisdom knew the value of empty spaces in music and design as well as in the art of living. Above all, there are different levels of efficacy; I say this in passing, perhaps I will get a chance to come back to this. The fact is that whatever is meant *only* for efficacy, a limitless efficacy, is precisely what is least really efficacious (because nature and life are a hidden order, not a mere unleashing of force), whereas what seems least efficacious (if it belongs to an order superior to that of activities bound to matter) is what most possesses genuine efficacy.

But the efficacy I am discussing here pertains to the energies man deploys and uses in the order proper to his nature as an animal endowed with reason, thanks to his brawn and especially to his brain. To neglect such efficacy would be a childish nonsense we needn't fear the world will be guilty of. Nor does the Church fall into such nonsense. That is why, at each great moment of her history, she renews not merely her means of action, but her awareness of the vital sources on which they depend (she takes her time with it; Aristotle remarked that the magnanimous move at a slow step). Today the Church is at one of these great moments of renewal. And she knows perfectly well the risks involved. (Have no fear, she will surmount them.)

Can we say as much for a number of her clerics and faithful? It is

32 *Rom.* 12:2.

toward them that I now turn my old hermit's gaze, not sorry more-over, to put aside for a moment the world and its false pretenses—but am I actually putting them aside that much? That's what bothers me. Nevertheless, the viewpoint I would now like to adopt is no longer that of the assistance and cooperation which Christianity brings to the world and the temporal order from on high, but rather what Christianity is confronted with in the spiritual order itself, which is its own proper order.

There is, nowadays, among a good many Christians and even, without their clearly realizing it perhaps, among an alarming number of priests and consecrated people (it is these clerics, above all, whom I have in mind), a marked tendency to give efficacy primacy over truth. What does it matter if the means one uses set the mind on a wrong course, ask group techniques and group psychology [33] to do better than the theological virtues, the gregarious instinct to do better than the gifts of the Holy Spirit, the flowering (*épanouissement*) of nature to do better than humility, the *engagements* or commitments (preferably made in common) to replace the "egocentric" search for intimacy with God, the joy of sharing in the world's labors to replace the search for the perfection of charity and for the love of the cross, mass action to take the place of that "go into your chamber and shut the door and pray to your Father who dwells in secret," [34] which Jesus Christ had prescribed—for another age, was it?—community celebrations to cast aside the search for silence and solitude—the lat-est fables and quackeries to give a little vitality to the catechism—and, above all, the generous expenditure of self in external works and in an incessant dialogue with everybody to free us from any attempt at intellectual concentration? What does it matter, once these means are supposedly dynamic—that's the only thing that counts—and serve *efficaciously* to gather men together in the fold of the Good Shepherd?

Precisely here lies the flagrant absurdity, since the Good Shepherd is precisely Truth itself; and since the means are nothing unless they are proportioned to the end—that is, in the present case, unless they

[33] Mind you, I have nothing against group psychology or the flowering of nature, nor against commitments, the joy of sharing in the world's labors, mass action, community celebrations or dialogue. I am speaking of the *use* (for which these things are in no way intended) *which certain people*, not too rare at this stage, *wish to make them serve.*

[34] Matt. 6:6.

are means of truth; and since, in the domain of the kingdom of God, it is truth which is the source and measure of efficacy itself.

Actually, in so far as the tendency I have pointed out prevails, the souls of men are being exposed to a fine case of inner disintegration, and there is a risk of their becoming spiritual cripples who cannot easily be cured.

There, carried to its extreme limit, you see the troubled and unhappy "faith" of pure fideism, and the supernatural Truth (or what's left of it) lying in poor people like a stone at the bottom of a pond, but no longer vitally *received* by a living being. In their intellect, every link with this stranger has been severed. Their dismasted reason, robbed of the inner formations and structures which it naturally demands, floats adrift in religious ignorance, and (when they are men whose cultural level would have normally required a few certitudes, however elementary, in the matter of knowledge) in a total skepticism or theological and philosophical indifferentism.

Who's talking about efficacy! The end result would be the defection of a great multitude. The day when efficacy would prevail over truth will never come for the Church, for then the gates of hell would have prevailed against her.

A FEW WORDS ON THE CAPACITY OF HUMAN REASON

It is normal that after all this, I should feel called upon to say a few words concerning the capacity of human reason.

How, in fact, poor imbeciles that we are, could we know through faith and with full certitude the supernaturally revealed Truth to which man's mind is not proportioned, if we were not able to know with full certitude the truths of a rational order to which man's mind *is* proportioned? I have in mind philosophic truths, which are purely rational—let us understand this "purely" in contradistinction to what lies above reason, but of course not to what lies below it (for all knowledge naturally acquired by man proceeds from sense experience, and, if there is an insane asylum among the pure spirits of heaven, it is only there that we can see Kant's Pure Reason in operation). I also have in mind theological truths, which are rational but whose object is superior to reason, and which proceed from the light of faith, but not without the theologian's having to use, in their service, philosophic truths which emerge from the experience of the senses through the agency of the intellect.

Grace perfects nature and does not destroy it. It is essential for man to aspire to truth, and he has the capacity to reach it by his own powers—even if it be in stumbling and zigzagging along the way, a way which is endless—in the things which depend on sense experience or to which such experience gives us indirect access. So much for philosophy and the swarming of sciences. Man also has the capacity—and here we are speaking of theology—to gain a still imperfect but genuine and authentic knowledge of divine things when his natural forces work in the light of faith, which quickens them and raises them above their ordinary level. This is my point Number 1. (Please excuse me for appearing to give a lecture. It's certainly not my intention.)

Let us move on to point Number 2. Since there are truths of a rational order in regard to which man's understanding can acquire certitude, does it not follow that an organic network of fundamental truths—in other words, a *doctrine* (why, certainly, so much the worse for the reigning prejudices), a doctrine which is essentially grounded in truth,[35] is *possible* (in the philosophical order, and likewise, when it is a question of acquiring in a rational way some understanding of the mystery revealed, in the theological order)? One can regard the thing as improbable, but that is not the point. The point is to know whether, of its nature, it is *possible*.

The affirmative answer compels recognition, if one is not too much afraid of professors. I know very well that all present-day philosophers (almost all, to be more precise) are speaking in the opposite way. But I don't care. Besides, they are not philosophers, as I will soon have occasions to explain.

We have surely to admit that—since man is made for truth—a doctrine essentially grounded in truth must be *possible* for our mind on condition, however (and this goes further than one thinks), that it not be the work of a single man (a thousand times too weak to

---

[35] Every doctrine, even the most erroneous, is based on some truth. I call essentially grounded in truth a doctrine grounded in truth in its essential or fundamental structure.

manage properly, in three or four decades, so enormous, and so enormously risky a business), but that it rely, with a proper respect for common sense and common intelligence, on the efforts of the human mind from the most remote times, and embrace the labor of generations of thinkers with contrasting views—all of this being one day brought together and unified by one or several men of genius (supposing they unexpectedly come along among the contingencies of history).

My present intention is not to quarrel with the idea, so widespread in today's world, that the pluralism of philosophic doctrines is something normal *de iure*. It is rather to dispel a misunderstanding and to show that, contrary to what is often imagined, what I have just affirmed, namely that a doctrine essentially grounded in truth *is possible*, can only be understood correctly if we recognize at the same time the pluralism of philosophic doctrines, I don't say as normal *de iure*, but as *bound to happen* or normal *de facto*: by reason of the conditions under which human subjectivity is working among philosophers.

On the one hand, it is, to be sure, nonsense to imagine that a philosophic doctrine grounded in truth would by the same token be, or pretend to be, a finished or perfect doctrine, nay more, that it would contain or claim to contain, all ready-made, the answers to all the questions which will arise in the course of time. Doubtless one can say (it is a suitable abbreviation—flattering, certainly, to the partisans of this possible doctrine; exasperating to the rest) that a doctrine essentially grounded in truth is a "true" doctrine. But we must quickly remove all risk of misunderstanding. What do the words "a *true* philosophy" or "a *true* theology" mean? They signify that since its principles are true, and ordered in a manner which conforms to the real, such a (possible) philosophy or such a (possible) theology is thus equipped to advance from age to age (if those who profess it are not too lazy or complacent) toward a greater measure of truth. But there are an infinity of truths that this possible true doctrine has not yet attained; and, such as it presents itself at a given time, it can itself admit of a number of accidental errors.

Assuming it exists, it is not enough to say that it is never finished and should always progress. In order to free itself from the limitations inherent in the mentality of a given cultural epoch, such a doctrine necessarily implies a perpetual process of self-remoulding, as is the case with living organisms. It has a duty to understand intelligently the various systems which develop from one age to another in opposition to it, to discover their generative intuition, and to rescue the truths which they hold captive. Now, given the conditions (hardly splendid, it goes without saying) in which human subjectivity is at work, it is certainly to be feared that the adherents of this possible doctrine grounded in truth will more or less neglect the duty I have just spoken of, and likewise the aforementioned process of self-remoulding.

On the other hand—given always the famous conditions in which human subjectivity is at work—it is inevitable that in every epoch a certain number of minds, devoted primarily to research, and fascinated by this or that particular truth they have discovered (with, ordinarily, the fresh supply of some error), will give rise to other systems which clash more or less violently with the admittedly possible doctrine grounded in truth and which will succeed each other from age to age.

The minds I am speaking of will be burned out by the particular truth they have discovered, and which it will be up to the possible doctrine grounded in truth to rescue and deliver in a coherent universe of thought. Yet they will have contributed effectively, at times splendidly (but then beware of the after-effects of their prestige) to the progress of philosophy.

Thus, as I just indicated, one sees how to recognize the possibility of a doctrine essentially grounded in truth, but which advances slowly (it is, by hypothesis, a common work, which embraces in its preparation a human experience that goes back to remotest times, and is called upon, by the same token—once formed, and supposing all goes well—to grow ceaselessly through some common effort), to recognize, I say, the possibility of such a doctrine essentially grounded in truth is, at the same time, to recognize as inevitable or normal *de facto* (by reason of the human subject) the existence of other doctrines which—each one an individual work, and, as such, ephemeral, though a Descartes or a Hegel was able to influence several centuries—

will mark, in regard to a certain aspect of the immense unknown, a more rapid advance, yet paid for at great cost.[36]

There is obviously a third point, which is no longer concerned with the *possibility* of a doctrine (philosophical or theological) grounded in truth, but (that is when they will attack me) with the existence of such a doctrine. Is the existence of such a doctrine probable? Certainly not, given the preceding considerations. But the improbable sometimes happens. I am saving this third part for the next chapter.

PHILOSOPHY AND IDEOSOPHY

I intend to speak now in a way that will perhaps seem a trifle arrogant. But when it comes to absolutely essential matters that have been ignored by an intellectually degraded epoch, and when one is dealing with the great idols of the day (venerated, moreover, by a great many thinkers, some of whom are first class and deserve esteem and respect, even admiration—a qualified admiration), it is one's duty toward what is highest in the world to use the knife (and there is no point in being too gentle). Now that I have pronounced this modest preamble, I will resume my natural tone, and the course of my reflections.

My few words on the capacity of reason have taken longer than I had wanted them to. I will now ask those who do me the honor of glancing at these pages to kindly re-read the Gospel texts I collected earlier on the subject of Truth.

The truth of which these texts speak, and which sets us free, does it push us back into the inner prison where we supposedly would be confined in company with the ideas of our mind? In fact, the truth of divine revelation throws us to the heart of He who is—and of what *is*, with an absolute violence which pulverizes any claim to make our mind the rule of what it knows, or to make what it knows a product of its own innate forms organizing phenomena (or indeed, as is

---

[36] In the same way we understand how those who see in the development of philosophy only a succession of individual works will be brought to consider as necessary *de iure* (as if it were demanded by the object itself) a doctrinal pluralism which is doubtless indeed normal (from the point of view of the philosophizing subject, and given the human condition), but only normal *de facto*, or in point of fact inevitable.

readily believed in our days, simply a phenomenon which makes sense for us through our experience of ourselves). The Bible and the Gospel radically exclude any kind of idealism in the philosophic sense of the word. I noted that in my first chapter.

The Almighty God who created the world, and whose voice Moses heard, was he owing his existence and his glory to the mind that knew him? And the people this God chose for himself, and the land to which he led them, with its vines, its olive trees and its corn—were all these men and all these things which the hand can touch and the eye see, objects which have shape or consistency only in dependence of the mind that knows them? And the Word which descended to take flesh and human nature in a virgin of Israel, does the Gospel ask us to believe in this Word, and the flesh and human nature it made its own, as in mere ideas of our mind? And Christ preaching along the roads, and the enemies through whose midst he passed, and the mountain from which they sought to hurl him, and the children he blessed, and the lilies of the field he admired, and the sins which he took upon himself, and the love with which he loves us, is all this grasped by our intellect as being, to say, like Schopenhauer, "my representation"? And when Jesus teaches his disciples and says to them, for example, "I and the Father are one",[37] or "when the Paraclete comes, whom I shall send to you from the Father, the Spirit of truth who proceeds from the Father, he will bear witness to me," [38] do the terms of these propositions come from *a priori* synthetic judgments subsuming the data of experience (no, that won't do), or do they express an Idea of Reason in which a postulate of practical Reason obliges us to believe? (That won't do either.) In what drawer of the Critique, then, must we put the terms of the assertions uttered by the Lord? Or should we see in the thinking-master who still reigns over the world of professors, what he in fact was: an elderly meditative clockmaker laboriously tracing, in his head and on paper, the outline of the mechanisms of a transcendental clock destined to make the stars move in their courses?

The Judeo-Christian revelation is the strongest, the most insolently self-assured testimony rendered to the reality *in itself* of being—the being of things, and Being subsisting by itself—I say being dwelling in the glory of existence in total independence of the mind that knows

[37] John 10:30.
[38] John 15:26.

it. Christianity professes with a tranquil impudence what in the philosophical vocabulary is known as *realism*. I said previously that a Christian can not be a relativist. One must say, and this goes much further, that a Christian can not be an idealist.

Nor can a philosopher be an idealist. I appear to be voicing an enormity, but it is an axiomatic truth I am stating. Of course I am not challenging the great thinkers of India, they lived in a mental regime where religion, rite, mystique and metaphysics were all mixed together. I am not thinking of Plato either, for whom reality in itself had passed into the eternal Ideas (this was but a displacement, though a formidable one, of the life-center of philosophy, and a great intuition wrongly conceptualized). To him philosophy owes the flash of lightning which gave birth to it, and the propensity to go astray from which it might have died. It is on Descartes, the father of modern idealism, that I have designs, and on the whole series of his heirs, who, while each of them subjected this system to some mutation, have followed an evolutive curve of an irresistible internal logic.

All these men begin with thought alone, and there they remain, whether they deny the reality of things and of the world (Descartes still believed in it, but on account of a wave of the magic wand by the God of the *cogito*), or whether, in some way or another, they resorb this reality into thought. What does this mean? They impugn from the outset that very fact in which thought gets firmness and consistency, and without which it is a mere dream—I mean the reality to be known and understood, which *is here*, seen, touched, seized by the senses, and with which an intellect which belongs to a man, not to an angel, has directly to deal: the reality *about which and starting with which* a philosopher is born to question himself: if he misses the start he is nothing. They impugn the absolutely basic foundation of philosophic knowledge and philosophical research. They are like a logician who would deny reason, a mathematician who would deny unity and duality, a biologist who would deny life. From the moment they set out, they have turned their back on philosophic knowledge and philosophical research. They are not philosophers.

In saying this, I certainly don't mean that a philosopher should dismiss them, or consider them charletans. Their contribution to the history of thought has been immense. They have rendered considerable services to philosophy. They have obliged philosophers to become more clearly aware of the care they should devote to the theory of knowledge and the critical examination of its problems. It is important to read and study them with the greatest of care, an eager interest in the way their minds work, a vivid curiosity concerning their enigmatic ways of approach, and an odd but almost tender sympathy for their research. I have spent a good deal of time absorbing what they wrote. Descartes was an enemy of whom I was singularly fond. I was charmed by Berkeley; I narrowly missed being won over by Spinoza (at twenty I didn't know how much he depended on Descartes). I have admired the implacable bitterness of Hume and the slightly too facile genius of Leibniz. I gave extensive lectures on Kant which taught me a good deal. Auguste Comte has given me some rather uncharitable joys for which I am always grateful. I cannot say as much for Hegel, even though I have passed long hours in his company and though he was the greatest genius among them—and the maddest, for he was certain of having brought himself and the Spirit to the pinnacle of wisdom. And then there was Bergson, who, contrary to the others, really was a philosopher and holds no place in the line of descent; he endeavored to break it. (As I wish to be polite, I would rather say nothing about the logical positivists, who hold a nice place in the line.) After Bergson, everybody readily reentered the Cartesian lineage, at the thin end of it: with Husserl first, of whom I will speak soon, and for whom, whatever the catastrophe he caused, I have a great intellectual respect. I also have intellectual respect for some of those who take after him, Heidegger in particular, and, among my countrymen, men like Paul Ricoeur (who, however, I am still far from trusting) and Mircea Eliade (a great explorer but one who does not want to be a guide, thank goodness). I have none for Jean-Paul Sartre, who seems to me too artful, and who besides (and here he pleases me) would be quite sorry to find himself respected. (Yet I like to imagine him elected to the *Académie Française*, an honor which he certainly deserves.) But he has offered a testimony we would be quite wrong to neglect.

Of all the thinkers—and great thinkers—whose lineage has its origin in Descartes, I contest neither the exceptional intelligence, nor the importance, nor the worth, nor, at times, the genius. In regard to them I challenge only one thing, but that I challenge with might and main, and with the certainty of being right: namely, their right to the name of philosopher (except, of course, for Bergson, and perhaps also Blondel). In dealing with those children of Descartes we must sweep away this name with the back of our hand. They are not philosophers; they are *ideosophers*: that is the only name which fits and by which it is proper to call them. It is in no way pejorative of itself, it merely designates *another* way of research and thought than the philosophic one.

I beg my readers not to take what I have just said for the whim of a crazy old man. I am old but not crazy, and never have I spoken more seriously. Exactness of vocabulary is always important; in the present case it is of essential importance. Thinkers who from the outset have placed themselves outside the field of philosophic knowledge and research are not philosophers. A lineage of idealist origin, which from mutation to mutation more and more radically impugns extra-mental reality and the absolutely primary foundation of philosophic knowledge, could not possibly be called a philosophic lineage. Whoever is careful to be precise in his language should consider it an *ideosophic* lineage. (We can note, parenthetically, that at the present time the very thinkers whom current language, with little concern for precision, still calls philosophers, do not seem overly anxious to claim the name. They value much more the name phenomenologist. And with a melancholy loyalty which does them honor, a number of them would prefer, it seems, merely to be a channel for the stream of research, a vanishing instant in its ever changing self-awareness. Their misfortune is not to have seen that thought is not the harlot of time . . .)

☆

Once the clarification to which I have just resorted has been effected in our ideas and vocabulary, and once we have recognized the fact that there is no properly philosophic knowledge or research without a realist conception of knowledge, we can ask ourselves how the situation of philosophy looks in this second half of the twentieth century.

The ideosophers being therefore left aside for a moment, we then realize, not without something of a shock, that we are confronted today with only two doctrines—yes (a thousand pardons), they are doctrines, and rather firmly planted ones (though far from cherishing one another)—which are, properly speaking, philosophic doctrines. For, while a good many different kinds of philosophic realism are surely conceivable in theory, in point of fact there are at present only two: Marxist realism and Christian realism. In other words, on the one hand there is Marxist philosophy, and on the other Christian philosophy, when it does not fall short of the demands created by the coupling of these two words, nor give love-tokens to idealism or ideosophy. It is fairly well known that there is a Christian philosophy which meets these requirements, and is not faring too badly, in spite of the wishes and predictions of a sizable number of clerics.

Here is a meeting point between Christianity and Marxism that M. Garaudy would have been well advised to take note of.[39] A pity his attention was not drawn to it by the authors he consulted before offering us that pious humanization of an old faith, pretty well demythized and at last converted to the hopes of the earth, which he terms "the fundamental" in Christians. One must praise the fidelity with which, in striving to depict this ancient faith, he has followed the directions furnished him by his informants, but still, when one undertakes to "dialogue" with Christianity, it is unfair not to take as one's interlocutor Christianity as it is, whatever the incorrigible alienations and superstitions one deems have debased it.

Whatever the case with M. Garaudy's book, for my part I wish to

[39] If I have read M. Garaudy correctly, I saw the name of Aquinas appear only once in his book (*Un Marxiste s'adresse au Concile*, p. 93), and it seems clear, in the light of this passage, that he is less interested in the basic principles of the philosophy of St. Thomas than in the latter's opinion of serfdom. Feudal society was very far (a little further than ours) from being a fully humanized society, which doesn't mean that it had to be condemned in the name of absolute justice, or that moral theology should have regarded the lord who owned serfs as being in a state of sin. One wonders that an author who has (as one expects of an eminent Marxist) a sense of history (and a healthy aversion to "moralizing") did not see this immediately, and could consider that a theologian of the thirteenth century, in regarding the feudal regime as a *de facto* situation sufficiently justified by history, thereby demonstrated an unfortunate resignation to evil. There are, alas, more conclusive signs of the indifference so long demonstrated by the Christian world in the face of social injustice.

It is likewise somewhat astonishing that, after having himself noted that St. Thomas lived at the time of serfdom, M. Garaudy, in the fragments he extracted from two articles of the *Summa*, translated *servus* not as "serf," which would have been normal, but as "slave."

call attention to the meeting point. For to be a philosophic doctrine, properly speaking, is no small thing, and we have to do justice to Marxism by recognizing that such is the case.

Thereafter we must also be quick to recognize that the meeting point is a point of irreducible disagreement. For, from the very first, Marxist philosophy identifies *extra-mental reality* and *matter*,[40] thus making of the spiritual a superstructure or "reflection" of matter in dialectical motion and perpetual evolutive change, and excluding the slightest possibility of admitting or even conceiving the autonomy of the spiritual and the liberty which is proper to it (as they see it, the spiritual is no doubt in interaction with the substructure, but as though begotten by it and determined by it at every instant).

Moreover, when we think of this matter in dialectical motion,[41] and which refuses every "substance" or "nature" of permanent constitution, we cannot help finding Marxist realism itself, however resolute it may be otherwise, nonetheless rather suspect. The famous "turning upside down" proclaimed by Engels itself invites us to do so. Hegel turned upside down, and put back on his feet, is still Hegel. . .

But this is not the place to examine Marxist philosophy. (I have done that elsewhere.) As for Thomistic philosophy, its turn will come in the next chapter. It is of the liberation of *philosophic eros* that I would like now to speak.

THE LIBERATION OF PHILOSOPHIC EROS

We are confronted today with only two philosophies. But there exists in man a philosophic eros and a nostalgia for philosophy. And since the theme of these last chapters is the inner renewals which the great historic springtide, the new Renaissance announced and ushered in by the Council primarily calls for, it is clear that with respect to

[40] "The notion of matter," wrote Lenin in *Materialism and Empiriocriticism*, "from the point of view of the theory of language, signifies absolutely *nothing but* the objective reality whose existence is independent of human consciousness and is reflected by the latter." On Marxism, cf. our recent work *Moral Philosophy* (Chap. X, "Marx and His School"), and also *True Humanism*.

[41] In reflecting also on what M. Garaudy (*op. cit.*, p. 60) calls the "Faustian primacy of action in Marx" and the practical criterion considered as "criterion of truth." In the eyes of this philosophy, the real *is* not before *acting*, it *acts* in order to *be*, which is rather suggestive of very ancient mythologies.

the demands and worries of intelligence it is toward this philosophic eros present in the depths of man that we have first to turn.

This poor philosophic eros is today in a rather bad condition, lying bound and gagged at the bottom of the soul. And what is worse, it is being *cheated*. It stirs in its jail, it yearns for liberation. Such a liberation implies two operations. The first of these, which I will discuss at length, answers to the need for liberating philosophic eros from every idealist or ideosophic shackle. In saying this, I turn to the man who, in our times, has played a role analogous to Descartes' in the seventeenth century, namely Husserl.

Yet in order to shed a little light on the subject, we must first briefly recall just where the mystery of knowing lies. As I have written elsewhere,[42] thought need not go out of itself to reach the extramental thing. This extra-mental thing, a being for itself posited "outside of thought," that is to say, fully independent of the act of thinking—thought itself renders it existing within thought, posited for it and integrated with its own act, so that henceforth thought and being exist within thought in one and the same supra-subjective existence. Thus, it is in thought itself that extra-mental being is reached, in the concept itself that the real is touched and handled; it is there, within thought itself, that the real is seized, and devoured, because the very glory of thought's immateriality lies in *not being* a thing in space external to some other spatial thing, but indeed a life superior to the whole order of spatiality, which, without going out of itself, perfects itself by what is not itself—that intelligible real whose fertile substance its own activity takes out from the senses, after the senses have first drawn it—in their (not yet spiritual) way—from material existants in act.

These things Husserl did not see. A man of greatness and fundamental integrity, he deserved the gratitude and affection Edith Stein continued to feel for him while freeing herself from his influence. But like so many others, he was a victim of Descartes and Kant. The tragedy of Husserl lies in this, that, after being given his start by Brentano, he made a desperate effort to liberate philosophic eros, and at the moment he was about to succeed, he hurled it back into its jail, binding it (because he was himself ensnared), with the finest of threads, stronger by far than those of the old *cogito*, to illusions

42 *The Degrees of Knowledge, op. cit.,* pp. 125–126.

much more deceptive than all the Cartesian illusions, and which were to bring ideosophy taken for philosophy to a refined form most treacherous for the mind.

Husserl's procedure involved an intrinsic contradiction which his idealist prejudice prevented him from perceiving. Believing, like Descartes, that a reflexive gaze turned back upon the thinking subject could be used to build a philosophy, he erected into a principle the *suspension of judgment,* the *épokhè* dear to Pyrrho, by positing, as the primary methodological rule for the philosophizing intellect, that the latter is obliged (as a result of an *a priori* dictate and an idealist postulate never critically examined) to put *in parentheses* the whole range of extra-mental being (the very bread by which the intellect lives) *at the very time when it performs the act of knowing.* Thus, by a detestable rupture, we must separate the "object" perceived by the intelligence—which we place at the interior of knowing—from the "thing" which it perceives—which we banish to the exterior of knowing, in the parenthesis. As if the *object* perceived were not the *thing* itself insofar as intelligibly perceived! The thing itself carried to the very heart of the intelligence in order to become one with its vital act! Henceforth, the intellect, violating the very law of its life, is supposed to stop short at an *object-phenomenon,* which severs it from itself as well as from *what is* in the real world.

What is the meaning of this? It means (at this point I am obliged to do violence to the English language) that the intellect should *think being (penser l'être) while refusing to think it as such;* in other terms, it means that in thinking "being" I think something that is *thought,* not something that *is(en pensant l'être, je pense du pensé, non pas l'être);* or, as I have already observed:[43] *I know being on condition that it is put in parenthesis and abstracted out of sight (je connais l'être à condition de le mettre entre parenthèses ou de faire abstraction de lui).* Thus one sees emerge the absurdity inherent in the first principle—let us call it the Husserlian Parenthesis, which cuts knowledge in two, or the Husserlian Refusal—on which the whole of contemporary phenomenology depends.

In this phenomenology, every regulation coming from being or the real is henceforth rejected, and thought must do all its work while leaving the real in the parenthesis, and with no other guide-marks

43 Cf. Chap. 1, p. 8.

than the variable and endlessly swarming aspects it discovers in subjectivity—either the subjectivity of the intellectual operation itself, if I may say so, or the subjectivity of the experience of man with all its riches which, enthralling as they may be, have only the value of mere fact seized by the good fortune of observation. As a result, the whole of thought is delivered in its interpretations to the rule of the Verisimilar and the Arbitrary, and the ideosophy is brought, come what may, to the state of Grand Sophistry. Protagoras had already formulated the great axiom: and that's the point to which they have all come—man as the measure of all things, even of the God he worships.

CONTEMPORARY PHENOMENOLOGY

Whether they honor Husserl, or disregard and disown him (Man is ungrateful), or dismiss the *Méditations cartésiennes*, all our phenomenologists presuppose Husserl and are the prisoners of his Refusal.

There are some—the existentialist theorists (have they chosen the name to compensate for some frustration?)—in whom philosophic eros struggles to free itself, and who thereby find themselves engaged in a blind drama. It is in what I have just called the subjectivity of the intellectual operation itself, with its infinity of aspects and psychological shifts (to which, for the sake of a small ecstasy, they claim to give an alleged "ontological" meaning) that they are attempting to find this impossible liberation. The great witness in this drama is Heidegger, whom an ardent metaphysical eros, but enchained too, relentlessly torments, and who, obsessed with anxiety for being, carries on a tragic struggle against the emptiness of thought implied by phenomenology, only to go and seek help now, it seems, from the poets and the theogonic powers of their language: thereby bringing, as has been said,[44] "the most significant evidence of the absence of philosophy in our time."

[44] Pierre Trotignon, *Heidegger* (Paris: Presses Universitaires, 1965), p. 66. Besides, Heidegger himself does not wish to be a philosopher—but doubtless in wishing to be or become something better (once more the Hegelian virus).

"Thomism," writes Etienne Gilson, "is a philosophy of *Sein* insofar as it is a philosophy of *esse*. When young people invite us to make the discovery of Martin Heidegger, they invite us, without knowing, to make them rediscover the transontic metaphysics of St. Thomas Aquinas. . . . It would be interesting to know

To the drama of which I am speaking our Sartre is, for his own part, a nauseated witness (and less liberated than he likes to believe), who has, I think, perceived, thanks to literature and something of the novelist's sixth sense, a crack in the Parenthesis—situated so low down that one can steal a glance at it without giving offense to methodology—and, through the sewer, catch a glimpse of real existence, but (there is an idealist for you) as a shapeless, enormous and obscene, unspeakable and monstrous insult to reason—the Absurd of pure and absolute contingency.[45] And he was very quick to fill up the crack in the Parenthesis and to bring back into his thought, in the capacity of "object-phenomenon," that loathsome Absurd, in order to work out with it an "ontology" of the phenomenon, or better still, "of the trans-phenomenal being of the phenomenon," [46] and to declare that "the world is *en trop.*" [47] Words put up with everything. Yet it is clear that Sartre too brings us, in his own way, a forceful proof of the absence of philosophy in our time. (Well, there are nevertheless two, let us not forget it.)

Some among our other phenomenologists, a good many it seems, have definitely renounced philosophic eros, and, with perfect peace of mind, leave it tightly bound in its dark cell. To be theorists of existentialism holds no attraction for them. What interests them is to scrutinize and interpret (while still keeping, of course, extra-mental reality in the Parenthesis, and conforming, good naturedly, to the Husserlian Refusal) the world of human things which we are thirsting to know—ourselves and our life and the whole mystery of our past, as well as of our present beliefs and anxieties, history, culture, art, philosophy (why not?), religion above all—which they submit to

what Heidegger would have thought had he known of the existence of a metaphysics of *esse* before making his initial decisions. But we will never know; it is too late. . . . How could we, since Heidegger himself will never know? I ask the question only to suggest to those who urge us to follow him that there is no danger in store. Perhaps we have but the handicap of our advantage: they are urging us to follow those we have left behind." (*"Trois leçons sur le Thomisme et sa situation présente,"* Seminarium, No. 4, pp. 718–719.)

45 On this Sartrian idea of contingency, see the remarks of Claude Tresmontant in *Comment se pose aujourd'hui le problème de l'existence de Dieu* (Paris: éd. du Seuil, 1966), pp. 130–144.

46 *Being and Nothingness* (New York: Philosophical Library, 1956), p. lxii.

47 Probably (it is but a possible interpretation) the author meant that the world is a meaningless, unwanted and disgusting surplus, offending both reason and man's freedom.

hermeneutics where it is forbidden to go beyond man and his measure, and where myths henceforth inevitably reign supreme. Since they
are quite intelligent thinkers, anxious to be thoroughly and precisely
informed and, more often than not, honest and sincere (although the
Grand Sophistry, hidden in the heaven of the mind, keeps them always under its wing), their investigations are remarkably instructive
and sometimes fascinating. Provided it is not so craven as to accept
everything uncritically, philosophy can greatly profit by them. But
these investigations still remain under the regime of the Verisimilar
and the Arbitrary, of *everything to the measure of man*, and thus, of
a kind of latent immanentism; and finally, they seem to, but fail to,
quench our thirst. And not just our thirst. If we had only them for
guides they would land us in illusion.

Phenomenology is enjoying an immense prestige. I wish (without
expecting too much) that my necessarily long discussion of this most
recent of the mutations of idealism has been able to help some
readers clarify their own ideas on the subject.

There are still two remarks left to make. The first concerns a
radical error which the mind, if it wishes to free itself from the chains
which have fettered it for so long, should squarely reject once and for
all. This is the Kantian error. I quote a few lines from a contemporary
philosopher, who says what matters most on the subject: "If reason
is, as it were, an *organon* constituted *a priori*, we can ask ourselves by
what chance does reason happen to accord with the real. But if reason
is not constituted *a priori*, if the principles belonging to reason are in
fact *drawn from the real* itself through our knowledge of the real, then
one need hardly be astonished if there is accord between reason and
the real. . . . Rationality is not an order or a structure constituted
a priori, but a *relation* between the human mind and the real. . . .
Rationality is not determined *a priori* and in a purely formal way, but
with respect to the real, and in terms of the real. Rationality is," in the
mathematical sense of the word, "a function of the real." [48]

My second remark concerns a truth (obvious but obscured by
generations of hair-splitters) which the mind, if it seeks to liberate
at last philosophic eros and liberate itself, should first of all recognize

[48] Claude Tresmontant, *op. cit.*, pp. 161–162.

and always respect. I mean to say that the human mind, although being a reason handling its concepts and held to the strictest logic (it owes this to its carnal condition), is also an intellect, that is, a power capable of *seeing* in the intelligible order as the eye *sees* in the sensible order, but with incomparably more certitude. Is it not through such an intuition that the intellect knows the "first principles" of every demonstration? I am by no means speaking here of intuition such as Bergson understood it—although I am not forgetting that there is a "Bergsonism of intention" much nearer than one believes to Thomistic realism, nor that Bergson toward the end of his life, said once that he and myself, that poor Jacques who had criticized him so severely, had met "in the middle of the road." I do not forget, either, that even when busy with its work or research of the most rational kind, the human mind (because it is an intellect drawing its sustenance from the sensible world), is helped and prodded, in order to work well, much more often than philosophers and scientists are willing to admit, by "intuitions," or flashes of the imagination—they come to it unexpectedly, with the luck of the road, from the vigilance of sense and poetic instinct, or are born in the night of the unconscious (let us say rather, of the preconscious or supra-conscious of the spirit).

But I leave all that aside. It is of a totally different intuition that I am speaking: and *intellectual* intuition, purely and simply intellectual, which is the proper and sacred good of the intelligence as such —the absolutely primary intuition without which there is no genuine philosophic *savior* or wisdom: *the intuition of being.* To wish for it is not enough to get it. Bergson got it through a substitute which deceived him—and it was masked, in his way of conceptualizing it, by anti-intellectualist prejudice. Neither Husserl nor any ideosopher has had it. But whoever goes far enough in meditation will experience it some day—I mean whoever manages to enter into that alert and watchful silence of the mind where, consenting to the *simplicity* of the true, the intellect becomes sufficiently available, and vacant, and open, to hear what all things murmur, and to *listen*, instead of fashioning answers. Many have actually had this intuition who were too distracted by everyday life or their own reasonings to become aware of it. And many more among the common people experience it in this way than among "cultured" people. And it is enough to look at the gaze of certain children to realize that, without their having in them any of the reflectiveness of adults, their gaze is directed more at *being* than at the toys with which one amuses them, or even at the world whose riches they constantly discover simply by taking the trouble to receive them.

I will not try and describe what escapes any restraint and is beyond any word (although the simplest of concepts and the simplest of words are a valid sign of it), nor to lead someone where access is given only in purest solitude of soul. But is it not possible to resort to the language of metaphor, as inadequate as it is, to convey, not, to be sure, that which the intelligence grasps, but an inkling of the experience of this grasping? Let us say then (I have said this before,[49] though somewhat differently): What I then perceive is like a pure activity, a consistency, but superior to the whole order of the imaginable, a vivid tenacity, at once precarious (it is nothing for me to crush a gnat) and fierce (within me, around me, mounts like a clamor the universal vegetation) by which things surge up against me and triumph over a possible disaster, stand there, and not merely there, but in themselves, and by which they shelter in their thickness, in the humble measure meted out to what is perishable, a kind of glory demanding to be recognized.

That is what I can say of the experience in myself, *faible roseau pensant*, of the intuition of the *actus essendi*. A soul who is very close to me once gave me this testimony: "It often happened that I experienced, through a sudden intuition, the reality of my being, of the profound, first principle which places me outside of nothingness. A powerful intuition, whose violence sometimes frightened me, and which has first given me the knowledge of a metaphysical absolute." [50]

The intuition of being is not only, like the reality of the world and of things, the absolutely primary foundation of philosophy. It is the absolutely primary *principle* of philosophy (when the latter is able to be totally faithful to itself and achieve all of its dimensions).

[49] Cf. *A Preface to Metaphysics* (New York: Sheed and Ward, 1940), p. 53.
[50] Raïssa Maritain, *We Have Been Friends Together* (New York: Image Books, Doubleday and Co. 1961), p. 116.

THE NEED FOR FABLES
OR INTELLECTUAL FALSE CURRENCY

I have already stated (pp. 104–105) that the liberation of philosophic eros implies two operations, and have discussed the first of these, which concerns idealism and its after-effects, at some length. There is still one other thing which it behooves the mind to get rid of in order to bring about this liberation. This time it is not only philosophic eros which must be set free: for we are dealing with *all* that of which the hunger for the real, co-essential to the human soul, is defrauded; and this hunger longs to be satisfied with the real insofar as philosophic knowledge can convey it to us, but it also longs for the real insofar as it can be conveyed to us through more exalted ways.

Frustrated by an unbearable fast, such a hunger can give way in us to a pathological need which is equally vast, and seems a perversion of it. We have now to examine this need, for it worries us a great deal and we must get rid of it. What need? *The need for fables and intellectual false currency*. It is enormous nowadays and its roots go deep.

As a result of prejudices at work for a century in our proud modern culture, we are convinced not only that metaphysical knowledge is entirely valueless, but that in the realm of non-metaphysical knowledge only one type is capable of unshakeable certitude: Science—either mathematical sciences or sciences of the phenomena of nature. (This is rather funny, because great mathematicians tell us that the poetic instinct and the sense of beauty play a great part in their business,[51] and because the more physics, the queen of the sciences of nature, advances in its admirable discoveries, the more its fecundity seems to depend on what M. d'Espagnat calls "the perpetual renewal of scientific perspectives," [52] on rapidly changing hypotheses, and on ways of mathematical interpretation which vary with the diversity of

[51] See Marston Morse, "Mathematics and the Arts," *Yale Review*, Summer 1951, cited in my book, *Creative Intuition in Art and Poetry* (New York: Pantheon Books, 1954), p. 93, n. 33.

[52] Bernard d'Espagnat, *Conceptions de la Physique contemporaine* (Paris: Hermann, 1965). This rigorous and lucid book offers philosophers concerned with epistemology a remarkable presentation of the actual state of the question in the case of theoretical physics.

cases, and even at times contradict one another. All this is quite normal, moreover, as far as this particular level in human knowledge is considered. But this in no way alters our general conviction that scientists are the only ones to perform a work of rational knowledge worthy of the name, and that Science, in the modern sense of the word, is endowed with an absolute privilege of intellectual certainty.)

On the other hand, it is clear that science as such has nothing to tell us about the problems which matter most to us, and about the idea of the world, of man, perhaps of God, which we cannot escape forming for ourselves, any more than about the torment of the absolute, the "why were we born?"; the "to what can we wholly give our hearts?"; the desire for that fire which will burn us without consuming us, which as hidden as they may be, are there, in our very depths. All of this remains completely outside the scope of science.

No one is more keenly aware of the limitations inherent in the very validity of science, and more scrupulously careful in observing them, than the scientists themselves, although they sometimes feel how desirable it would be, if it were possible, to go beyond these limitations in order to work out a *de natura rerum*, and reach, in a rational synthesis in accordance with their findings, an overall view of that world on which they work in their closely guarded precinct. A few of them, Julian Huxley for instance, have tried their hand at it by extrapolating the concepts of science—that is, by carrying them outside the field where they are valid. (How could they do otherwise, since no one has furnished them—supposing they wished to learn how to use it—with the only instrument adapted to such an enterprise: philosophic knowledge with the approach and concepts proper to it?) The attempts in question have all been unhappy. Without being in the least aware of it, these perfectly honest minds had issued bad money, though not very harmful. This kind of bad money has a circulation as restricted as it is short-lived, and hardly deceives anybody but those who naively coin it.

With the phenomenologists it is quite another story. Mixed in with the good copper coin of psychological observation and the human sciences whose treasures they are exploiting for us, the highbrow fables and false currency they issue (in perfect good faith, I am not forgetting) enjoy a very widespread circulation, and succeed in making philosophic intelligence come to grief. That's a fine achievement.

Because of their very renunciation of attaining reality in itself, such ideosophers cannot, however, launch the mind on miraculous dreams or enthralling adventures in which its living forces will blaze in vain.

Of course, there are also counterfeiters, the quacks, and their clientele. But these don't count, even for our precious intelligentsia which leaves them where they belong, in the gutter.

When we bring all this data together, what sort of balance sheet should we draw up? Nothing but a blank: a blank rather innocuous, as far as the pseudo-philosophical ventures of a few scientists are concerned; an immense void with respect to philosophical intelligence snared and deluded by phenomenology; an absolute blank when it comes to the aspiration of the spirit for that supreme wisdom which Hegel sought in vain.

Except for the quite restricted province of science busy with interpreting measurable phenomena and achieving mastery over matter, the great hunger for the real, co-essential with the human soul, has absolutely nothing to allay what it longs for. Why be surprised at the enormous need for fables and intellectual false currency which has developed within us? This need is limitless. What it craves for is not any kind whatsoever of fables or false currency even enjoying a widespread circulation; it is the great Fable and the great False Currency, which will cheat our great hunger, and will be current in the entire world, controlling the entire market of our hearts' and minds' demands.

That bad money chases out good is a familiar adage, and it applies equally to the false currency of the intelligence, at least for a while. This spell was very short for the early Christian Gnostics, however sublime the Logos they claimed to represent may have seemed. Far from answering a need for fiction, they were in front of truth itself, and the reaction of faith was too sharp, the offensive of the Apologist Fathers too vigorous, for their influence to be lasting. History has witnessed the appearance of other superior minds with a passion for the truth, who deluded themselves and uttered the great Fable and issued great intellectual False Currency—the latter has never been the work of purveyors of fiction or counterfeiters,[53] it demands perfect sincerity, at least to begin with, great intellectual power, and the en-

[53] A counterfeiter is one who makes counterfeit money on purpose, with the intention of deceiving.

raptured devotion of noble spirits led astray in spite of themselves. (Not completely in spite of themselves, for there is at the outset a sin against the intellect: the refusal to recognize the intrinsic order of the human intelligence, with the essential distinction it requires between the typical forms of knowledge of which the mind is capable. From the start one mixes everything together: since, scanty as it may have been in such and such an age, philosophy of nature, metaphysics, theology, natural mystique, even touches of supernatural mystique, all of which are made to contaminate and corrupt one another in a powerful high-soaring lyrical flight—unnatural and deceptive because it is pseudo-angelic.) The Moslem Gnostics have a particular interest for us because they were monists who clung nevertheless (hence a tremendous and stimulating inner tension) to faith in the one and transcendent God of Islam. I am speaking of them without scruples, despite my lack of scholarship because conversations with Louis Gardet have given me the necessary information on the subject. He made me share his admiration (the most guarded) for the genius of Ibn 'Arabī, that great wondrous synthesizer of the thirteenth century, fascinated by a world in the process of emanation which came from God, manifested God to God himself, and returned to him.[54] The remote and contrasted analogy which my friend pointed out between the thought of Ibn 'Arabī and certain views of Teilhard seemed to me quite remarkable. Before Ibn 'Arabī there had been Nāsir e-Khosraw, and, after him would come Mulla Sadrā. In the Christian world there was Jacob Boehme, Fichte perhaps, and some other great names. But none of the men dedicated to Gnosis I have just referred to were answering a general need for the great Fable, any more than were the Christian Gnostics of the first centuries. This privilege was reserved for our time.

As far as the history of culture is concerned, the great Fable or great intellectual False Currency, taken in itself, is not as dangerous as it appears. What is infinitely more dangerous is the need for this counterfeit money because, as long as it is with us, it will insist on being served. After each issue, it will require another, it is never satisfied. In spite of everything, it is a piece of good luck for our age that Teil-

[54] Cf. Louis Gardet, "Expérience et Gnose chez Ibn 'Arabī," an article soon to appear in a collective work in honor of Ibn 'Arabī, under the auspices of the General Secretariat of Arts, Letters and Social Sciences, U.A.R.

hardism—whatever disastrous simplifications may always accompany the enthusiastic popularization of a great impassionate conception—owes its origins to a genius as lofty as that of Père Teilhard de Chardin with so tenacious, so ardent, and so artlessly pure a faith. After Teilhardism, something new will be demanded, and after that something else, which will be worth even less.

As superfluous as it is for any sensible person, I am here inserting a parenthesis. For there are things which are self-evident, but on which, nevertheless, it is worth our while to insist. The offensive terms which I have had to use in this section refer to ideas that are in circulation, not to the person who conceived them. The solitary, painful, obstinate research of Père Teilhard, his patient courage in the face of the hardly very noble obstacles set up in his path, his zeal for truth, his total gift of self to a mission which he considered prophetic, the pure sincerity which shines from one end of his work to the other, and the extraordinary personal experience which he underwent, are all things which deserve deepest respect. He was a paleontologist of great worth, a Christian whose faith never wavered, a priest of exemplary fidelity. I said earlier that none of the varieties of the great Fable or great intellectual False Currency exemplified by history was ever the work of dealers in fiction or counterfeiters. Nobody will do me the wrong of imagining that words I have explicitly ruled out with respect to the person of the great Gnostics, could ever be applied by me to the person of Père Teilhard de Chardin, nor that outrage and self-contradiction form part of my arsenal. And yet, when I consider, not Teilhard certainly, but the ideas which he put in circulation, and especially Teilhardism, with its literature of propaganda and its enraptured ecclesiastical retinue, no matter how hard I am striving, it is impossible to avoid offensive terms if I look for exactness. And the fact is, I pledged at the beginning of this book to call a spade a spade.

TEILHARD DE CHARDIN
AND TEILHARDISM

I had the honor of meeting Père Teilhard de Chardin a few times. When I saw him for the first time—it was at Paris a long time ago—I was struck by the total isolation in which he carried out his research.

He asked himself a good many questions and, on leaving him, I wondered how, in a great religious Order such as the one he belonged to, he was not helped by a few friends, good philosophers or theologians, who would form a team with him. Maybe he didn't want such a thing. (Just why, after years of study under teachers no doubt wisely chosen for their mission, he remained in perfect ignorance or forgetfulness of the *Doctor Communis*, is another mystery, which has astonished Gilson.)

In the course of another meeting, he spoke in a moving way of the scientists among his friends with whom his language permitted him to broach the problem of religion without obstacles or the feeling of their being pushed out of their own home ground, and I had the impression he found this a valuable encouragement. During the war, he sent me from China a pamphlet [55] whose contents confirmed me in certain of my views, and which I cited in one of my books.[56] It was toward the end of the war, in New York, that I saw him for the last time. He did not conceal a certain bitterness (understandable enough) toward the ecclesiastical authorities. For my part, I can't say I liked the way, a few years later, his papers circulated anonymously in the seminaries.

There is a justice to be rendered to him, which is that he was always at the opposite pole from idealism or ideosophy. He never stopped believing with an unshakable certitude in the reality of the world. With respect to realism, in the sense this word has for epistemology, and to the primary foundation of philosophy (it is, nevertheless, only the foundation) he was, without realizing it, in full agreement with St. Thomas. It is their only meeting point; and yet it left room, all the same, for a serious ambiguity. For while St. Thomas was perfectly certain of the reality of the world, he didn't put so much fervor into it; he had only to open his eyes. Whereas "faith in the world" and "faith in God" were, so to speak, the two poles of Teilhard's thought. Everybody knows how he spoke of these two types of faith.

And finally did he not state once that his effort to discover a "better Christianity" (the "meta-Christianity" which he mentioned to Gilson) was directed toward a religion in which the personal God would

[55] *Réflexions sur le progrès*, Peking, 1941.
[56] *The Rights of Man and Natural Law* (New York: Charles Scribner's Sons, 1942).

become "the *soul of the World* that our religious and cultural stage of development calls for?" [57] (something to delight the ancient Stoics . . .)

At the very root of Teilhard's thought there was, I believe, a poetic intuition—extremely powerful—of the sacred worth of created nature: a worth to which no limits could be assigned. I am imagining a Lucretius who would have been Christian.

This intuition had to be reconciled with a faith in the one and triune God and in the Incarnate Word—and simultaneously with a religious awareness, extremely powerful in its own right, of the presence of God in the world. (In this religious awareness, natural mystique must have played the greater part, for it caused the soul to experience in some way the created effects of the Presence of immensity, but, in a soul living from grace, it could no doubt include also touches of supernatural mystique, mingled, as this whole experience was, with a singular human exaltation.) I am thinking of the great text of Teilhard, *The Mass on the World*.

How realize such a reconciliation, and attempt to conceptualize it? By taking hold of the idea of evolution, which biology, astrophysics, microchemistry have made familiar to science, so as to give a mystical sense to it (to it too), and make of it a great Myth of the universal reality: we have thus to contemplate a sacred Evolution carrying through a series of threshold-crossings a matter endowed with spiritual potentialities, and infinitely humble at the outset, to the very glory of the sons of God, and the throne of that personal God whose incarnate

---

[57] *Lettres à Léontine Zanta* (Paris: Desclée De Brouwer, 1965). The italics are mine. I reproduce here the entire sentence: "What is coming to dominate my interests and inner preoccupations, as you already know, is the effort to establish within me, and spread around me, a new religion (let us call it, if you like, a better Christianity) in which the personal God ceases to be the great neolithic proprietor of old in order to become the soul of the World which our religious and cultural stage of development calls for."

In this text, it is fitting to underline not merely "the *soul of the World*, which our religious and cultural stage calls for," but also the words: *"the effort to establish within me and spread around me."* This *"spread around me"* obliges us to conclude that Etienne Gilson allowed himself to be carried away by an impulse of the heart when, noting that the doctrine of Teilhard "was hardly a doctrine, but rather a way of feeling," he added, "one could not possibly maintain that he did anything whatever to spread it." See his Article *"Le cas Teilhard de Chardin,"* *op. cit.*, p. 735. He never stopped trying to spread it.

Son is, at the heart of the cosmos, the principle motor of the whole of becoming.

Thus, it seems to me, may be outlined, as to its essentials, the bare trajectory of Teilhard's thought. This thought gives to Science a dazzling primacy. Actually, the science of the scientists has been entirely outpaced, nay more, swept along and absorbed into a great torrent of ardent meditation, in which science, faith, mystique, theology and philosophy in a diffused state, are inextricably mingled and confounded. And in this we are forced indeed to recognize the sin against the intellect to which I have already drawn attention.[58] Doubtless it was in all innocence that Teilhard committed it, since the idea of a specific distinction between the different degrees of knowledge was always completely foreign to him. Yet even so, it was a sin against the intellect in its own right, and, as such, an irreparable one.

That is why, if we place ourselves in an authentically theological perspective in order to consider the doctrine ("hardly a doctrine, rather a way of feeling") of Teilhard de Chardin, we must say with Gilson that, in the poetic world in which he introduces us "whoever has followed the history of Christian thought finds himself in familiar country. The Teilhardian theology is one more Christian gnosis, and like gnoses from Marcion to the present, it is a *theology-fiction*. We recognize all the traditional earmarks of the breed: a cosmic perspective on all problems, or perhaps we should say a perspective of cosmogenesis. We have a cosmic material, a cosmic Christ,[59] and, since the latter is the physical center of creation, we have a Christ who is basically an 'evolutor' and 'humanizator,' in short, a 'universal Christ' as an explanation of the universal mystery, which is but one with the Incarnation. Cosmogenesis thereby becomes Christogenesis, giving rise to the Christic and the Christosphere, an order which crowns the noosphere and perfects it through the transforming presence of Christ. This nice vocabulary is not cited as blameworthy in itself, but merely as symptomatic of the taste which all gnoses show for

---

[58] Cf. pp. 114–115.

[59] In support of his views, Teilhard appealed to St. Paul by assimilating the thought of the Apostle to his own in a way which only the "transports of passion," as is said in famous criminal cases, can excuse. At the conclusion of this book there is a long *Note on a Text of St. Paul* which I have written on the subject. [J.M.]

pathetic neologisms, hinting at unfathomable perspectives and heavy with affectivity." [60]

In the matter of doctrine, we are here in the regime (impossible to invent another word nor one less offensive to pious ears, nor more exact) of the Great Fable. While it is true that Teilhardism—I say *Teilhardism*, the ideology fabricated by the initiates and given circulation by the popular press—presents itself as a doctine (which we must describe for what it is); on the contrary, what matters essentially in Teilhard himself is a personal experience, and, truly speaking, incommunicable, although he never ceased looking for ways to communicate it. This accounts for the title chosen by Etienne Gilson for his excellent study; [61] since it unfortunately appeared in a publication which is not easily come by, I will offer a few extracts from it in the course of my own reflections. I would like first to have cited the pages where Gilson pays tribute to the person of Teilhard, but I was pleased to pay such a tribute myself just a few pages ago, and I see no point in repeating myself.

The core of Gilson's study, it seems to me, is the part where he accounts for that meta-Christianity about which Teilhard, on the spur of the moment, once spoke to him in New York. The term "left him nonplussed" at first, but on further thought, Teilhard's meaning was not slow in dawning on him. The key was furnished by a passage in *Christianisme et Evolution, Suggestions pour servir à une théologie nouvelle*: "Roughly speaking," Teilhard writes, "we can say that while the main preoccupation of Theology during the first centuries of the Church was to determine, intellectually and mystically, the position of Christ in relation to the Trinity, its vital concern in our day has become this: to analyze and specify the relations of existence and influence connecting together Christ and the Universe." [62]

Teilhard believed that "in the first century of the Church, Christianity made its definitive entry into human thought by boldly as-

---

[60] Etienne Gilson, "*Trois leçons sur le Thomisme et sa situation présente*, *Seminarium* (No. 4, 1965), pp. 716–717.

[61] "*Le cas Teilhard de Chardin*," *op. cit.*, pp. 720 ff.

[62] Quoted by Claude Cuénot, *Teilhard de Chardin* (Paris: éd. du Seuil, 1963), p. 141. "I don't believe," Gilson remarks, "that any text of Père Teilhard is more significant or expresses more clearly and simply the meaning of his enterprise." "*Le cas Teilhard de Chardin*," p. 730.

similating the Christ of the Gospel to the Alexandrian Logos." [63]
Here he was wrong, for as Gilson puts it, what happened was "exactly
the opposite. The Apologist Fathers did not boldly assimilate the
Jesus of the Gospel to the Alexandrian Logos"; it was the Alexandrian
Logos which, even more daringly, they "assimilated to Christ the Savior of the Gospel." [64] Be that as it may, what was called for today, in
Teilhard's view, was the reverse of what he believed the Fathers had
done. It involves, then, a "complete transposition of Christology," [65]
a "generalization of Christ the Redeemer into a veritable Christ the
evolutor." [66] We must "integrate Christianity with cosmogenesis"; [67] for it is imperative that "today's theology assimilate Christ to
the cosmic force, origin and end of Evolution. What a revolution! We
are simply invited to bring back our faith in the Redeemer to its
proper place." [68]

In this way, Teilhard "can in one stroke speak of that 'elevation of
the historical Jesus to a universal physical function' and that 'ultimate
identification of cosmogenesis with a Christogenesis.' Note the
word *elevation!* We thus obtain the 'neo-logos of modern philosophy,'
who is no longer primarily the redeemer of Adam, but the 'evolutory
principle of a universe in motion.' Look how careful he has been to
preserve Christ, they will tell us! Yes, but what Christ?. . . I am not
sure whether an omega point of science exists, but I feel perfectly
sure that in the Gospel, Jesus of Nazareth is quite another thing than
the 'concrete germ' of the Christ Omega. It's not that the new function of Christ lacks grandeur or nobility, but that it is something utterly different from the old. We feel a little as though we were before
an empty tomb: they have taken away Our Lord and we do not know
where they have laid him." [69]

We would be making a mistake, however, if we thought that Teilhard ever wished to substitute for the historical Jesus of the Gospel a
Christ "elevated to a universal physical function," and to replace the

[63] *Teilhard de Chardin, op. cit.*, p. 141 (Gilson, p. 731).
[64] Gilson, p. 732.
[65] *Ibid.*, p. 731.
[66] *Teilhard de Chardin, Christianisme et Evolution*, p. 142.
[67] Claude Cuénot, *Teilhard de Chardin* (Paris: éd. du Seuil, 1963), p. 143,
(Gilson, p. 734).
[68] Gilson, p. 731.
[69] *Ibid.*, pp. 732–733 (all the formulations of Teilhard de Chardin quoted there
are found in the work of Claude Cuénot, *op. cit.*, p. 142).

Christ of faith by a cosmic Christ—in whom, as Gilson remarks, "no scientist believes," [70] (although he was imagined for their sake). The turning upside down of Christianity which Teilhard's "meta-Christianity" amounted to is an operation of much vaster scope. What is to be done is to make the very Christ of history into the cosmic Christ. It seems to me I can catch a glimpse of the manner in which Teilhard was able to conceive such an enterprise, when I consider what is implied in a *purely evolutive* conception where being is replaced by becoming and every essence or nature stably constituted in itself vanishes.

If the truth of this conception be granted, does not *being man* lie in being or having been the cosmos itself throughout the whole immense process by which it was hominized? Could the Word take flesh in Mary without having "taken matter," if I may say, in the entire cosmos and throughout the whole extent of its history? Could he become Incarnate one day, at a certain moment in history, without having first been (why should I be the only one afraid of neologisms?) Immaterized and Encosmicized during the whole course of the evolution which led up to that point? If he made himself *man*, it is because he also made himself *world*. There you have the "generalization of Christ the Redeemer into a veritable Christ the evolutor," or at least the only way I can find to give such a formula an intelligible meaning. (Did I say intelligible? My tongue has tripped me up: let us say rather, almost thinkable.)

This Christianity turned upside down would be for religious thought, if religious thought were to become purely imaginary, a grandiose vision, enchanting it with the spectacle of the divine ascent of creation toward God. But what does it tell us of the secret path which matters more than any spectacle? What can it tell us of the essential, of the mystery of the cross and the redemptive blood? or of that grace whose presence in a single soul is worth more than all of nature or of that love which makes us co-redeemers with Christ, and those blessed tears through which his peace reaches us? The new gnosis is, like all gnoses—a poor gnosis.[71]

If, moreover, we wish to get a more complete idea of the Teilhardian gnosis and of the "reversals of perspective" which it calls for, I

[70] *Ibid.*, p. 732.
[71] See Appendix II, on *The Theology of Teilhard.*

must cite once more (I do so reluctantly, but the texts are there and, though taken from a private letter, they disclose the thought of the author with an unquestionable exactness) the aforementioned letter to Léontine Zanta, which brings us a few clarifications offered by Père Teilhard himself: "It is not a question," he wrote, "of superimposing Christ upon the world, but of 'panchristizing' the Universe. The delicate point (I have partly touched on it in *Christologie et Evolution*) is that, in pursuing this line of thought, one is led not merely to an enlargement of views, but to a reversal of perspectives: Evil (no longer punishment for a fault, but 'sign and effect' of Progress) and Matter (no longer a guilty and inferior element, but 'the stuff of Spirit') take on a meaning diametrically opposed to the meaning *habitually* considered as Christian.[72] Christ emerges from the transformation incredibly exalted (at least I think so—and all the worried ones to whom I have spoken of it share my view). But is this still really the Christ of the Gospel? And if it is not he, on what, henceforth is based what we seek to build?" [73]

One will observe that to regard matter as a guilty element is a *platonic* notion held to be senseless by the thought "habitually considered as Christian." And although Christian thought believes that our condition of fallen nature is the result of original sin, it has never held that evil (illness, the loss of a child, any kind of affliction) is always "punishment for a fault." The Lord said just the opposite apropos of the man born blind. One will notice also that "transformation" from which (because it panchristizes *"the Universe"*) Christ emerges *"incredibly exalted"*—he, the Word Incarnate, whose grace, causing streams of eternal life to gush forth, raises us to the very life of God. Finally, one will note that at one point Père Teilhard asked himself apropos of his cosmic Christ, the question: "Is this still the Christ of the Gospel?" (without which, he added, and here we recognize the fidelity of his heart, his construction would lack all foundation). But his faith in the Christ of the Gospel was too strong—and his faith in the world too—for him not to be inwardly convinced that the question he asked could only be resolved in the affirmative. "One thing

[72] In the same letter, p. 129, apropos the *Esquisse d'un Univers Personnel*, which he was soon to draw up, he added: "Gradually everything is being transformed: the moral is fused with the physical, individuality extended into Universality, matter becomes the structure of Spirit."

[73] *Lettres à Léontine Zanta, op. cit.*, pp. 127–128.

reassures me," he continues in the same letter, "it is that the growing light within me is accompanied by love and by self-renunciation in the Greater than me. This could not possibly mislead." Would that such proofs, alas, as noble as they are, could never mislead. The *this* with which Père Teilhard set his mind at rest did much to confirm him in his worst illusions.

Gilson is probably right in reminding us that the religious experience of Père Teilhard actually counts for much more than his doctrine. "Scientific illumination and the cult of evolution, in a manner somewhat similar to the confused evolutionism of Julian Huxley, invited him to conceptualize, in a language that was imprecise although it wore a scientific look, a religious experience of whose depth there can be no doubt" [74] and which, whatever the tenor of its spiritual authenticity or the illusions it may have fostered, was the life of his life,[75] but which has been absolutely personal to him, and without which moreover, his "doctrine makes no sense." [76]

"That is why," Gilson continues, "I see no danger in store." [77] On that point, I am less of an optimist. The religious experience of Père Teilhard was not transmissible, that's perfectly true, but Teilhardism is transmissible, and it transmits itself extremely well, with words, confused ideas, a mystico-philosophical imagery, and a whole emotional commotion of huge illusory hopes, which a good many men of good faith are ready to accept as a genuinely exalting intellectual synthesis and a new theology.

Yet I have a hunch that this Teilhardian gnosis and its attempt at a metachristianity received from the Council a rather heavy blow. For when all is said and done, it was nothing for Marx and Engels to turn

[74] Gilson, pp. 735–736.

[75] Thus, to quote Gilson again (*op cit.*, p. 727), "like a nugget of pure gold, his piety and childhood faith" remained always in him, in spite of everything, "intact and almost miraculously preserved beneath ceaseless alluvions of science and the rest. He himself underlined this continuity. . . . For him the cosmic Christ was first of all the Child Jesus, and was always to remain so. The newborn of Christmas is exactly the same who became 'the Child of Bethlehem and the Crucified One, the Prime Mover and the collecting Nucleus of the world itself.' " (The passage of Teilhard reproduced here is cited by Claude Cuénot, *op cit.*, p. 65.) Teilhard felt all this in a spiritual experience in which a good many heterogeneous elements were mingled, before attempting to express it in the conceptualization we have been dealing with above (pp. 115–122).

[76] Gilson, p. 728.

[77] Gilson, p. 736.

Hegel upside down, but to turn Christianity upside down so that it is no longer rooted in the Trinity and the Redemption but in the evolving Cosmos is quite a different matter. No theologian, mystic, or meditative scholar, no matter how hard he tries, is equal to that—nor even a wonder-worker. It would require the one whom the Creed calls the *unam, sanctam, catholicam et apostolicam* (when you come right down to it, it's the Church, isn't it, who teaches Christianity, whether "better" or not better Christianity). This means that it would require a Council. It is possible that certain Teilhardists, when they heard there was to be a Council, looked, if not for a dogmatic confirmation of the cosmic Christ (it was obviously too soon for that), at least for some encouragement, be it only the shadow of an encouragement, for their doctrine. But read the texts of the Council, study them with the aid of a magnifying glass, and you won't find there the ghost of a shadow of such an encouragement. With a magnanimous serenity, the Council utterly and completely ignored this great effort at a *"better Christianity."* And nothing could be more classical than its two dogmatic Constitutions. If the partisans of Teilhardism did not have their head in the clouds, they would realize a little just what this means for them. They will have to wait for a new Council, and another, and Lord knows how many after that. Or else, if their patience wears thin, they will go so far as to form themselves into a separate sect, as did Marcion and his disciples, at the risk of making Père Teilhard rise from his grave to condemn them? All that is none too pleasant.

Getting back to Père Teilhard himself, I would merely like to say in conclusion that he has not been well served, either by his friends, his enemies, nor in the first place, by himself. What he strove to translate into rough drafts or suggestions of a system—and what both friend and foe hastened to harden into a doctrine sure of itself, and of its power to renew everything—were ideas at work in the very fire of a quite peculiar kind of spiritual experience, where the faith of his childhood, ardent and vivid until death, struggled with great scientific dreams: an experience which, by its very nature, remained strictly incommunicable.

Whatever Teilhard may have done or hoped to do, such ideas, in reality, could only find expression as fragments of a vast poem which he would have written. One doesn't expect a poem to bring us any kind of rational knowledge whatever, be it scientific, philosophical, or theological. One expects it only to give us a glimpse of what, in an obscure contact, the poet has seized in himself and in things at the same time. But we can admire such a poem for its boldness and its beauty. And it can awaken in those who love it—particularly the poem I am speaking of—fertile ideas and lofty aspirations, and can likewise serve to overcome their prejudices and defenses, opening their mind to the flame of living faith which burned in the soul of the poet. For it is the privilege of poetry to be able to transmit an invisible flame, and through the grace of God, a flame of such a nature.

Well, this poem which Teilhard would have written, and which he actually gave us in a kind of travesty, is what his work really was. If Teilhard's work had been taken for what it truly was (but which he did not want it to be), both his overly zealous friends and those enemies who were over-anxious to condemn him, would doubtless have been disappointed, and he himself the first to protest. But this work would have retained its most authentic nobility and dignity, and Teilhard and the Christian world would have been spared not a little turmoil and unfortunate misunderstanding. But then there would have been no Teilhardism, or mad hope for the advent of a better Christianity celebrating the glories of the cosmos.

There are many, I surmise, whose hearts have been opened to the grace of faith by Père Teilhard de Chardin, or the reading of his books. Not only is it fitting that they acknowledge and revere the memory of one who was of such help to them, but one can also understand the respect and admiration they harbor for his works and for what Gilson and I call his gnosis, which no doubt appears to them as a well-founded doctrine. Yet it is not to it that they actually owe the gift of the truth which sets one free, but to the flame to which I have just alluded, and which, from the heart of Père Teilhard, and through the channel of a "theology-fiction," reached them, thanks to the holy grace of God and thanks to the grace of poetry, which is not supernatural, but descends also from the Father of lights.

March 31, 1966

6 THE TRUE NEW FIRE

THE REQUESTS AND
RENEWALS OF GENUINE
KNOWLEDGE

A GREAT WISE MAN

In the first part of the previous chapter I tried to show that human reason, infirm as it may be, is not, of itself, precluded from the possibility of attaining some day a *doctrine essentially grounded in truth,* with respect to the highest problems man may grapple with in his quest for truth, and which pertain to philosophy and theology. Such an attainment is something possible, I wrote, it is certainly not something probable. I added, however, that the improbable sometimes occurs.

The Catholic Church—who is entrusted only with the deposit of faith, but who, in order to maintain it both intact and progressive (for here too there is progress, I mean as far as the revealed dogma becomes more and more explicit) needs solid judgment and has received a gift of discernment unquestionably superior to that of all her professors—seems convinced that, thanks to a singular good fortune, the improbable in question has actually occurred as regards theology (and philosophy).[1] And an old peasant like me, who, having not been entrusted with any sacred deposit, is obliged to no particular prudence, and feels perfectly free to say all he is thinking, has a firm

---

[1] "So heartily do we approve the great praises accorded this most divine of geniuses," declared Pius XI in 1923, "that we think Thomas should be called not merely the Angelic Doctor, but the Common, or Universal Doctor of the Church, for the Church has made his doctrine her own." (Encyclical *Studiorum ducem*)

certitude that such in fact was the case: thanks to a long historical development in which Eastern and Western Christianity (even, at a given moment, through Islam) were equally engaged, and thanks to the exceptional genius—exceptionally favored by the historic moment (and by graces from on high)—of a European (alas, one cannot avoid being born somewhere) who could never speak any language except Neapolitan and Latin (no time for Berlitz) and who never believed he had a prophetic mission—but he had read all the Fathers, and "all the books," [2] and he knew the Bible by heart (who knows? that's perhaps the case for Bultmann and Vögtle, and our other biblicists). And not without weeping and trembling, he found himself invested with the gravest of responsibilities: to set in order and integrate the immense labor of knowledge and wisdom by means of which the ages of faith had sought to acquire some rational understanding of the divine mystery which had been proclaimed piecemeal by the prophets, and in its fullness by the Incarnate Word. "What is God?" the child used to ask his teachers at the Abbey of Monte Cassino where, at the age of five, he had been presented as an oblate by his parents (who already saw him Abbot-Bishop). He never did anything but ask this question.

Thomas Aquinas was a man of extraordinary humility; Guillaume de Tocco, his first biographer, makes a big point of this. We know that at the Convent of Saint-Jacques in Paris he listened to Albertus Magnus without once opening his mouth, and that the students dubbed him the great Dumb Ox of Sicily. Shortly after, at Cologne, where he had followed his teacher, they pitied this silent one until the day when a student who had been moved "by compassion" to repeat a difficult lesson for him, stumbled all of a sudden, and the Dumb Ox serenely explained the whole business to him—truth is first served, isn't it?

It was owing to his meekness of heart and humility, writes Tocco, that he was given in contemplation the knowledge of what he taught. At the moment of becoming Master in theology, so appalled was he by the magnitude of his new responsibility that he could not stop his prayers and tears, "because I am forced to receive the dignity of Master and I lack the necessary learning." At the end of his life,

---

[2] *La chair est triste, hélas, et j'ai lu tous les livres.* (Mallarmé) "The flesh is sad, alas, and I've read all the books.")

whatever he had written seemed to him "like so much straw." His Master's cap was never for him a matter of the least pride, nor did he feel he was failing in his duties toward this cap when, in Bologna, panting for breath (he was quite stout) he hurried to keep up with a fellow friar whom he accompanied in town and who had called him a dawdler.

Each time he set to work, this Doctor wept and prayed a good deal. It was near the altar that he would go seeking guidance. With his head pressed against the tabernacle, "he would remain there with many tears and great sobs, and would then return to his cell and continue writing." He has been above all a contemplative, great among the greatest, constantly in touch with heaven through a very pure and very humble *oraison. Contemplata aliis tradere,* is a motto of the Dominican Order and it's from St. Thomas that the phrase derives. He took it seriously.

He had, along with that, a good sense of humor, drawing donkey heads in the margins of his manuscript when his pen reached the name of some particularly esteemed author. Once, when a brother beckoned him (for he was thought to be naive) to the window to see an ox flying by, he hastened to do so, only to say to the sly one: "It is less surprising to see an ox fly than to hear a friar lie."

Why have I begun to go on about his character and personality? Because I love him. And also, with a hope it will help prepare me a little to say something about his doctrine, which I don't feel worthy to speak of.

For here we actually have it, that improbable doctine essentially grounded in truth, which, instead of remaining in a state of mere possibility, as a virtual goal to which the contrasting efforts of human thought tended without attaining it, found itself *formed* and organized at a privileged moment in history, and thanks to a privileged genius, in keeping with the habits I have already alluded to of a Providence as ironic as it is generous. The doctrine equipped by St. Thomas is possessed of all the properties, highly exceptional, one may wish for so hazardous a success. It is not the doctrine of *one* man, but the whole labor of the Fathers of the Church, the seekers of Greece, and the inspired of Israel (without forgetting the prior stages crossed by the human mind—nor the contribution made by the Arab world) which it brings to unity. And certainly not as though to a dead end! For it is an intelligible organism meant to keep on growing always, and to extend across the centuries its insatiable thirst for new prey. It is a doctrine *open* and without frontiers; open to every reality wherever it is and every truth from wherever it comes, especially the new truths which the evolution of culture or science will enable it to bring out (an achievement presupposing that the mind is able to transcend for a moment its own conceptual language in order to enter the conceptual language of another, and to return from this voyage possessed of the intuition by which this other one has lived). It is, too, a doctrine open to the various problematics it may see fit to employ, whether in the course of time it give rise to them itself or whether it goes to seek them out—while renewing them in the light of its own fundamental intuitions—in other universes of thought formed under other heavens.[3] I like to imagine all that could be brought to us by a Hindu who had become a Christian and a disciple of St. Thomas, and who would thoroughly know, with a kind of piety and filial connaturality, the Vedantic schools of thought and their particular ways of intellectual approach.

And because it is such an open doctrine, a hunger and thirst for truth that can never be sated, St. Thomas' doctrine is a doctrine indefinitely *progressive*, and *free* of all save the true, free with respect to itself, to its own imperfections which need correcting and its own

[3] The above can be found excellently stated in a page of Olivier Lacombe. "We will not surprise anyone," he wrote some years ago, "when we say that in our eyes St. Thomas Aquinas is, in the age of Doctors, the Doctor par excellence. We think his doctrine rests on definite foundations, while remaining progressive and faithfully open to all the increases of truth in man. We do not pretend that the disciples of St. Thomas have a right to despise the avenues of discovery, nor the fruitful zeal, or the contributions to truth of thinkers and schools who do not accept our premises. On the contrary, we are convinced that it is incumbent upon us to be that much more attentive to all of this, since we consider these premises most certain and most comprehensive. We believe that twenty centuries of the life of human reason in the climate of Christian grace have confirmed it in this powerful source of truth. Thus hallowed, it affirms itself eminently fruitful. To the degree that it stands faithful to an intellectual tradition which has been able, by its fullness and depth, to liberate and give a permanent place to the intelligible treasures accumulated by Western civilization, we would like to be simply the useless servants in whom it will carry out, with respect to the great oriental cultures and the new world in the throes of development, the process of creative assimilation which will reveal to these systems the great human movement their most authentic meaning, both for themselves and for the entire human race." Olivier Lacombe, *Sagesse* (Paris: Desclée De Brouwer, 1951), pp. 33–34.

gaps which need filling, to its formulators and its commentators, and even to the very master who founded it; I mean, free of him as he was himself, and ready, like him, for the changes and remodelings required by a better view of things, and for the enlargings and deepenings demanded by an inquiry that is always going forward. (Good Lord! I am speaking of the doctrine of St. Thomas such as it was in him and is in itself—the way in which it has sometimes been taught is another story.)

This doctrine comes from the greatest master in realism—an integral realism, as aware of the reality of the spirit as of the body—who ever lived. In St. Thomas himself (although he was obliged, in order to initiate his pupils, to use the methods of the rational a–b–c), this doctrine presupposes an inexhaustible center of intuitivity. Its definitions and its great architectural profiles could not have had such *justesse* (unfailing accuracy, as of one who has been born with a true ear and sings in tune), had he not been also the poet to whom we owe the liturgy of the feast of Corpus Christi. And even as regards his conclusions, one often feels he had seen them before demonstrating them.

What I have just called a rational a–b–c—questions, articles, numbered objections, the body of the article, numbered responses—is actually (for intuitivity never suffices) the innocent externals of a marvelous living network of intellectual rigor (yet simpler when one reads St. Thomas himself, than his successors had led one to believe) which taught the modern world what *scientia* and the uncompromising honesty of the ways of knowing are.

So much for the properties which even our well-bred contemporaries could discern in his doctrine if they deigned to come near it. I am told that they are repelled by his vocabulary. Why be astonished that men who understand Hegel, Heidegger and Jean-Paul Sartre so well find themselves somewhat terrorized by scholasticist rigor, when they however know perfectly well that every science has its technical vocabulary? Let us hope that instead of reading the *Summa*, they don't run into some Thomist textbook; this time we would sincerely sympathize with them. But I will come back to this point. For the moment, I would simply like to note that the properties I have just been discussing derive from something much more profound: what the doctrine of St. Thomas is in its purest flame, and about which I can-

not avoid trying to say something, however clumsy (this is no rhetori-
cal apology, believe me; the old philosopher knows himself a little
better than that).

THE INTUITION OF BEING
AND THE CONTEMPLATION OF
BEING ITSELF SUBSISTING BY ITSELF

St. Thomas was a theologian, absorbed all his life in *sacra doctrina*,
and his whole work is essentially a work of theology. It wasn't his job
to say "I'm right" where another man is wrong, but, on the contrary,
to preserve and assimilate the whole truth (with a fair amount of
junk and blunders which had to be weeded out), carried along by an
immense tradition. Hence his sacred respect for all the Fathers—in
particular for St. Augustine, whose ways of approach, however, were
not his, and consisted more in a loving meditation on the things of
God than in the search for an elucidation strictly grounded in reason.
His relation to St. Augustine is particularly worth examining. "It can
be said of Augustinianism that its substance passed completely into
the *Summa*." [4] With a good deal of touching up, we need hardly add.
Indeed St. Thomas simply busied himself, in keeping with his office
as a theologian, in bringing to light and saving the truth which was
concealed in such and such a thesis stated in terms he did not accept.
The task which fell to his lot was to save all truths which had been
asserted (often badly asserted) prior to him.

And yet he overturned all the habits and routines of the School-
men, and struck his contemporaries by the astonishing novelty of
his teachings. "A new method," wrote Tocco, "new reasons, new
points of doctrine, a new order of questions." Here was a first-class
aggiornamento.

How is this paradox to be explained? Oh, it's no conjurer's trick. It
is enough that we should think of the extraordinary *philosophic*
genius of St. Thomas. St. Thomas was a theologian, that is, someone
who uses his reason to acquire some understanding of the mysteries
of faith. And what instrument does such a task call for? A philosophy.

---

[4] Etienne Gilson, *op. cit.*, pp. 697–698.

And not any kind of philosophy, but—especially when it is a question of bringing theology to the state of a genuine *scientia* or articulated knowledge grounded in truth—a philosophy which is itself grounded in truth. In the hands of a theologian, philosophy is only an instrument, an *ancilla*. But this instrument is very necessary—just as a rocket is for an astronaut who seeks to explore interplanetary space. Without the appropriate instrument, nothing good can be done.

St. Thomas knew that perfectly well. And he knew, likewise, that Plato, in the course of the preceding centuries of Christianity, had not done such a good job of it. *Because St. Thomas was a theologian, he was careful in choosing, and choosing well, his philosopher* (here he was helped by Master Albert and a singular good turn of history—the introduction of the works of Aristotle into the medieval schools through the intermediary of the Arabs); *and he was not content with choosing his philosopher; he made him over from head to toe.*

It is St. Thomas' connection with Aristotle that it is now worth our while to consider. To say, as so many professors are fond of doing, that the philosophy of St. Thomas is the philosophy of Aristotle is a gross error, as Gilson has rightly insisted. The philosophy of St. Thomas is that of St. Thomas. And it would be as big a mistake to deny that St. Thomas owes his philosophy to Aristotle, as Dante owes his language to the fine raconteurs of his country. Such an extraordinary conjunction of swift insight (one must be something of a poet for that) with ironclad logical rigor may be found in Aristotle too; because he was, in the world of philosophers, both the greatest realist and most perspicacious discoverer of the first apperceptions of the intellect, and the strictest instructor in the unforgiving exigencies of a rigorously rational work, the founder of metaphysics furnished the principles. He missed, however, those conclusions whose object is the loftiest and which matter most to us. But St. Thomas did not just sift out or rectify conclusions—which would, after all, have been a minor contribution. He was possessed of an incomparably deeper vision of the principles themselves; his metaphysical intuition impelled the one he was always to call "the Philosopher" infinitely beyond Aristotelianism and the whole of Greek thought.

St. Thomas did not stop short at *ens*—the "be-ing" (*"das seiende," "l'étant"*)—but went straight to *esse*, (*"Sein," "l'être"*), to the *act of existing*. (A pity, I've already observed, that Heidegger

couldn't see that.) I apologize for having recourse to a technical vocabulary, but for once it is necessary. A metaphysics of the "be-ing"
(*"das seiende," "l'étant"*) stops on the way; a metaphysics of *the
good* or of *the one*, both of which are *passiones entis* or "transcendental properties" of being, remains in an inevitably partial or fragmen-
tary perspective, and is thus put on a wrong track from the outset.
Quite another thing is required. The metaphysics of St. Thomas is
not the metaphysics of Aristotle, because it is the metaphysics of
Aristotle *entirely transfigured.* In other words, St. Thomas the theologian has, in the service of theology, humbly and without putting in a
claim, brought metaphysical wisdom to the most basic and universal
degree of intuitive grasp possible to reason. A metaphysics of *"Sein"*
(*esse*), a metaphysics born from the intuition of the *act of existing*—
and whose primary object is this primordial and all-embracing intelligible reality—has the capacity to welcome, recognize, honor, set to
rights all that is.

And it is because that faithful servant, human wisdom, instrument-
ally used—*the metaphysics of St. Thomas* (not that of Aristotle)
—had the intuition of being and saw in *esse* her chief object, that the
higher wisdom—*the theology of St. Thomas*—was able to contemplate in the trans-luminous obscurity of the mysteries of Faith the
Uncreated Cause of being as *Being itself subsisting by itself, ipsum
Esse per se subsisten,* to which the handmaid had already lifted her
eye as toward her ultimate end.

"To conceive God," writes Gilson, "as the Act of being pure and
subsisting by itself, cause and end of all other beings, is by the same
token to give oneself a theology that can do justice to whatever is
true in other theologies, just as the metaphysics of *esse* has what is
needed to do justice to whatever is true in other philosophies. Because it includes all of them, this theology of the uncreated Act of
being, or of the God whose proper name is *I Am*, is as true as all of
them together and truer than any one of them taken separately. Here
is, if I am not mistaken, the secret reason for the choice the Church
has made of St. Thomas Aquinas as her Common Doctor." [5]

As for the metaphysics which supports such a theology, and without which the latter would not have been (it is this metaphysics
which, from the side of reason, provided the indispensable spark), let

5 "Trois leçons sur le Thomisme," *op. cit.*, p. 700.

us cite further the lines of our friend: "For those who live on it, the metaphysics of the Common Doctor accepted in its fullness is a *ne plus ultra* for the understanding. At once unsurpassable in its own right and inexhaustible in its consequences, this metaphysics is the human understanding itself in its permanent work of rational interpretation of man and the universe." [6]

That brings us to a final consideration which deserves a word or two, however nonsensical this may seem to those who think (if one dare use the word with respect to them) that the only conceivable capacity of being up-to-date is that with which topical gazettes, stop-press news, or news reels are endowed, let us say that only such *actualités*, as they say in French, have the attribute of up-to-dateness. Well, we are thus led to consider briefly the relation of St. Thomas with time. Please pardon me for being myself out-of-date: there is an *up-to-dateness* which, while bound to manifest itself in time, is, of itself, above time, that's the up-to-dateness of truth. The Doctrine of St. Thomas, being essentially grounded in truth, and therefore, as I have already pointed out, open to the whole future, has, of itself, a supra-temporal up-to-dateness.

Alas, I just said that the up-to-dateness of truth, which is, of itself, above time, must manifest itself in time. In other words, the doctrine of St. Thomas was bound to manifest in time—after St. Thomas —its supra-temporal truth. If it fell short of this somewhat too often, it is not the fault of St. Thomas, who was dead. It's the fault of his disciples, for which we are paying today. But this needs looking into more closely and I will come back to it later.

THE PHILOSOPHY OF ST. THOMAS

Another fault of St. Thomas' disciples (I am speaking of "disciples" in general—*with certain exceptions*, of course) lay in not striving to sift out, for its own sake, the philosophy of St. Thomas, by expounding it in its own nature and with its own gait, which by definition have nothing theological about them. (In him, it was present in the most real and deepest manner, but as underlying his theology and enveloped by it.) St. Thomas' disciples have, to be sure, spoken a

[6] *Ibid.*, p. 707.

good deal about Thomist philosophy, and have taught it, in magisterial commentaries, courses, and textbooks where, more often than not, they were content to pick up, in the theological exposition of St. Thomas, the philosophical substance which can be found there—brought there to the light of theology and enveloped in theology: a substance splendidly rich, but all theologized in the use St. Thomas had made of it. Once one had extracted this substance from the theological exposition of the master, one had only to trace off the formulas, often the very order of exposition, to offer in handsome syllogisms some philosophical thesis or other, nay, "the philosophic doctrine" of the Angel of the Schools.[7]

This "Thomist philosophy" was no theology, since they had withdrawn it from the light proper to theology to transfer it into the kingdom of reason using only its natural powers. Still less was it a philosophy, since it remained structured after the theological treatise from which it emerged, and possessed neither the gait and method, nor the light characteristic of philosophical research. Without the characteristic light of theology, and that proper to philosophical research, it had practically no light at all. The *via inventionis* or way of discovery, which is essential to philosophy, was ignored; so too, was the procedure proper to philosophy, which has its starting point in experience and a prolonged intercourse with the world and with sensible reality. The characteristic atmosphere in which philosophy takes shape, which is the atmosphere of curiosity where it dwells with its fellow sciences, and from which it raises itself to the purer and more rarefied atmosphere of what comes *meta ta physica*, was equally absent. Most important was the absence of the light from which philosophy originates, which is intuitive before being and in order to be discursive, and is transferred point by point all during the reasoning process.

Leaving in the oblivion they deserve a number of more or less mediocre textbooks, let us choose instead a work of great merit, drawn up

---

[7] There were certainly, as I have observed, exceptions, although rare to my knowledge. When it comes to overall expositions which have genuine philosophic value, I will name here old Kleutgen, from whom, at one time, I benefited, and in particular two excellent books: Père Garrigou-Lagrange's *La Philosophie de l'être et le Sens commun*, and Gilson's *The Spirit of Medieval Philosophy*.

It is Brentano, a somewhat aberrant disciple, who in the last century had taken the most remarkable initiative; but, because he neglected what mattered most, it took a sharp turn with him, and a very bad turn in Germany, with those who made what they had received from him veer in the direction of phenomenology.

in the most precise and conscientious fashion. We will find a perfect model of the genre—this kind of Thomist philosophy—in the *Elementa philosophiae aristotelico-thomisticae* of the good Père Gredt. It is a precious repository of information, which we have only to consult should we want to know what St. Thomas thought on some given point. But how it was ever possible to have worked out such a conclusion, that's another story. We have in our hands an aerolite which has fallen from the sky, with everything we need to know written on it.

Given a chance to reveal its own nature, Thomistic philosophy exhibits the gait and demeanor characteristic of all philosophy; a demeanor and gait fully at liberty to confront the real. The philosopher swears fidelity to no person, nor any school—not even, if he is a Thomist, to the letter of St. Thomas and every article of his teaching. He is sorely in need of teachers and of a tradition, but in order for them to teach him to think when he looks at things (which is not as simple as all that), and not, as is the case with the theologian, so that he can assume the whole of this tradition into his thought. Once this tradition has instructed him, he is free of it and makes use of it for his own work. In this sense, he is alone in the face of being; for his job is to think over that which is.

As for the method he must follow, it is obvious that the statement of problems, the research, and the discovery come before systemization. Even, before he undertakes direct research (and the struggle with things, and discussion, and controversy, and finally the doctrinal synthesis toward which he tends, all of which go to make up his characteristic work) the most normal way for approach for him is by historical inquiry—yet not simply historical, for he already has, to be sure, his own idea and perhaps his system of reference in the back of his mind (and history alone is not enough to bear judgment); his most normal way of approach is *historical and critical* examination of what has been thought before him. (Here too we can take lessons from Aristotle.) This method of procedure is merely introductory, but it is very necessary both for teaching and for research.

Finally, the root principle on which everything hangs for the philosopher, assuming he is a Thomist, and a metaphysician, is that intellectual intuition of being about which I have already had a good deal to say. Here I would like to make two remarks. The first concerns this intuition itself. It has, as I observed earlier, nothing in common with Bergsonian intuition, and it presupposes a more strenuous, at least quite resolute intellectualism. Nor does it have anything in common with any kind whatsoever of charismatic intuition. It takes place in the heart of the most natural exercise of the intellect, and its only charisma is its *simplicity*—the mysterious simplicity of intellection. There is nothing simpler than to think *I am, I exist,* this blade of grass exists; this gesture of the land, this captivating smile that the next instant will hurry away, *exist;* the world *exists.* The all-important thing is for such a perception to sink deeply enough within me that my awareness of it will strike me some day sharply enough (at times, violently) to stir and move my intellect up to that very world of preconscious activity, beyond any word or formula, and with no assignable boundaries, which nourishes everything within it. Such a descent to the very depths of the soul is doubtless something *given,* not *worked out*—given by the natural grace of the intellectual nature.

And then, if luck should take a hand, and if the eye of consciousness, sufficiently accustomed to the half-light, should penetrate a little, like a thief, this limbo of the preconscious, it can come about that this simple *I am* will seem like a revelation in the night—a secret revelation which will awaken echoes and surprises on all sides and give a hint of the inexhaustible ampleness it permits one to attain.

And there can be instances, as I noted in the foregoing chapter, where this experience is genuinely present in someone who takes no notice of it, either because it remains involved in the more or less superficial layers of consciousness, or because, as with children, it takes place only in the preconscious of the spirit.

It is in a judgment (or in a preconscious act equivalent to an unformulated judgment), and in a judgment of existence, that the intellectual intuition of being occurs. The philosophical concept of the *actus essendi,* of the act of existence, will only come later. And the more profound and pure the intuition, the more accurate and comprehensive (barring accidents) will be the conceptualization of the various discoveries philosophy will be able to make by scrutinizing the real in the light of this absolutely fundamental principle.[8]

8 "The more vital and central the intuition, the more chances its conceptualization has to express it uprightly; the more it is limited, the more conceptualization risks betraying it," writes Louis Gardet (on the subject of primary intuitions in general), in his penetrating study, "Plurality of Philosophies and Unity of Truth," *Nova et Vetera,* IV, 1965, p. 268.

My second observation has to do with Bergson. I have stated that the intellectual intuition of being has nothing in common with Bergsonian intuition, which was spoiled by a quite accidental, I think, anti-intellectualism, and which Bergson described as a kind of ineffable sympathy demanding a torsion of the will upon itself. Furthermore, this Bergsonian intuition did not focus directly on being, but only on *duration* which is but one of the aspects of being, and which served him as a kind of substitute for being. Having said that, one must add that through the experience of duration it was actually *being, esse*, which, without being aware of it, he attained. In any case, Thomism is greatly indebted to him; for if the intuition of being has nothing to do with Bergsonian intuition, it is nevertheless thanks to the impact of the latter, and of Bergson's metaphysical genius, on modern thought (Père J.-H. Nicolas observes that the "real knowledge" of Blondel also played its part in the matter) that contemporary Thomists have at last recognized (not without opposition, nor yet unanimously; there are not that many metaphysicians in the world) the essential and absolutely rockbottom importance of the intuition of being in their own philosophy.[9] From this point of view, one ought to consider Bergson a great liberator.

To wind up my reflections on Thomistic philosophy restored to its proper nature as philosophy, let me say that in my judgment, even though, in this last third of the twentieth century, it does not enjoy the favors of fashion, it is actually in pretty good shape. In saying this, I am thinking of its intrinsic development and of the various kinds of research it has stimulated. I have in mind particularly the progress which is owed to it (thanks to the investigations of Olivier Lacombe and Louis Gardet) in the understanding of Oriental thought (and a good understanding, too, with its representatives) and in an authentic theory (the only one) of natural mystique. Nevertheless,

---

[9] I am pleased to be able to invoke here the authority of the Rev. Jean-Hervé Nicolas. See his remarkable article in the *Revue Thomiste* (1947–I) "The Intuition of Being and the First Principles"; where he notes, in particular, the important text of St. Thomas on metaphysical knowledge (*in Boet. de Trin.*, q. 6, a.i.) in which the word *intellectus* must be translated as "intellectual intuition." His conclusion is that by obliging Thomists "to become more keenly aware of this overly neglected aspect of their metaphysics, the new philosophies which have developed alongside of theirs . . . have rendered them an immense service from which, along with Thomism, Christian thought in general has profited. These new philosophies have awakened them from their abstractive slumber."

we must admit that at the moment it is suffering from a great lack; it has not yet re-elaborated the *philosophy of nature which is one of its indispensable* ingredients. It's no consolation to tell oneself that the whole of contemporary thought is afflicted with the same lack; nor that the scientists, whose very achievements have confronted them with so many problems (and whom no intellectual counterfeit money, moreover, can fool for very long) are clamoring the loudest, though in vain, for this philosophy of nature, which stubbornly refuses to appear. As for Thomism, its philosophy of nature has needed reshaping for a long time. The task (a vanished dream of my youth) is certainly not impossible, but it is difficult in the highest degree. Yet I am confident it will be done. It would require a team in which scientists and philosophers would work together, and which would be led by a competent philosopher. Such a philosopher seems to be improbable? I don't think so, his name is on the tip of my tongue.[10]

Even then, a fair amount of patience will be required. What will also be needed—and here is the *diabolus in musica*—is an uncanny sense of the requirements of that "subtle and delicate" art which consists in *distinguishing in order to unite*. I am not about to launch out here into the intricate problems of epistemology. I will simply note that the sciences of nature, all of them, have a hold on the real insofar only as it can be observed (or within the limits of the observable). Although very far from forming a whole company of the same tenor from the epistemological point of view, they are all, therefore, equally dependent upon an intellection of an "empiriological" order (whether simply empiriological or empirio-mathematical).[11] They are "sciences of phenomena." The philosophy of nature, by contrast, is dependent upon a type of intellection which, through the observable, or through signs apprehended in experience, attains the real in its very being, and must be called an intellection of an *ontological* order (the most natural kind of intellection, to tell the truth; the other kind requires a more particular sort of mental training and discipline). The functioning of thought, and the conceptual vocabulary, then, are typically different in the sciences of nature and in the philosophy of nature. The error of antiquity was to believe that the functioning of thought and the conceptual lexicon proper to the philosophy of na-

10 The author was thinking of Claude Tresmontant. [Trans.]
11 I am using here the vocabulary of *The Degrees of Knowledge*.

ture extended to the sciences of nature. The error of certain modern scientists, insofar as they are in search of a philosophy, is to believe that the kind of thinking and conceptual vocabulary proper to the sciences of nature can serve to build a philosophy of nature. We are faced here with two different keyboards. If a Thomistic philosophy of nature should some day take shape, as I hope, it will only be by having a clear awareness of this distinction. It is first and foremost through such an awareness (even more than from the novelty of the scientific material employed, completely transformed by the advent of modern science) that it will be a philosophy of nature *entirely re-newed* (although retaining the same philosophical perspective) with respect to that of St. Thomas and his age. In the team which will work at such a renewal, each man must be able to use (with relative ease) two typewriters, one equipped with a certain keyboard, the other with a quite different keyboard—one that his discipline has made familiar to him, and the other which, as a man of good will, he will have to learn how to use rather late in the day.[12] The philosophers should know how to use, at least as amateurs, the machine equipped with the scientific keyboard, and the scientists the one equipped with the philosophic keyboard. May the angels of true knowledge be there to help them!

PHILOSOPHY AND THEOLOGY

Between faith and reason, as between grace and nature, there is an essential *distinction*; and one sometimes tends to lose sight of it. (Much more often today because we are too dull, now that we have been so well instructed, to understand what to distinguish really means. With dialectic and the elimination of "natures" in behalf of becoming, isn't it as plain as day that everything is different because everything is the same, and that the more thresholds there are to be crossed along the discontinuous, the more the continuity of the universal movement which goes on by itself becomes obvious and axiomatic?)

But between faith and reason, as between grace and nature, there is no *separation*. One tends sometimes to overlook that, too (much

12 See, at the end of the book, Appendix 3, *Short Epistemological Digression.*

more often in the old days; quite a few of our ancestors were as dull as we, and once two concepts were seated on the chairs of a reliable distinction, they found it too tiring to raise those concepts from their seats and make them embrace one another).

Whatever the dullness of our ancestors and of a good many of us, things are that way, and so is life: there is distinction without separation.

Reason has its own domain, and faith hers. But reason can enter the domain of faith by bringing there its need to ask questions, its desire to discover the internal order of the true, and its aspiration to wisdom—that's what happens with theology. And faith can enter the domain of reason, bringing along the help of a light and a truth which are superior, and which elevate reason in its own order—that is what happens with Christian philosophy. (Conventional words like "Christian philosophy" and "Christian politics" are rather annoying, for they seem—people like to be misled—to clericalize a thing secular by nature, and to pin a denominational label on it. "Philosophy in faith" sounds a little better perhaps than "Christian philosophy," but also lends itself to misinterpretation. In the last analysis, whatever word you use presupposes some intelligence in the hearer.)

Let us leave aside the somewhat incongruous name by which the *Christian Scientists* are designated. Apart from this rather odd sect, one could not possibly speak of "Christian science," because science is concerned only with phenomena, and the latter, as Pierre Termier said, "don't look Christian," any more than does the eye or the microscope which observes them. But philosophy is concerned with *what is* beneath phenomena. And faith, with *He who is*. Metaphysics is concerned with prime truths, and faith with others more prime still. Why should it be normal for them to ignore one another?

After all, a Christian can be a philosopher. And if he believes that, in order to philosophize, he should lock his faith up in a strongbox—that is, should cease being a Christian while he philosophizes —he is maiming himself, which is no good (all the more as philosophizing takes up the better part of his time). He is also deluding himself, for these kinds of strongboxes have always poor locks. But if, while he philosophizes, he does not shut his faith up in a strongbox, he is philosophizing in faith, willy-nilly. It is better that he should be aware of it.

When one becomes aware of it, then one is forced to admit that there is a "Christian philosophy." It is philosophy, and its work is a *work of reason*; but it is in a *better position* to perform its work of reason. Not only does faith place in our path certain signals ("Danger: Winding Roads," etc.), thanks to which our little saloon-car runs less risks. But, above all, faith can help us from within to overcome allurements and irrational dreams to which, without assistance coming from a source superior to reason, we would be disposed to yield. In all honesty, then, given the general conditions, hardly very promising for reason, in which our fallen nature finds itself, the state or "situation" of Christian philosophy should be regarded as the most desirable state or "situation" for philosophy among the children of Adam. Which doesn't mean that a Christian philosopher cannot err as seriously as any other—faith may cause philosophic minds insufficiently robust to run other risks. Nay more, the remnants of ancestral faith (but then it is a question of philosophies which falsely proclaim themselves Christian, or are no longer Christian at all) throw into most serious dangers strong-minded rationalist doctrinarians, who fancy, like Hegel and some others after his pontificate, they have to assume the whole burden of old theologies now supposedly dispossessed.

St. Thomas had a sound mind, and it was he who really taught us to distinguish without ever separating. If we think of the various traits of his philosophy I have been trying to recall, and of how, in building this philosophy for himself, he transfigured the metaphysics of Aristotle—with no intention of curbing reason before faith, but in order to goad reason into a better control of its own realm, and a decisive awareness of the absolutely basic principle of the *opus philosophicum*—perhaps we will begin to suspect that the philosophy of St. Thomas (and especially his metaphysics) is not merely a Christian philosophy, but is *the* Christian philosophy *par excellence*.

People who, for all their intelligence, are inclined to believe that everything repeats itself, are naturally tempted to grow impatient with the privilege thus conceded to a philosophy about which, moreover, they know little or nothing. Shouldn't theology do with the modern philosophers what St. Thomas did with Aristotle? That's obvious, isn't it? One hears this inept question today on all sides. It is inept for a good many reasons. The first is that to do with Hegel what St. Thomas did with Aristotle would involve, in the first place, taking on the job of making over Hegel from head to toe. Just let them try it, they will break their teeth. One can make over from top to bottom a philosopher who, while he fell short of his goal, was well on his way, i.e., was truly *in the axis* to look at the real. With a philosopher (ideosopher) who is only in the axis of the Idea, it's surely not so easy; especially if this ideosopher regards himself as the summit of the whole of human thought and the revealer of ultimate wisdom. Nor is it any simple matter with a crowd of philosophers (ideosophers who, unaware of any tradition other than that of their immediate predecessors in a given line, offer us only individual attempts and, like a good many of our contemporary thinkers, grow increasingly resigned to vanishing into thin air like fireflies that glow for but an instant. There have, in fact, actually been attempts at Cartesian theologies, Malebranchian theologies, Kantian theologies and Hegelian theologies, and they didn't shed much light within the Church. For the time being, it is with any run-of-the-mill kind of phenomenological product that our creative geniuses are working. It would be no small job for theology, assuming it continued to believe itself charged with teaching men how to gain some rational understanding of the eternal Truth revealed in faith—to be forced to re-design its models every season like manufacturers of motorcars.

But none of this has much effect on the clerics and the friars, or indeed on the innocent laymen who are at grips with the question: why not repeat with the thinkers of today what St. Thomas did with Aristotle, so as to be rid of those two spoil-sports? To tell the truth, the matter is more serious than it seems. Let us try to discern what, fundamentally (and unconsciously, doubtless, for a good many) lies concealed beneath this question. It is what, with a completely changed idea of theology, one could call a fideism gone astray. I will sum up in three points what I mean by this.

Primo. According to this fideism, theology is not, as we have been led to believe for so long, a *rational knowledge* through which human reason humbly penetrates, as far as it can (and always progressing, as it should), the Truth which came out from the mouth of God in the mysteries of faith. For not only does faith transcend reason, but reason is powerless to do a genuine work of knowledge (that is, a work of rational knowledge solidly enough established—on a rock—to go on progressing forever) by scrutinizing in some fashion, in their eternal and intrinsic depths, the truths which faith conveys to us and whose custody belongs to the Church. The theologian, however, lifts his eyes toward faith.

Secundo. Does this mean that in order to contemplate these mysteries, he already is in the mystical transforming union? No, apparently not. He is a scholar, and, even while lifting his eyes toward faith, he makes use of reason, and thus also of philosophy (and the treasures of an erudition as vast and caviling as possible). But since faith is supposed to be, of itself, averse to reason, and to a work of knowledge accomplished by means of reason, the theologian can and should, in looking at faith, make use of any philosophy whatever, once it is that of his times. For it isn't at all a matter of understanding better, thanks to reason, or of managing in some way (always and indefinitely progressive) to *know* the things (immutably true) faith reveals to us. It is a matter (what a much humbler attitude for reason to have, isn't it?) of *reinterpreting* for each age, by means of the philosophy of the age, faith itself, with the things (mutably true) it brings us to know. This time, the *handmaid* becomes mistress. And the original fideism of theology conceived in this way is taken in tow by a dynamic philosophism which gives theology the bliss to which it aspires: to be a child of its times. What better fate could one ask for a theology essentially "pastoral"? (The blame is not mine if this venerable word has been prostituted by so many zealous journalists.)

Tertio. Why then all the fuss? Because, while the object of theology continues to remain the truth of the mysteries of faith (but a truth henceforth mutable in its intelligible value and meaning, at times mythical if necessary)—and also, of course, the truths of erudition (absolute, these ones, if only for the moment)—nevertheless, the ultimate purpose of theology, finally, has become no longer Truth but Efficacy. Here we are at last. Thus it is that with the new notion of theology which underlies the grand question I have irreverently, though not unreasonably, described as inept, we are dealing with a fideism *gone astray.*

At first glance, this analysis may seem somewhat harsh. But if one gives it a little serious thought, one will find it hard to challenge its accuracy.

Theology should be of its time, yes, that's true, but in an entirely different sense, and provided one preserves it or re-establishes it in its very essence: an effort to understand, as far as one can, and to connect together in a rational whole the truths of faith, in view of that supreme end which is Truth, not Efficacy. Besides we must also bear in mind that the object of any knowledge is one with its end.

"For us to repeat what Thomas Aquinas did" means, in reality, "to descend once more from revealed truth to the philosophies of our time in order to enlighten them, purify them," and ransom the truths they hold captive. "An immense task," as Gilson [13] wrote, "but one in which Thomas Aquinas has gone before us and can still show us the way."

☆

In this immense task, he can of course show us the way, provided we go forward with him. And this is dreadfully urgent. This is one of the most necessary renewals called for by the *true fire* that the Holy Spirit has kindled, and with which the flame throwers of the Council have disturbed so many slumbers. A few Thomists did not wait to set out en route (a small flock, yet fairly robust indeed, and where young searchers are not lacking, but, as always, *operarii pauci*, operatives are few). The fact remains that if one wishes to be led by someone, one can't afford to stay put, and when it comes to this particular task, it is true that Thomists have too often remained comfortably seated in their magisterial chairs.

I don't much relish talking about this because, when one speaks in general terms, as I have been forced to do in this book, it is impossible to avoid a certain amount of injustice. I'm not much, but what would I be without the undeserved luck of having been taught by masters like Père Clérissac, Père Dehau and Père Garrigou-Lagrange, and, among those still with us whose names I will omit out of respect for their modesty, a humble Cardinal to whom I owe everything I know about the Church, and who would still be an unassuming priest and seminary professor (he still is a seminary professor) but for the perspicacity of Pope Paul VI?

Why then should I go out of my way to pick a quarrel with the Thomists? Because the old peasant spares nothing, that's why. Espe-

[13] *Op. cit.*, p. 706

cially not the immobilism which, since the canonization of St. Thomas (prior to that, his doctrine had, of course, been attacked and slandered by his brothers at Oxford and by the bishop of Paris, Étienne Tempier), has allowed Thomism to become learnedly ossified.

If one speaks ill of the past, especially in the precious and ungrateful world of today, there is a certain fear of being what Sartre calls *un salaud*, a dirty dog. Yet we must recognize that glory has its dangers, and so does the lofty mission of recognized defenders of the truth. A great School, with celebrated teachers and renowned universities, was hard put to maintain the studious humility which had played so essential a role in the life and work of St. Thomas. The doctoral cap which St. Thomas set so little store by soon became a sacred emblem, crowning teachers whose word was law. (Yet they were, after all, only professors; and how much good it might do them —as, in principle, it would every professor—to go every now and then and refresh their experience of reality by milking cows or by pushing a plow.)

All that I just said is in no way concerned with the matter of personal humility. It is the office to be filled which knew too well its own greatness. To be in the retinue of the queen of sciences includes of necessity lofty duties, and it is only fitting that a Master of theology be penetrated by these feelings. I once had occasion to meet a most worthy theologian, plain dealing, childlike, humble and charitable, and who was not lacking in a sense of humor, about whom I was told a good story. In a course on moral theology (on the question of the lesser evil, I suspect) an example suggested itself to him. "Let us imagine," he told his students (his skill in mimicry used to delight them), "that I am on a ship which is about to go down and there is only one lifeboat. Naturally, I say to myself: it's up to me to sacrifice myself, for the man standing next to me is the father of a family. . . . But I think it over for a moment, and it occurs to me: I am a Master in theology, *valde utilis sanctae Ecclesiae!* Then, it is a matter of duty, isn't it, to get into the lifeboat before the others. . . ."

This story is told only in jest (but it is true). The haughtiness with which a great lord of the mind like Cajetan addresses "apprentices" remains inscribed in his Commentary on the *Summa*. When one's function is to teach the loftiest wisdom, it is difficult to resist the temptation to believe that until you have spoken, nothing has been said. As a *dispositio animae*, this is hardly conducive to restless inquiry, or progress, or the wish to examine the feeble efforts of the common herd. I number among theologians a good many dear friends of whom exactly the opposite would have to be said; their humility, even their "professional" humility, has won my admiration. But the history of the brotherhood gives one no reason to think that such has generally been the case. The most curious aspect of the matter is that those who today are throwing out St. Thomas and the rest, and nourishing themselves with the bread of existentialism or demythization in order to come up with hypotheses in the grand manner, seem to have inherited from their ancestors only an instinctive persuasion of the *professional* superiority of their own pronouncements.

There were, in the past, a good many excuses for this. I like to think back to the age of the great jousts and controversies when it was up to the Thomists to trade blows with the Scotists or Suarezians. These nice tournaments made it possible to safeguard precious truths and to deepen doctrine (sometimes in hardening it, or making it labyrinthine). Those men knew their business. How pleased I am with that Dominican—his name, I think, was Thomas de Lemos—who, in the course of the celebrated debates *de auxiliis* held in the presence of the Pope, so ardently flung his arms about *scientia media* that he had to be shut up in a glass cage. Yet, the fact remains that scholastic disputations, oratorical argumentation, the play of concepts, the victorious art of *distinguo*, and didacticism gained the upper hand so well that Thomists made little advance in their own line, hardly daring to change classical positions when the need arose, as St. Thomas would have done had he been present. As a result, when modern philosophy and modern science began (and continued) to make a noise in the world, most of St. Thomas' disciples remained almost deaf to these wretched murmurs, except to refute them. (And however necessary that may be, it's not refutation I'm concerned with here.) Gradually the Thomism of the schools lost that openness, that feeling for research and progress, that zeal to go to the rescue of truths wherever they were held captive, that commerce with the real and with experience, which quickened it in its original source—and, above all, that intuitivity which is the life of its life (this is verified in theology too; for although theology, unlike metaphysics with the *actusessendi,* lacks an intellectual intuition of its prime object, it has, nevertheless—to advance step by step, as reason does, in the mysteries of Being itself subsisting by itself—the light of faith, which in the experience of contemplation quickens the theologian, as well as any contemplative soul, in a more piercing, almost intuitive fashion: so that the *sacra doctrina* might actually become what it is *de iure,* "a certain impression in us of the divine knowledge, *quae est una et simplex omnium,*" which knows all things in its perfect unity and simplicity).[14]

The loss of potential due to this loss of ever-alert intuitivity is the underlying cause of the baneful deterioration which has taken place in the direction of notionalism and a fixation upon abstract essences (hence, a metaphysics unmindful of the intuition of being) for which Gilson is doubtless right in regarding Cajetan as particularly responsible. (It is not without a certain ruefulness that I admit this since, in other respects, I'm an admirer of this incomparable reasoner; he was, alas, a partisan of Aristotle in the very sense St. Thomas was not, and yet for all of that, a theologian of extraordinary power. But the Commentator with whom I fell in love—without being afraid to depart from him whenever I have to—isn't Cajetan, it's John of Saint-Thomas, who, despite his interminable sentences and his charming fondness for logical technicalities, was himself basically an intuitive.)

It is hardly surprising that Thomism should finally have entered into the "abstractive slumber" denounced by Père Jean-Hervé Nicolas. What can one say of the prudent ignorance in which theologian and exegete have so long remained in respect of one another? Or of the isolation in which our masters remained for so long regarding the new conceptions of the world with which science, and especially its popularizers, captured the attention of the *vulgum pecus?* It helps explain a little how so many of our intellectuals still imagine that whoever takes interest in Thomism is stepping out of our age.

What's more, if one were to turn, no longer with special reference to the kind of teaching in which the Thomists too often indulged (its lacks were particularly serious in proportion to the living treasure it

[14] As Père Clérissac wrote, "The joys and vital energy which theology dispenses are incomparable, because this knowledge is nothing else than the baptismal illumination become conscious of itself and progressive." *Le Mystère de l'Eglise* (Paris: ed. du Cerf, 1917), p. 6.

should have transmitted), but to the ordinary teaching which, too often also—this time in bland doctrinal indifference—prevailed in Christian schools, things would appear still worse. At this point I remember that pious offense to the intellect, the Latin textbook of theology of the venerable M. Tanquerey.

It is all that that needs changing—and is in the process of changing at top speed. That is where the true new fire should bring its flame.

☆

All that should change. But it risks changing for the worse.

In actual fact, the result of all the setbacks I have enumerated has been an even greater misfortune. The immense work of discernment and integration, of interpretation, reconstruction, purification and liberation, which the adventures of thought and culture in the modern age called for and which needed to be done *within* the truth—always up-to-date by nature but above time, and demanding to be manifested in time—of the great doctrinal wisdom St. Thomas gave to the world, this immense work has not been done by his disciples.[15] Thus it was left to theologians of good will but unsteady head, to carry out, instead of this work, a completely different one—designed not to save captive truths, but to try to adapt them to the very thing which holds them captive. Such a work is performed under the spur of the moment, and accomplished *outside* the ever up-to-date (but above time) truth of a doctrinal wisdom which they either don't know, or scorn, or betray, by following the petticoats of any philosophy dressed out in the latest fashions, which becomes their servant-mistress. As if an ambitious and phenomenologist *ancilla*, which is positive of knowing more than they, could help them do anything but transform theology into a kind of exegesis, at once bold (why, of course) and modestly conjectural, of the truths in which our fore-

---

[15] There is a certain amount of injustice in putting it this way, but, as I have already said, I am speaking in general terms—leaving aside a number of Thomist scholars who in the course of the last century have shed light on a good many problems or opened up a number of new lines of investigation. I would have preferred to name names, but I don't wish to seem to be drawing up a list of honors. Besides, the scholars to whom I refer (particularly Père Schwalm) contributed more to the deepening of Thomistic thought than to the work we are discussing. It is in exegesis that such an effort has been undertaken, in particular by the admirable Père Lagrange.

fathers believed, duly reinterpreted and provided with a new set of
clothes, without forgetting beret, spectacles, and mutinous look, so as
not to appear at a disadvantage in international conferences and col-
loquies where modern mentality makes itself comfortable.

To the foregoing reflections on the faults and omissions which, in
the past, have gradually encrusted Thomism, and the price we are
paying for them today, one could add similar ones on a number of
other subjects, and, generally speaking, on the progressive sclerosis
which, in the course of recent centuries, has afflicted the mores, if I
may say so, or the ways and customs of Christian thought. The main
question had to do with the practical aftereffects of ideas upon human behavior; Churchmen's prudence played a great part in the
matter. A sacred trust and venerable traditions of exalted wisdom, although always at work wherever there were blood and life, gradually
found themselves half embedded in routine, narrowness of mind, and
a kind of vigorous and suspicious refusal to think which served as
preventive medicine for a host of threatening contagions. The inevitable result was to turn the Christian people in upon itself (many
kept alive wonderful riches of faith and piety, but many also sank in
indifference or an unfathomable ignorance) and to divorce, not
Christianity, certainly, nor the Church, but the mass of average
churchgoers and their ordinary concerns, from the world of culture,
with its nice progress in shamelessness and the experience of un-
reason, but its genuine progress, too, in the experience of beauty,
poetry, intelligence, freedom of mind, and the knowledge of man.

Léon Bloy, Bernanos, Mauriac, each from his own standpoint, have
said all that needs to be said on this subject. In spite of everything, it
had become the custom to look at all this with a kind of resigned
indulgence, as the inevitable weaknesses of every great human institution, or the unavoidable squalor and routine of departments which
prepare the equipment for some heroic venture. One lost sight a little
too much of the foot-sloggers and the poor common people whom
the toil and worry of earning a living kept prisoners of the force of
habit and who did not read the great mystics. One forgot, above all,
that it wasn't a case of a human institution or a military venture. The
Church was well aware of it, and she didn't forget the common people either. Everybody was surprised by the Council because everybody
is little concerned with what the Church is. She has said at last that

she is fed up with routines and unnatural isolation. She has marked out the road of renewal and liberation. And she will manage well enough, have no fear.

The fact remains that, when worm-eaten barriers begin to snap, a horde of bewildered souls are quick to take advantage of it and disperse in nature—or "culture," and blithely follow the prevailing winds, in other words, the lastest fashion. This too is inevitable. And if we are seeing right now a good many outlandish things, and a curious unleashing of Christian tomfoolery (it's the same old tomfoolery, only turned upside down) where a certain number of priests and consecrated people take care not to forget their role as leaders—"firemen who catch fire," as Degas used to say of certain painters—we should look back over our shoulder, with a little suitably disillusioned wisdom, and recall the gross errors and omissions of a not-too-distant past (it is mainly a case of the nineteenth century) for which we are now paying the price.

Having said that, we are forced to admit that the spectacle enjoyed by our contemporaries has a good many questionable allurements. It is not merely the brilliant theological work already alluded to that they behold without a murmur (save for compliments). They have also to contemplate the work of reconstruction expected on all sides of statistical and scientific devices, and, first of all, to admire the general substitution of techniques—especially the psychological—which are now flourishing, not only for pious practices which are more or less obsolete, and the routines and antiseptic precautions I have already mentioned, but even for the traditions (still alive, in spite of hardening of the arteries) of exalted wisdom which I have also mentioned, and especially the humble and noble disciplines of what is still occasionally referred to as the spiritual life.

Some of my friends are afflicted with this phenomenon. There are, moreover, a good many things that the Chinese proverb I invented as an epigraph to this book advises us never to take too seriously. For my part, I plead guilty to being particularly struck by the comic aspect of the spectacle, which it seems permissible to poke a little fun at. In spite of everything, it is very funny to imagine countless Christian families poring devoutly over copies, not of the *Spiritual Combat*, but of treatises on Sexology; or to think of that Mexican monastery whose sturdy pioneering zeal prompted it to have the whole community psychoanalyzed, with the not unforeseeable result of a number of happy marriages, and new Christian families whose children will, one hopes, be psychoanalyzed first thing after the tragic event which made them come out of the intra-uterine paradise. It is also pretty amusing to picture to yourself superiors of seminaries or of religious houses, masters and mistresses of novices, or crack students who are being prepared for this function, studiously and eagerly attending courses in dynamic psychology which initiate them in projection tests, Rorschach, and the psychodrama of Moreno. In this way, they will acquire the science of human behavior, and will be able to tell souls who are or will be confided to their care "what to do," or, in embarrassing cases, send them to the psychiatrist, the man who really "knows" (*Domine, quid me vis facere*). They will have been taught, too, how to spot the *other meaning* hidden behind the confidences of those who speak to them, and how to practice on them the *counseling* of Rogers, thus giving proof of an "unconditional consideration" of which old-fashioned charity had no knowledge. My only regret is that I am too old to look forward to being comforted by the young generations who are being prepared in this way to dedicate themselves to the Lord—fully flowering in their nature, poised, de-complexed, socially conditioned, spontaneously adapted to group reflexes, and, at last, happy to be alive.

A visit to the psychologist is no more attractive to me than a visit to the dentist, but I realize that in certain cases it can be necessary. Psychologists are able to offer important services to those who really need them, and whom the conditions of modern life make probably numerous. In any case, it would be ridiculous to underestimate the value of their work, and I have no intention of falling into this error. I have a good deal of admiration for Freud, if not for the Freudians, and I heartily value the discoveries of contemporary psychology, however incomplete. What tickles my funny bone is the rush of consecrated persons who, in spite of an incurable incompetence, can't wait to have themselves indoctrinated with the most pious (and least scientific) enthusiasm.

Who knows? Maybe all this bustle is needed to put an end to certain absurd routines,[16] and to teach people to steer clear of errors that a bit of intelligence and a fair amount of fraternal care and com-

[16] Here, too, we are paying a *penalty* for the terrible errors due to an ignorance that good faith failed to make any less frightful, which once led to the stake, as "witches," so many unfortunate victims of mental illness.

passion would have sufficed to avoid. Furthermore, the elementary psychological knowledge which has today become normal for everyone, can help persons in charge deepen their insight in the case of candidates for the priesthood or the religious life whose perserverance is open to question. But much fonder hopes are being entertained. We are to learn better than with the Gospel and the love of charity how to lead a human community to the service of God and our neighbor. We are to improve with a technique that is at last foolproof the manufacturing of souls efficaciously devoted to this service. Clearly, all such pieces of foolery will pass away as quickly as they have appeared.

It is certain, also, that for her part the Church will find—a bit late perhaps—a cure for the dangerous new forms of enslavement which we owe to the empire of technique. (I cannot say as much for the world or the State, if I can believe the picture sketched by M. Jacques Ellul in his book, *The Technological Society*. [17]) Let me say it once more, it is Christianity which will doubtless be the last resort for the human person, and for those poor adults who, after a too well educated childhood, will have nevertheless retained concern for freedom, and will struggle to break from the universal conditioning.

☆

If now we turn again in the direction of theology, we will find that the masters of the new schools of theological re-interpretation have still other joys in store for us which, if not the purest, are at least bracing and of a rare quality. I read a little while ago in an estimable and widely read Catholic periodical,[18] an article in which the Reverend Robert T. Francoeur, praising the creative genius of the Reverend Père Schoonenberg, voices the hope that one of his books recently translated into English, *Man and Sin*,[19] will be considered— although it by no means presents itself as definitive—as a classic work. The *creative genius* I'll buy. But it is worth taking a closer look at a book on original sin before holding it up as a classic work. That's why

[17] New York: Alfred A. Knopf, 1967.
[18] *Jubilee*, February 1966.
[19] *Man and Sin: A Theological View* (Indiana: University of Notre Dame Press, 1965). The original title is *De Macht der Zonde*, L.C.G., Malmberg, Hertogenbosch, 1962.

I couldn't wait to get hold of *Man and Sin*. My reading of this work (brimming over, as you might expect, with erudition), which the author is at pains to stress he is presenting as a hypothetical or conjectural essay, but whose high renovating value he certainly makes no attempt to conceal, has given me joys of a very special kind.

As we all know, the *ancient church* [20] considered original sin as a fault committed once in the past by the first human couple. We experience its effects in the loss by our human nature, along with the supernatural and preternatural gifts of Adamic grace, of the internal order which it owed to this grace. Every man, then, was born in a state of fallen nature which, unless he was delivered by the redeeming grace of Christ, made it impossible for him to enter into supernatural beatitude and the vision of God. [21]

As for myself, I have always believed, and still do, that this doctrine is of faith, and that one should be prepared to suffer death rather than deny it. But views other than those of *the ancient church* are possible today, aren't they?

The author admits neither the preternatural gifts nor the grace proper to the state of innocence, both of which seem to him somewhat nearing fairyland; he does not admit their loss, either, nor the too "essentialist" notion of fallen nature. [22] Without following Teilhard throughout (he criticizes his conception of evil as a simple, statistically necessary penalty for progress) he adheres to the perspective and "spirit" of Teilhard, and seeks, therefore, a total reinterpretation, in keeping with our evolutionist view of the world (which is beyond contest, of course). We know that in this view Christ did not come primarily to save; his "first function is that of fulfilling." But the minds renewed by the metaphysics of evolution have too often neglected the "other functions" of Christ: "restoration, salvation, and the destruction of sin." It was to remedy this shortcoming that Père Schoonenberg boldly set out. [23]

[20] *Ibid.*, p. 197.
[21] St. Thomas added that children who died unbaptized—before being able, in an act of freedom, to accept (or refuse) the grace of Christ offered to all— were doubtless deprived of beatitude and the vision of God, but would enter into a state of natural felicity exempt from all pain and sorrow. This doctrine of Limbo, scorned by so many of today's theologians who don't know what they are doing, should be recognized as a precious treasure by every intelligent Christian.
[22] Schoonenberg, *op. cit.*, p. 198.
[23] *Ibid.*, pp. 193–194.

The reinterpretation he proposes would substitute an "evolutionary and historical" picture for a "static" one.[24] The sin known as original (because someone—or ones—among the anonymous primitives must have one day begun and set in motion the history of sin),[25] is actually an historical sin. Original sin, or the sin of the world (which the author considers identical) is spread all through evolution, growing continuously. For the world advances at the same time in the acceptance of grace and in perdition; "both salvation and doom grow apace," [26] in such a way that "sin is directed against the history of salvation rather than against any law of being."[27] In the history of sin as in the history of salvation, what we are dealing with is a series of "being-in-situation" in which we find ourselves by reason of prior historical evolution: either those kinds of "being-in-situation" which are leading to salvation because our human environment disposes us to receive grace, or those kinds of "being-in-situation" which are leading to sin, because our human environment disposes us to sin.

Original sin is thus a "being-in-situation" in which—on account of the history which has preceded us and the refusals of grace to which our human environments have been subjected by the fault of a long series of forbears—we are placed prior to any personal decision on our part,[28] but which inclines us to sin.[29] Thus, thanks to the new theology, we are rid of the state of fallen nature. But this state affected us in our individual nature, so that a child coming into the world was in an intrinsic state from which only the grace of Christ could draw him. With a succession of "being-in-situation," there is no longer an intrinsic state of deprivation of grace in which we are placed at birth. It becomes easier to understand why the word "redemption" has passed out of fashion and why the *primary function* of Christ is not to save.

24 *Ibid.*, p. 192.
25 *Ibid.*, p. 195.
26 *Ibid.*, p. 196.
27 *Ibid.*, p. 195.
28 *Ibid.*, p. 198.
29 *Ibid.*, p. 181. As with every being-in-situation, this situation in which we are placed before any personal decision on our part or any freely chosen attitude of the person (p. 198) "is in some way assumed by the person in the process of self-development . . . , and accompanied by some faint foreshadowing of a personal decision, probably a personal sin." (p. 181)

Whatever the advisableness of this remark, what is to be kept in mind is that the fall occurred through a long "history of sin," [30] where we are nevertheless permitted to assume that before Christ certain human groups, which, as luck would have it, history had left fully open to primeval grace, could thus be free from original sin. You can see we have made progress since *the ancient church*, and since that St. Paul who pretended to maintain that the sin of one single man had *"passed into all men* for their condemnation" [31] and that likewise the justice of one man worked in them for their justification.

Those who were born in the fortunate groups in question were in a state of "immaculate conception" [32] (with this difference, noted by the author, that it is not to the foreseen merits of Christ the Redeemer, as in the case of Mary, that they owed their condition). What is one to say then? Has not this clause, *"intuitu meritorum Christi Jesu Salvatoris humani generis,* by the foreseen merits of Christ Jesus, Saviour of the human race," been expressly placed in the definition of the dogma of the Immaculate Conception to maintain a point of faith—the impossibility of any human being being born exempt from original sin, with the sole exception of the grace thus bestowed on Mary? Let us, to be polite, simply say that being Professor of Dogmatic Theology at the Catechetical Center of Nijmegen must be a remarkable "being-in-situation" of daydream.

In any case, the crucifixion of Christ has put an end to the possibility of those immaculate conceptions prior to Mary's which were permitted by history. And if, until then, the universality of original sin "must not be taken strictly," [33] the putting to death of Christ, because it cast out of the world the Author of life,[34] has an importance and a seriousness greater by far than any possible first sin in the

---

[30] *Ibid.,* p. 178.

[31] *Rom.* 5:18. (Yes, this is the sense of the Greek text.)

[32] *Op. cit.,* pp. 189–190. "In that hypothesis more people may have engaged in 'immaculate conception' not in the way in which the Church professes it for Mary—that is, as a gift proceeding from Redemption—but as it may be said, and is sometimes explicitly said, of Adam and Eve, that is, as a gift coming from primeval grace."

[33] *Ibid.,* p. 190.

[34] *Ibid.,* p. 196.

human race.[35] It is this supreme culmination of the sin of the world
—the rejection of Christ from the world where he dwelt among us—
which, completing the measure of the sins of the fathers, brought it
to pass that thenceforth the universality of original sin would admit
of no exception. From that time on no one can escape from it except
through the grace of baptism and the outpouring of the Holy Spirit
which followed the Resurrection. Since the death of Christ, therefore,
every man enters the world simultaneously in the disastrous situation
of original sin and (because of the Resurrection) in a situation of salvation.[36]

Here, then, is why the Word was made flesh. The stroke of genius
is to have seen that the death of Jesus on the Cross brings us perdition right along with salvation. It places each man at birth in the
situation of being lost through original sin—a situation which has now
become universal—and simultaneously in the situation of being
saved through the grace of the risen Christ after his crucifixion. (It's
the Resurrection that matters: in this "Theological View" I read
nothing about the redeeming sacrifice or the merits of the Passion.)
In truth, the cross itself, the blessed cross, is hardly, for our author,
the *spes unica*. It is "only from God's point of view, for whom nothing is impossible, that salvation comes to us through the cross of

[35] That is the essential point for Père Schoonenberg. We used to believe that
the sin of those who condemned Christ and who failed to recognize the Messiah
of Israel and the light of the world consisted solely—and that was enough!—in the
putting to death of the Lamb of God: *felix culpa*, we might say, as Adam's fault
had been, thanks to which Christ accomplished the redeeming sacrifice for which
he came. Not so! The sin of those who condemned Christ goes much deeper than
that. What must be seen first of all in the death of Christ is the physical or
cosmic fact which resulted from it: the Author of grace was excluded from the
world and from this earthly existence where he had come to share our life and
offer us salvation. By that very fact "our whole existence on earth" is "deprived of
the life of grace, so that everybody starts his own existence with the lack of it."
(*Ibid.*, p. 190.)

The reason this is true, we are told, is that before the Incarnation the com-
munication of grace was "interpersonal, charismatic" (how nice to hear that), but
now this road is "closed for all," since Christ is no longer among us. Hence the
necessity of baptism. That is only one of the gems in this precious "Theological
View."

[36] *Ibid.*, pp. 196, 197. "Since Christ's death on the cross, every man enters the
world in the disastrous situation of original sin. Everybody enters the world in that
situation of perdition, but the opposite, too, is true. Every man enters the world
in a situation of salvation, for the Lord has risen and his spirit fills the earth."
(p. 197)

Christ, in connection, of course, with the Resurrection. From man's point of view, the cross of Christ means the greatest disaster." [37]

The Lamb of God burdens us with the sin of the world at the very time he is taking it on himself. As far as dialectic is concerned, nothing could be better and everything is finally clear. But it is damn strange all the same.

☆

The judgment deserved by the works of the renovators who season their theology either à la Teilhard or with the sauce of the phenomenologists is not hard to reach: they are the product of an impassioned fatuousness anxious to serve the idols of the times. However ephemeral they may be, these choice writings threaten to disconcert completely Christian consciousness and the life of faith. Instead of the true new fire called for by our era, they bring us only the smoke from rotten wood which cannot catch fire. The would-be renewers we are discussing are hapless stragglers who would like us to return to a zero

---

[37] "From man's point of view the cross of Christ means the greatest disaster. Only from the point of view of God, for whom nothing is impossible, salvation comes to us through the cross of Christ, in connection, of course, with the Resurrection, for if Christ has not risen, we are still in our sins" (1 *Cor.* 15:17). (*Ibid.*, p. 197.) The author apparently considers the Cross only a preface putting an end to the life of Christ here below (while seeming to forget completely that he sacrificed himself and laid down his life of his own free will), so that salvation could be achieved through the Resurrection. This is a rash re-interpretation—and in my view a disastrous and intolerable one—of the whole of Christian thought, which has always held to the belief that the sacrifice of the cross and the merits of the Passion—victory over sin—have accomplished the work of saving and redeeming mankind, and that the Resurrection—victory over death—has consummated this work by inaugurating the kingdom of glory to come, and by making possible— for us, here below—the sending of the Paraclete by the risen Son ascended to the bosom of his Father; so that "as Christ is risen from the dead through the glory of the Father, in *the same way* we too might enter in newness of life." (*Rom.* 6:4.) Does not the sacred liturgy itself declare this explicitly? One has only to read at one go what is said in the Preface of the Holy Cross and of the Ascension: "*Qui salutem humani generis in ligno crucis constituisti*"; "*Qui post resurrectionem suam est elevatus in coelum, ut nos divinitatis suae tribueret esse participes.*" Père Schoonenberg twists from its obvious meaning the text he invokes of First Corinthians. What St. Paul tells us here is that if the Resurrection—which, by making manifest the divinity of Christ, is the proof and pledge of our faith in the redemption accomplished by him on the cross—has not taken place, this faith would be in vain. If our faith in the Redemption is vain, then obviously we are "still in our sins."

point so that we can begin all over again. In other words, they wish to make our thought retreat across the centuries and bring us back to the gropings of childhood (a modern childhood, of course, brought up on audio-visual techniques and trying its hand at typewriters and computers). That is not how one makes progress.

It is desirable, surely, that serious theologians should take the trouble to refute the assertions, constructions and hypotheses of these stammering stragglers who see themselves as pioneers. Yet this is likely to prove a waste of time. For one never gets very far launching frontal assaults on what Léon Bloy, referring to the right-minded cleansings with which the Abbé Bethléem tried to make innocuous the literature of his day, and which now appear antediluvian, liked to call an "extraordinary flood of foolishness." What the people of God expect of theological wisdom is for it to take the lead and cut the grass right out from under the feet of the vain Doctors of Divinity by renewing, where necessary, its own problematics and discovering, in total fidelity to truths already acquired, new truths which will take their place alongside the old ones and new horizons which will enrich and enlarge our knowledge. Nothing will be achieved by an idiotic attempt to break everything in order to do up everything to the taste of the day; what is needed is an effort of the mind to see more deeply into the mystery which it will never finish probing.

The truth is that the silly things of our day are quite often a biological phenomenon (to call them intellectual would be saying too much) of reaction to the silly things of the past, particularly the recent past. Thus, another conclusion emerges from a study of the pseudo-renewals which a chronolatrous fatuity is causing to swarm before our eyes. We see a remarkable confirmation of something we knew all along: namely, that what goes by the name of integralism is an ill of the mind disastrous on two counts. First of all, in itself; and secondly, for the consequences it entails.

First, in itself. Integralism is, of itself, an embezzlement, an abuse of trust committed in the name of truth—that is, the worst offense against divine Truth and human intelligence. It takes hold of true formulas which it empties of their living content and freezes in the refrigerators of a restless police of the minds. In these true formulas it is not *truth* that integralism actually sets its heart on and places above everything—truth which demands to be understood in its precise balance and exact meaning and is never something to go to sleep on. (It always involves the dangerous desire to go further and to engender as well as integrate new truths, whether they are truths of the speculative order which the progress of thought gives rise to, or those of a practical order whose discovery is required by the new historical stages through which human societies are passing.) In the formulas which it freezes, integralism sees and cherishes *human means of security*—whether for the convenience of intellects which immobility reassures by giving them, at cut-rate, a good bedrock of fidelity, inner coherence and firmness—or for the equally cheap protection these frozen formulas offer persons in authority, sparing them any risk when they brandish them, prudently as regards themselves, and rudely when it comes to others—or for the ease of government they provide as instruments of prohibition, more or less covert threat and intimidation. In sum, the primacy thus passes to human security and the need for self reassurance, whether it be psychological or social, thanks to the various protective devices called for by this primacy of security, the chief of which is a vigilant ardor in denouncing whatever threatens it: all that, and here comes the abuse of trust, in invoking God and the blessed Truth! The net result is to inhibit the search which the intellect, when it is straight, loves not for the pleasure of seeking but for the joy of discovery and as a means of entering into possession of more of the truth.

It is integralism taken in itself I have been describing here. Of course, a good many minds more or less tainted by it are in good faith, and some even of great value. It is in their unconscious that integralism is at work and spreads its poison. But that's not the question.

As for the consequences which integralism entails, they are all the more dangerous since, as a rule, it is tied to a political and social philosophy which is itself dominated by a secret need for security above all. Confronted no longer with the movement of ideas but with the movement of history, this philosophy takes refuge in utopian claims of restoring order (it's been upset, hasn't it, by this cursed fever for justice of which men should be cured); it cherishes force and a brutal authoritarianism, especially when they derive from a usurped power; it distrusts the people and freedom, and, in spite of occasional demagogic trappings, helps to buttress the interests of the mighty ones and a regime of protracted social injustice which, shaken in the end, stops at nothing to insure its survival in the midst of a world in turmoil but in development. Why be surprised when the consequences entailed by integralism with its usual political and social implications, and by the frustrations thus produced in Christian intelligence and sensibility, lead inevitably, owing to the pendulum movement of human affairs biologically considered, to an explosion of childish anarchy in the opposite direction? Why should we be surprised when in some of our spiritual guides, unstable guides carried away by vainglory, but also in many generous souls who readily follow them—mingling together religion and politics, and mistaking genuine doctrinal rigor for the integralist abuse of trust—the consequences I just pointed out take the form of the fine outburst of theological, philosophical and exegetical nonsense which today greets us at every turn? And it is a fact that integralism, in quite various degrees and under more or less veiled forms, has been spreading among us during the nineteenth century and the first decades of our own. Now, with a crash, the pendulum is swinging to the opposite extreme.

Acknowledging such historical misfortunes is in no way an excuse for the neo-modernist flood I have mentioned, or for the fatuity, mental weakness and mental cowardice which are responsible for it. We have simply to acknowledge also that, in the final analysis, the amount of foolishness and intolerance in human history remains relatively constant, merely passing from one camp to the other, changing styles and having significance in terms of opposite algebraical signs. If I use the word intolerance, it's because, at this stage of the game, whoever gets out of line and refuses to believe in the "latest" fables to hit the market is treated as a reject, good only for the scrap heap. I have suffered more than a little myself from the integralist methods, accusations and denunciations. But I hope I haven't lost my head over it and have kept my reason sufficiently free of the traumas of resentment not to yield to the delicious and so "consoling" pendulum movement which is sweeping along so many of my dear contemporaries.

☆

The crisis in which theology is involved today is obviously a passing phenomenon. In the *Dasein* there is doubtless the human infatuation, but there is also the Holy Spirit, for theology is a necessary ingredient of the mystical Body. The conjectural and imaginary theologies will go as they have come, and so will the vain hopes put in psychological techniques.

Let us rest assured, too, that Thomistic theology—this will take a bit of time—will recover whatever ground it has lost. It will, where necessary, renew itself and likewise its methods of teaching. And it will undertake at last—within the truth (ever up-to-date above time, but demanding to develop in time) of the great wisdom of St. Thomas—the vast work of discernment and integration which the Church and human thought both need. Let us rest assured, too, that the Order of St. Dominic will surmount its present crisis, (whatever way you look at it, it's better to be in a crisis than to cut a fine figure by carrying water on both shoulders), if only those of its members who are clear-sighted don't let themselves be too intimidated by the stars of the intelligentsia and the precious students.

What, from his humble hut, the peasant of the Garonne would now like to bring to attention is that in the great and true renewal we are looking forward to, Christian philosophy will doubtless—this too will be something new in history—have its own role to play which will be of no small importance.

I stated earlier that the metaphysics of St. Thomas is the Christian philosophy par excellence. In St. Thomas himself this metaphysics (not Aristotle's, but St. Thomas', we must go on repeating), as decisive as its part was, remained in the role of a servant, because it was an instrument entirely committed to the service of theology. It was not established in the autonomy which its nature as philosophy requires. It had no roof of its own, nor had it installed its workshops on its own account.

The question is whether it will do so today, faced with so much opposition, unjustified but only too natural, on the part of philosophers (if there still are any) and of theologians (who sometimes seem to prefer employing someone who isn't one of the household). Still, Christian philosophy remains philosophy. And, in this capacity, when it works for its own ends and on its own account, it too is a queen, although of a profane and less lofty kingdom, which depends only on the natural powers of reason. Despite the autonomy suitable to its condition, it recognizes, since it is Christian, the superior rights of faith and of the queen of sacred knowledge.

Under these circumstances, Christian philosophy, if it is sufficiently versed in theology, may happen—with no intention, of course, of settling the matter definitively—to become interested in questions which, by themselves, fall within the province of the theologian. In so doing, it will not consider such questions from the theological standpoint and in the perspective of theology, but in its own philosophical perspective. It is risky but it can be done. As I have observed elsewhere,[38] the light of Christian philosophy is not the light of faith using reason in order to get at some understanding of revealed mysteries, but the light of reason assisted by faith so that it may better perform its own work of intellectual inquiry. And this very fact authorizes Christian philosophy, at the summit of its possibilities, to concern itself in its own way with matters belonging to theology. In such a case it is in a free, though subordinate, capacity that philosophy can eventually be of service to theology, since, by its own nature, it is more available for a work of research and discovery. At this point the *ancilla* becomes research-worker. The last word will, of course, belong to the theologian. But it is the philosopher who will have presented the theologian with the research hypothesis.

Here, it seems to me, is one particularly remarkable aspect of the role reserved for Christian philosophy in the future. One can already detect something of this kind in the investigations, to which I have already alluded, of Olivier Lacombe and Louis Gardet on natural mystique. If Christian philosophy is, by nature, more available than theology for a work of research and discovery, this is because it doesn't have the same responsibilities, nor the same obligation to guide itself according to the chart of a long and venerable tradition and always, each step of the way, with an eye to the revelation transmitted in the Scriptures. In an age when there is so much to renew, this greater availability of Christian (Thomistic) philosophy for a work of research and discovery, if it is given access to the workrooms of the theologian, may possibly provide appreciable help in the work of renewal which (Thomistic) theology has itself to perform.

[38] Cf. my book, *"De la grâce et de l'humanité de Jésus"* (Paris: Desclée De Brouwer, 1967).

Yet this is obviously, for Christian philosophy, an exceptional and slightly dangerous task. In its ordinary behavior, when it labors in realms which belong only to itself, the role assigned to it has a good many other aspects.

In the first place—this goes without saying and is fundamental—its task is to advance in philosophic truth and to perform the work of discernment and liberation so often mentioned in these pages with respect to the various currents of contemporary thought.

And there is something else I should like to point out—as an aside, but its importance, in view of the ecumenical perspectives opened up by the Council, should not be discounted. It seems clear that in its very capacity as philosophy, Christian philosophy is, on its own level, better "situated" than theology for the dialogue (the true dialogue, of course, not the one which takes place on public platforms). From the very fact that it depends, by nature, on reason, not on revelation, philosophy, unlike theology, does not need to engage in a dialogue with the theological systems of non-Catholic Christian families or non-Christian religions, which, fraternal as it is, inevitably runs against painful and sometimes insurmountable mutual oppositions. Dogmatic differences are not philosophy's concern, at least not directly. The object of its investigation belongs to the natural order and has to do with that natural ecumenism the desire for which, however frustrated, naturally haunts the human mind. Not only is dialogue with non-Christians much easier for philosophy, since each of the parties can more easily receive from the other valuable contributions for his own thought, but the possibilities for intellectual agreement in this field are also of much vaster scope. The spontaneous interest Moslem and Hindu thinkers are now taking in some of the research of Thomistic philosophy is proof of this.

Finally, if philosophy is of itself even less the private preserve of the laity than theology is of the clergy, the fact remains that for roughly three centuries laymen have enjoyed a numerical advantage in this field. Let us suppose that Christian philosophy should succeed in fulfilling its development. The work (not too bad a job, let's also assume) of the laymen taking part in its endeavors would, in its own way, be a small sign of the appreciable change history can discern in the Catholic notion of the laity since the days when Conrad de Megenburg said, in so full-flavored a manner, that the "genre" proper

to laymen was to be "an ignorant people, who ought to be ruled by
the clergy, in accordance with the principle that it is up to the wise
man to rule." [39] Without contradicting this principle, and while
being careful to pay due respect to the superior wisdom of theology,
Christian philosophy is perhaps in a position to bring its own modest
contribution to what current-day jargon calls "the up-grading of the
laity."

TRUTH AND FREEDOM

It's a well known fact that the Church has made St. Thomas her
Common Doctor, and that, particularly since the time of Leo XIII,
the Popes have never ceased recommending his doctrine in the most
urgent of terms.[40] Paul VI, in a letter to the American Dominicans
(March 7, 1964) quoted, like his predecessor, Pius XI, the remarkable
words of John of Saint-Thomas: "In St. Thomas, it is something
much greater than St. Thomas which is being received and de-
fended." [41] We know too that Canon 1366, §2, of the Code of Canon
Law enjoins professors who hold their function from the Church to
treat philosophical or theological matters *ad Doctoris Angelici ra-
tionem, doctrinam et principia*, according to the principles, doctrine
and rational approach of the Angelic Doctor.

As a matter of fact, this canonical injunction and all the exhortations of the sovereign Pontiffs don't seem to have made too deep an
impression on the professors who have been given the responsibility
of teaching by the Church. Yet I suspect that those who do the best
they can to follow these directives are somewhat more numerous
than is generally believed. That doesn't alter the fact that not a few
others pay no heed at all to such directives, judging that all of this
stuff is today out-of-date, and that the supreme authority continues

---

39 *"Genus laicorum est populus ignarus. . . . Debet regi a clero, quoniam
sapientis est regere."* Quoted by Jerzy Kalinowsky and Stefan Swiezawski in their
book, which I like so much, *La philosophie à l'heure du Concile* (Paris: Soc.
d'Editions Internationales, 1965).

40 Cf. p. 127, n. 1, the celebrated text of Pius XI, stating that St. Thomas
should be called "the *Common* or *universal* Doctor of the Church, for the Church
has adopted his doctrine as Her own."

41 *Cursus theol.*, ed. Solesmes, I, p. 222 (Vivès, I, p. 289): *"Majus aliquid in
sancto Thoma quam sanctus Thomas suscipitur et defenditur."*

its exhortations only by virtue of a saintly routine (the wind has changed, that alone is the decisive argument for the creative geniuses who are in the wind). And a good many other professors—I'm afraid this has been the case for years—feel ill at ease teaching things whose truth escapes them. For them, the *ad Angelici Doctoris doctrinam* means first of all invoking every now and then the name of the Common Doctor, by selecting from his works, in a brand of eclecticism of sterling quality, whatever seems to keep pace with the thought of other masters (or textbooks) much dearer to them.

Even were the dead to rise again in support of the recommendations of the Church, the situation would remain unaltered. Is it because a number of professors would resemble those people the Gospel tells of in the parable of Lazarus and the evil rich man? No, that's not my idea. For we should not forget, no doubt, the age-old attachment for rival doctrines, nor, of course, the demon of fashion and the itching in the ears. But there is something else we should not lose sight of: namely, the nature and laws of the intellect, for which, at least in the realm of human inquiry, the argument from authority is, as St. Thomas said, the weakest of arguments.

In the hands of the Church, nothing less than the requirements of the truths of faith itself and the preservation of the revealed deposit has the power to put minds under obligation. When the Church recommends a human doctrine, however energetically, she obviously could not possibly do so in the name of divine Truth, as is the case with a dogmatic promulgation. She does so—in the name of her divinely enlightened but human wisdom—only to bear witness to a doctrine which, in the words of Pius XI, she has made her own and in which she sees the sole worthwhile philosophical and theological guarantee of the preservation and spread of faith in men's minds. This witness borne by the Church is surely enough to cause many souls who are in love with truth to feel inclined toward the doctrine thus brought to their attention, and to set to studying it, fervently and hopefully; but it doesn't carry much weight with the professors. Such trust in the Bride of Christ and such love for her wisdom appear to them something rather mystical, and what they require is something legal. So they have been given Canon 1366, §2, which brings them a disciplinary regulation, which, being unable to impose anything on them in the name of the truth of faith, makes it their duty, in the name of prudence, queen of the moral virtues, to teach the doctrine of St. Thomas because it is the *safest one*. That's why I have little sympathy for this canon. Such a procedure is certainly legitimate in itself, but in practice it threatens to give rise to the very opposite of what is intended. For it is truth, not security—and the "fair dangers" of which Plato spoke, more than prudence—which draws the intellect on in its striving toward knowledge.

Although I have little sympathy for this canon, I refrain from wishing for its abrogation, which would be taken up quite wrongly, and, as a result, would be deplorable on all counts. But it seems to me that we are confronted here with a very serious drama, which goes well beyond the Canon in question. As disrespectful as I am toward the general run of professors,[42] I am aware that for all of them, even the most infatuated, truth is the object of their search (when they are seeking) and of their teaching (when they are not fooling around with conjectures). Even those who today, by virtue of an unnatural divorce between the *end* and the *object* of knowledge, see their fondest goal in Efficacy, do so because they mistakenly believe it's truly better that way. If they don't exactly shine in their love for Truth, still they burn with a love for the truths of scholarship. Besides, it's not love which is at stake here, but intelligence. And however misguided the latter may be, truth always remains its object. (Let us recall, for the philosophers, that the object is related to "formal causality," not to "final causality.") And truth keeps pace with freedom.

Doubtless professors of theology have a special duty toward the Church, since theology is a thing of the Church, while philosophy is a thing of the world or of culture. But to have as professors of theology men who, being utterly in doubt about the truth of St. Thomas' doctrine, would merely parrot it out of obedience is hardly an ideal state of affairs. The problem is to get them to see the truth of St. Thomas, and this presupposes a host of conditions for which the cult

---

[42] I am speaking here of professors and their own intellectual life (which plays a central part in the matter); I'm not speaking of their students for whom, obviously, it will always be true that *oportet addiscentem credere*. Still less am I speaking (heaven forbid!) of the thorny question, totally different and much more general, of publications, about which it will always be desirable that the public be enlightened (exactly how, now that the old Index is happily defunct, is no concern of mine).

of today's mentality makes them unfit. But this also presupposes that they move in a climate of freedom.

I am aware I am here trespassing on preserves which are in no way mine. But perhaps an old hermit will be allowed to express a humble wish. I am dreaming of a day when the Church would turn, even in these most delicate matters, toward the roads of freedom. Of her own intellectual life she has a particularly keen awareness (because particularly assisted by the Holy Spirit) in the person of the chief who here on earth is responsible for her universality. It is in exercising the liberty proper to the mystical Body of Christ that she has adopted the doctrine of the Angelic Doctor. Could not a kind of reversal take place in the practical manner in which she recommends this doctrine? More fervently than ever, but by appealing less to obedience and docility than to the freedom of the intellect in its pursuit of truth and by relying less upon her disciplinary authority than on her own unfailing confidence in the truth of this doctrine?

Is there any reason to fear that in such a climate of freedom the number of teachers either ignorant or scornful of St. Thomas would proceed to increase? This number is so great right now that it is difficult to imagine it getting any larger. It would be nice enough if the opinions they hold and teach contained nothing which, on the theological level, would present too much of a danger to the content of revelation, and, on the philosophical level, would come close to respecting the truths of a natural order which have a necessary connection with this content. But were there an explicit statute of freedom, wouldn't they become less concerned with the constraint (and the weakness) of legal injunctions and more appreciative, at least some of them, of the witness given by the Church to the *truth* of her own rational discernment, enlightened by her faith, when she recommends with extraordinary insistence a doctrine which is human, no doubt, but which, in her divinely assisted mind, she holds to be essentially grounded on truth? If for her part, the Church, while continuing to maintain her canonical regulations in such a way as to give them, as far as Thomism is concerned, the value of a simple counsel (besides, that's the way they are at present generally considered), were to decide to use those supreme maternal resources, which it is permissible to consider the most efficacious, and which involve imploring rather than commanding; if she were to address an urgent appeal to all who have ears to hear, and loudly declare how eagerly she wants—she, the blessed mother anxious for the salvation of her children—the living tradition of St. Thomas to go on growing and expanding from age to age, is it too much to believe that such an appeal would be heard by a good many of the faithful, and even by a sufficient number of professors, sufficiently intent, moreover, on studying the Common Doctor, and thereby sufficiently convinced of the truth of his doctrine to ensure, however feeble a proportion they might be in the beginning, its preservation, progress and expansion?

Such is the dream of an old hermit who may possibly have lost his way. If that is the case, he asks only to be put back on the right road.

VITAÏ LAMPADA TRADUNT

Little teams and small flocks have always been the ones who performed the great work. It looks as if this will be truer for our age than it ever has been, precisely because it will be (it already is) an age of massification through technique. Doubtless it is possible to massify completely all our activities and pleasures, our imagination, our unconscious, and, indirectly, the intellectual habits of a great many. But one will never succeed in completely massifying the spirit (and the supra-conscious of the spirit), or in totally alienating from himself the individual person, that mysterious and scandalous beggar who insists on existing and has means of his own (a poor blighter utters, even if only in silent prayer, a few words, naming a friend and pleading with heaven for him, and behold, that *operates*). Assuming (which I don't, in spite of the ways in which the world is going on these days) a total massification of mankind, it would remain for the individual person, in those cases (which will always be met with) where he had not become completely alienated from himself, to flee either into neurosis or into God: which would give promise of a great many lunatics and a few saints.

Yet I don't think we will ever reach that point. In his rather pessimistic book on technique, which I have already cited, M. Ellul points out somewhere that in actual fact the technician (who in addition to inventing new techniques is able to modify existing ones) matters more than technique itself. And it seems to me that this observation (a passing remark of the author) has a considerable bearing on the subject. For the technician is a man, and in a better position to question himself on technique than are those who receive the blessings of the latter. I am not unaware that among technicians there are a good many victims of the commonplaces to which we are treated about Technique in the service of Man, the Liberation of Man through Technique, technological Humanism, etc. But if I can believe what I am told by trustworthy friends, the best representatives of the world of technicians feel much more concern for the mystery of the *true* man, and are much more open to a genuine realism, than are those who belong to the world of the intelligentsia. What they lack is a thorough idea of man, which no one in the intelligentsia furnishes them, and which it would be up to philosophers and theologians worthy of the name to propose to them.

In other words, assuming a day would come when they find the intellectual guidance they are seeking, and assuming also that in such a case the better of them (which is not unlikely) would take the lead, it will be less with politicians or business men than with (enlightened) technicians that, as far as temporal activity and the temporal order are concerned, the world would have its best chance of escaping complete massification and the other servitudes to which the empire of technology is, of itself, dragging us off, as long as revolutionary changes don't occur in the management of techniques with respect to human life. All this seems rather obvious, since technicians play so dominant a part in our world. And all this presupposes, I repeat (perhaps as a utopian), a day when technology would be at least taken in hand by technicians who, having found the intellectual guidance for which they at present seek in vain, and being inspired by an authentic humanism careful to respect *all* that is in man, would then be in a position to overturn a good many things in the kingdom they govern and bring about the necessary revolutions.

In other respects, when we look at the process of technical massification that is going on before our very eyes, it seems that the realm of the spiritual should also, and first of all, have its role to play in a matter of such consequence to mankind. From this point of view, at least for the moment, the prospect, frankly speaking, is scarcely reassuring. By employing mass means, Christians will unquestionably obtain a certain number of immediate results of a kind to gratify their shepherds. But to resort in the first place, and on a grand scale, even for the loftiest goals and with the purest intentions, to the very things which depend on the empire of technique is to contribute by the same token to strengthening this empire, with all the threats of which it is at present chock-full, and which, moreover, are all the more redoubtable as one allows it to have a hold over things that, of themselves, belong to the realm of the spiritual itself, and of the freedom of the spirit. Under such circumstances we should regard the long-term outcome as rather doubtful.

If we take all of the foregoing into account, it clearly appears, methinks, that it is more than ever the task of the little teams and small flocks to struggle most effectively for man and the spirit, and, in particular, to give the most effective witness to those truths for which men so desperately long and which are, at present, in such short supply. For only the little teams and small flocks are able to muster around something which completely escapes technique and the process of massification, and which is the love of wisdom and of the intellect and the trust in the invisible radiation of this love. Such invisible rays carry far; they have the same kind of incredible power in the realm of the spirit that atomic fission and the miracles of microphysics have in the world of matter.

So here we are back once again at our reflections on Christian (Thomistic) philosophy and theology. To perform a mass action is, as far as these are concerned, a forbidden dream. And even if, in the teaching of the Church, it is to be hoped that one day they will resume (if they ever had it) or at last assume the decisively quickening role the kingdom of God on pilgrimage would like so much to see them play, they will never have in the world, I say *the world*, which has such need for them, a publicity success or a great multitude of workers.

Once the living waters of common human thought, which were running underground for centuries, were brought together by the angels of God to gush forth as a spring on the surface of the earth, a day came when there surged up from them a life-giving river which will never run dry, even if now and then it becomes very thin in size (though not in inner strength). What is absolutely needed is the very existence and activity of this current. We are sure they will hold out.

To transmit through the world and all the tribulations of the age the flame of the wisdom of St. Thomas and to make this wisdom progress as, here too, it demands to do, it is not a great crowd of carriers, sometimes a little drunk and stumbling, that is required. The little teams and small flocks, who work at their own risk with no object or goal but truth, and are counting quite a lot on the help of the Paraclete, will suffice. For the assistance of the Holy Spirit does not only help men when they are working within the precincts of the mystical Body and in the Councils of the Holy Church. The Spirit is active in the world, too, in an entirely different and apparently more hazardous way, amid all the clumsy efforts and *faux-pas*, and also in the passionate striving for truth and the loving prayer of men (even if they belong to the *genus laïcorum*) who stammer here: don't we know that He will renew the face of the earth? *Et renovabis faciem terrae.*

April 28, 1966

7 THE TRUE NEW FIRE

THE AFFAIRS OF
GOD'S KINGDOM

The One and Holy

Perhaps because I have spent my life philosophizing—and even an old peasant has trouble forgetting this—I have spoken at length of the demands and worries of the human intellect; I needed two chapters to bring out my package. And because I am just an old philosopher, and one who approaches only in fear and trembling a subject far above him, I promised myself that I would be more brief in this concluding chapter. Alas, it is longer than all the others. I might have done well to drop it, and yet since I started disserting on the true new fire, I could not omit those things in which its flame leaps highest.

Since this chapter treats with the affairs of God's kingdom, it is naturally advisable to begin with a section concerning the Church. I first had the idea of putting together a sort of anthology of the principal texts of the Council's Constitution on the Church, to which I would have joined, by way of illustration, other texts drawn from trustworthy theologians (there are still some around, and there always will be). I quickly perceived that such a project would fill too many pages and I would be starting a lengthy business, too weighty for this book. I will therefore limit myself to setting out as simply as possible some ideas which have come to me in readings and meditations over the years, and which have been reinforced further by the teaching of *Lumen Gentium*. I apologize to theologians for having occasionally resorted to a vocabulary which is not theirs at points where, trying to avoid too technical a language, I have chosen words within easier reach of most men.

Many people too frequently see the Church only as a vast juridical

174

administration charged with the duty of reminding them that God exists, and they look no further than its external apparatus. They do not know what the Church is. The Church is a mystery as profound as the Incarnation, and that is why the title of the first chapter ("The Mystery of the Church") of the dogmatic Constitution *Lumen Gentium* was chosen by the Council the way it was.

THE PERSONALITY OF THE CHURCH

"In the second century Hermas [1] was already depicting the Church as an old woman, and giving this reason for doing so: 'She was founded before all things, and it was for her that the world was created.' " [2]

The Church, Père Clérissac, wrote, has a mysterious personality which is underlined for us in the four-fold definition of the Nicean Council: *Unam, Sanctam, Catholicam et Apostolican Ecclesiam,* a personality which reflects "the divine Being, the most universal and the most personal of beings." [3] It was this personality that St. Irenaeus had in mind when he said: "Having received this [apostolic] preaching and this faith, . . . the Church, although spread throughout the world, guards that deposit with constant solicitude, as if she really dwelt in but one house; and to those things she adheres in the same way, I mean as if she had but one soul and one heart; and it is with that same oneness that she preaches and teaches and transmits them to generation after generation, as if she had but one mouth." [4]

And it is with the same unity that she pronounces the Lord's prayer: "The Lord's prayer is pronounced by the common person of the whole Church." [5]

Nothing could be more important than to try to form some idea of this personality, which goes infinitely beyond any purely human notion of personality, since it concerns a multitude spread out through the whole world and through all ages, and has nevertheless, to a su-

[1] *The Shepherd*, Vis. II, Ch. IV.
[2] R. P. Humbert Clérissac, *Le Mystère de l'Eglise* (Paris: éd. du Cerf, 1918, 5th ed.).
[3] *Ibid.*, p. 43.
[4] *Adv. Haer.*, Book I, c. 10, 2. (*Ibid.*, p. 49)
[5] St. Thomas Aquinas, *Sum. theol.* II–II, 83, 16, ad 3.

preme degree, the marks of personality—unity of being and of life, consciousness, memory, perception, voice ("the audible Voice of the Church is the Pope" [6]), and a task to accomplish—which, also, is one, through all times and places.

To designate the Church in such or such of her aspects, there are certain accepted names—all true, and all synonymous in spite of their great diversity, in the profundity of the mystery, but all inadequate inasmuch as they are images drawn from things of this world. The Constitution on the Church has enumerated all these names. I would like to talk about only a few of them here.

THE CHURCH, BRIDE AND MYSTICAL BODY

The Church is the *Body of Christ* and she is his *Bride*.

"St. Paul calls the Church a 'Body' that has Christ for its 'Head.' From this it would appear that Christ and the Church complete one another in the manner that the head and the body do in man; Christ being, on the one hand, the (formal) completion of the Church: 'You have come to fullness of life in him who is the head of all principalities and of all power' [7]; and the Church, with her greatnesses of hierarchy and sanctity, being on the other hand, the (material) completion of Christ: God 'made him the Head over all things for the Church, who is his Body, the fullness of him who fills all in all.' [8] Accordingly, St. John Chrysostom could write that 'the pleroma (that is to say, the fulfillment, the completion) of the Head is the Body, and the pleroma of the Body, the Head.' "[9]

Personality presupposes oneness; there is no personality without complete oneness of being and of life. It is by reason of her complete oneness that the Church or the mystical Body has her personality; in other terms by reason of the complete oneness in which her members are bound together by the unity of apostolic faith, Baptism and the other sacraments, and obedience to Peter. Thus in possession of her

---

[6] Humbert Clérissac, *op. cit.*, p. 55.

[7] *Col.*, 2:10.

[8] Cf. Constitution on the Church, Ch. I, Par. 7.

[9] Charles Journet, *L'Eglise du Verbe Incarné* (Paris: Desclée De Brouwer, 1951), II, p. 53. The passage from St. John Chrysostom is taken from *In Epist. ad Ephes.*, cap. I, hom. 3.

complete unity and her personality, the Church is at the same time mysterious and visible. She is visible or outwardly recognizable by the three signs which I have just mentioned: profession of the same faith, regeneration through the same Baptism, recognition of the authority of the bishops, successors of the apostles, and of the supreme authority of the Sovereign Pontiff. At the same time, the grace and charity that are her very life make her "mysterious." May I suggest that in place of this term "mysterious," which has been traditionally preferred (doubtless to avoid misunderstanding, and the heretical idea of the "invisible Church" as opposed to the visible Church), it might be better to say that the Church (who in her very essence is a mystery), this same Church *visible* in her structure, her preaching, her rites, and in the extraordinary fecundity with which she engenders saints, is also *invisible* in that which is principal in her and in her deepest reality: since grace is something invisible, and since, as St. Thomas writes, "that which prevails in the law of the New Testament, and constitutes all its virtue, is the grace of the Holy Spirit given by faith in Christ. The new law is, as to what is principal in it, the very grace of the Holy Spirit diffused in Christ's faithful." [10] The baptised who are in a state of mortal sin are still members of the mystical Body, members alienated from the life of this whole Body (the charity [11]) but who are still tied to the whole and still belong to it by virtue of a very special relationship with that life; for by reason of the sacred character with which they were marked by Baptism, God lays special claim to them, and the faith that dwells within them, however dimmed it may be for many, demands of itself to be

10 *Sum. theol.*, I–II, 106, I. Cf. Charles Journet, *op. cit.*, pp. 39–40. "It is the principal part of the Church—that is, her supernatural being—that is invisible," comments Bañez, "but she manifests herself to the world and she is visible." (*Ibid.*, p. 42)

11 Can they be called, as they sometimes are, "dead" members, like a "dead" or rather paralyzed member in a living body? This metaphor runs the risk of leading us into error. In effect, while they are undoubtedly "dead" members since they lack grace and charity, they are not merely *called* to live again, they are also being *worked upon* by life: because that which gives life to the whole Body still works from within them (through all the holy things that remain in them, which are mentioned in my text), and from the outside through the influences they receive from the collective charity of the Church. That is why theologians say that they are members of the Church *re, non voto*, "in act," but only through an "influx" which does not convey grace (cf. *L'Eglise du Verbe Incarné*, v. II, pp. 1072, 1080).

perfected by the virtue of charity. These two elements would already suffice for membership in the mystical Body, provided that the sinners did not separate themselves from that Body by an explicit denial of the faith. But there are many other holy things in them which connect them indirectly to the life of the whole: grace always solicits them, if only through the wounds which the loss of it has inflicted; and a loneliness of soul bitterly reminds them of God. Repentance and hope bring an immense number of them back to the sacrament of penance (a sacrament which was instituted *for them*). Because Hope, too, is there; as is also Suffering accepted. And, like messengers of the memory that the Head of the mystical Body keeps of them, actual graces, with the inner movements they entail, are passing in them; in great sinners such singularly profound movements can at certain moments give rise to quite unforeseen actions. And there are also the secret influences through which (are they not the favorites of mercy? Did He not come for them?) the charity which collectively animates the Church continues to reach them. The life of the mystical Body is grace and charity. "In the holy Church everything is to love, in love, for love and from love," said St. Francis de Sales.[12] Considering us, average Christians, it does not always look like it. And yet what tokens we have of that love! St. Francis de Sales saw with the eyes of faith, which seek the invisible beneath the visible; he spoke of the Church in terms of that which is her life. The uncreated Soul of the Church is the Holy Spirit;[13] her created soul, is charity.[14]

[12] Preface to *Traité de l'Amour de Dieu*.

[13] Cf. Constitution on the Church, Ch. I, Par. 7.

[14] Cf. Charles Journet, *Théologie de l'Eglise* (Paris: Desclée De Brouwer, 1958), pp. 193–213. (This work is an abridged version of the first two volumes of the great treatise *L'Eglise du Verbe Incarné.*) Cardinal Journet specifies that the created soul of the Church is charity "as *cultual, sacramental* and *oriented* (by the teaching and directives of pastoral authority)." In other words, I would say that it is charity as capable of making the body which it animates *sufficiently one* to be able to receive, together with it, a collective supernatural *subsistence* that is absolutely proper to the Church, or the seal of the Church's personality. "The mystical Body finds its accomplishment only there where the hierarchy is complete and the primacy of Peter is recognized" (*Ibid.*, p. 246). Only there do we find the personality of the Church.

I apologize for the technical nature of the remarks that follow; I believe they are necessary, because on this point I intend to go—in the same direction—a little further than Cardinal Journet (*L'Eglise du Verbe Incarné*, v. II, pp. 492–508).

Here, then, are what seem to me to be the true positions: the oneness that binds the faithful together is obviously not a substantial unity, it is the unity of a

And "the body of the Church is coextensive with her soul; where the soul of the Church is, there is her body. Where the Church is, there also is her uncreated Soul, the Spirit of God; and where the Spirit of God is, there is the Church and all grace." [15]

One can thus understand better that where the perfect unity of the mystical Body is lacking, that unity required by personality, and where

multiplicity. Contrary to what takes place here on earth, and which is the province of the philosophers (in the sphere of nature the complete) unity which is presupposed by personality is the unity of an individual substance, "rationalis naturae individua *substantia*")—the subsistence of which I am speaking does not inform and therefore does not perfect (with respect to the act of existing) a substance. It informs or perfects a *multiplicity*, the soul of which is charity (with the characteristics mentioned by Cardinal Journet) and the unity of which (one and the same Baptism, one and the same faith, one and the same jurisdiction) is complete—a multiplicity which by virtue of charity bears supernaturally the image of oneness of God. The subsistence in question presupposes (in place of substance) that complete or perfect oneness of the multiplicity whose life is charity. And it transcends the personality of each member of this whole, because what it informs and perfects (with respect to the act of existing) is supernatural life as received from God *in the complete or perfect unity of the multiplicity itself* (and not, obviously, in each of its members). That subsistence is given by the Holy Spirit, with and through the outpouring of grace and charity whose source is Christ—but it is a *created subsistence* (required by the created soul of Church as well as by the created body that it animates), a *supernatural created* subsistence. We find ourselves here face to face with the mystery of the Church in all its profundity, a mystery which cannot be *explained* (the more one might try, the more one would miss it), but which we must accept in faith; for reason can only establish that no contradiction is implied here. God save me from denying that infinitely holy assistance of the Spirit of God by reason of which my teacher and friend looks on the Holy Spirit as "the extrinsic and efficient personality of the Church"; nevertheless I can see there only a constant influx of the Holy Spirit—supreme fountainhead of the life of the Church, whose action is such that, as St. Irenaeus said, "where the Church is, there is the Spirit of God, and where the Spirit of God is, there is the Church and all grace." The Holy Spirit could not constitute the personality, in the proper sense of the word, that we ought to recognize in the Church, because personality, properly speaking, is an *intrinsic* and *formal* perfection—not an extrinsic and efficient support, as the assistance and the action of the Holy Spirit are for the Church.

Nor am I forgetting that the personality of Christ *marks* the personality of the Church in an incomparably profound manner. (There is an analogy of this—weak as it may be—in marriage.) But the personality of the Bridegroom, however profoundly it impresses itself on that of the Bride (to the point that they become—*spiritually* or *mystically*—but one person), cannot constitute the personality of the Bride, nor can the intellectual and moral support of the Bridegroom dispense the Bride from having her own personality.

[15] Charles Journet, *L'Eglise du Verbe Incarné*, v. II, p. 951–954; *Théologie de l'Eglise*, pp. 272–276.

charity is not in a fit state to receive the seal of the Church's personality, there are two distinct cases to consider. The first is the case of the
non-Catholic Christian religious families. I am thinking in particular
of the Eastern Churches separated from the Apostolic See. In the case
of these Churches, which still adore the same Christ, use equally the
baptismal rite, are blessed with the saints that they have engendered,
and certain of which possess an authentic hierarchy, we find ourselves in the presence of men who are *visibly* members in act of the
Church, but in a way that not being crowned with perfect unity,
remains imperfect and uncompleted. (I add that if, in the orthodox
Churches, the body and soul of the Church do not bear the seal of the
Church's personality, they are, nonetheless, if I might say so, strongly
attracted by that personality; this is proper to the particular example
that I have chosen. With respect to other non-Catholic Christian confessions, the remarks made above still apply analogously, but to a
lesser, sometimes to a much lesser, degree.)

The second case to be considered is that of the non-Christian
religious families, as well as of the diaspora of the unbelievers and
atheists. There, too, there are men who belong to Christ and to his
Church. In spite of the adverse positions of the religion or anti-
religion that they profess, but aided no doubt, by their natural righteousness and their own spiritual experience, they have not refused
the divine gift offered to all. They live—without knowing it—in the
grace of Christ. They are members in act of his Church, but this time
in a way *invisible to men, and to themselves,* a way that depends
solely on the freedom of the Spirit and that of individual human
beings. In other words, the body and the soul of the Church spread
out together—very far from the center where they have their perfect
unity, and not only deprived of the seal of personality they bear only
in the fully-formed Church, but withdrawn also from its attraction—
everywhere in the world where there are hearts that open themselves
to the grace of Christ, even if they do not know his name. Because
"we know that there is no soul that God does not call to himself by
name." [16] Those who have the grace of Christ and charity in this way
—not outside of the visible Church, but as belonging to her only in a

---

[16] Charles Journet, *Théologie de l'Eglise*, p. 351. On the "latent" membership
to the Church, whether "normal" before Christ or "abnormal" after him, see the
same work, pp. 360–364.

"latent" way—are invisibly [17] members of the visible Church.[18] They are living members of the mystical Body, but members in an abnormal and imperfect state; they are not integrated in act [19] into the personality of the Church, the invisible effulgence of which they nevertheless receive, and which reaches them through the secret influences of prayer or sacrifice, borne by the Spirit of God who alone knows their immeasurable power.[20]

☆

The Church is the mystical Body of Christ. And she is also his Bride.

I will betroth you to me in righteousness and in justice
in steadfast love and in mercy. (Hos. 2:11)

Fear not, for you will not be ashamed. . .
For your Maker is your husband. (Is. 54:4-5)

[17] In the visible behavior of these men, who have grace and charity within them, there is certainly (cf. *op. cit.*, p. 374) a quality which, of itself, is a sign of their belonging to the Church, but among men no one knows it—not even they. Those around them attribute it rather to some particular greatness or personal virtue; and if they make saints of them, they see them as saints of their own spiritual family. In other words, they themselves, as well as their acts, are no doubt something visible—and which belongs to the body of the Church; but no one sees this fact save God and his angels—neither they themselves nor anyone else (except perhaps, here and there, some Christian friend who has an inkling of it). Thus it is in a manner *invisible to men* that the body of the Church is spreading in the scattered ones who, not embraced in her perfect unity, are not united in act to her personality. (Further and more complete explanations may be found in Appendix 4.)

They are like petals of a rose perfectly one and beautiful—the normal flower of a rosebush planted and cultivated by God—which would sprout elsewhere in the middle of a flower blooming on such or such wild rosebush.

[18] See Appendix 4 in the back of the book, *On the Unity and Visibility of the Church.*

[19] I would say that they tend (without knowing it) to be integrated into it, since they belong invisibly to the body and soul of the visible Church, which of themselves ask for their normal fulfillment, that is to say, to be included in her personality.

[20] "The witness of the saints of the Orthodox Churches, or the Protestant Churches, or of Judaism, or of Islam, or of India, if their sanctity is genuine, would dim the brilliance of the sanctity of the Catholic Church only if the latter taught that genuine supernatural life and sanctity can be found only among those who belong to her visibly and bodily, and that there is neither supernatural life nor authentic sanctity in those who belong to her invisibly and spiritually, without knowing it, by virtue of the grace that they have received from Christ. The Church teaches the contrary." Charles Journet, *op. cit.*, p. 247.

"Christ," says the Council, "loves the Church as his bride, making himself the model of the bridegroom who loves his bride as he loves his own body." [21]

It is in the bringing together of these two names that the unsoundable depths of the mystery of the Church become perceptible to the heart. When we say that she is the mystical Body of Christ, or, using Bossuet's phrase, "Christ spread out and communicated," we are insisting that she is the Body and the members whose Head is Christ, he whose divine personality cannot, however, be communicated or spread. It is therefore in a spiritual or mystical sense—and by virtue of the graces through which Christ pours out and communicates his own life beyond his own person—that the Church and Christ make one person; it is not in the sense in which, among those living here on earth, head and body make but one. For at the same time the Church has her own personality, that created personality of which I am trying to speak here, which is not the uncreated personality of Christ. It is this created personality, distinct from the personality of Christ, that we stress when we say that she is the Bride of Christ. Truly *a single mystical person* with Christ, and truly *a person in herself* (on earth and in heaven)—that is what the Church is, and like all mysteries hidden in God, this mystery confounds the mind. Truly flesh of the flesh of Christ, and truly distinct from him.

"The Church as the Bride of Jesus Christ," Bossuet wrote, "is his by choice; the Church, as mystical Body, is his through an inmost operation of the Holy Spirit of God. The mystery of the election through the engagement of promises appears in the name of spouse; and the mystery of unity, consummated by the infusion of the Spirit, is seen in the name of body. The word 'body' shows us how much the Church belongs to Jesus Christ; the word 'bride' shows us that she was a stranger to him and that it was of his own free will that he sought her out. Thus the name of bride makes us see unity through live and free choice; and the name of body brings us to understand unity as natural. Something more intimate, then, appears in the unity of the body, and something more felt and more tender appears in the unity of the Bride—the name Bride distinguishes, in

[21] Constitution on the Church, Ch. 1, Par. 7.

order to then unite; the name body unites without mingling. . . ." [22]

The Church, says the Council, "is the Immaculate Bride of the immolated Lamb, the Bride whom Christ has loved and for whom he has delivered himself up in order to sanctify her, whom he unites to himself by an unbreakable covenant, and whom he unceasingly nourishes and cherishes, whom he has willed, having purified her, to be united with him and subject to him in love and fidelity, whom he filled for ever with heavenly gifts, in order that we may grasp the love of God and of Christ for us, a love which surpasses all knowledge." [23]

THE CHURCH, KINGDOM OF GOD BEGUN HERE ON EARTH

The Church is the *kingdom of God*: the kingdom Jesus came to announce, and mysteriously inaugurate—begun now on earth and advancing through the sufferings of the cross toward the plenitude it will achieve in the world of glory and of the risen.

Christ "inaugurated on earth the kingdom of heaven and revealed to us the mystery of that kingdom, and through his obedience he worked our redemption. The Church, or the kingdom of God already present in mystery, grows visibly in the world, through the power of God." That is what the Council teaches. And it says further, "This kingdom shines forth to the eyes of men in the word, the works, and the presence of Christ. . . . The miracles of Jesus are the proof that the kingdom has already arrived on earth: 'If it is by the finger of God that I cast out demons then the kingdom of God has come upon you'" (Luke 11:20; cf. Matt. 12:28).[24] And the Church, who "received the mission to announce the kingdom of Christ and of God and to establish it among all nations," constitutes on earth "the germ and beginning of that kingdom."

It matters indeed, is it not so, to all of us who are asking every day that it come—and to all the hopeless who hope despite everything, in the anguish and the shadows of that existence which they received without having been consulted—and even to the neo-Christian think-

---

[22] *Lettre à une demoiselle de Metz sur le mystère de l'unité de l'Eglise et les merveilles qu'il renferme.*
[23] Constitution on the Church, Ch. I, Par. 6.
[24] Constitution on the Church, Ch. I, Par. 3, 5.

ers who have discovered that the World has a right to our raptures—it does matter, in spite of our silly flutterings, to think that it is there, this kingdom of God is there, as hidden as it may be to our carnal eyes in the profound life of the mystical Body, behind the necessary episcopal chanceries and codes of Canon Law.

"The kingdom is already on earth and the Church is already in heaven." [25] "The kingdom, like its king, experiences two phases, one in which it is veiled and in pilgrimage, the other in which it is glorious and definitive." [26] To make use of the decisive formula of Cardinal Journet, the kingdom here on earth is "in a state of pilgrimage and crucifixion." For "the Church of the Cross" must precede "the Church of glory." [27] And why is the kingdom here on earth crucified with Christ, if not to do with Christ the work of Christ, to accomplish that mission of coredemption the importance and necessity of which has been marked for all centuries by some words of St. Paul ("in my flesh I complete what is lacking in Christ's afflictions for the sake of his body, that is the Church," Col. 1:24), a mission that comes from "the superabundance of the merits of Christ spreading in his living members?" [28] Because "from One only and through One only, we are saved and we save others," [29] as Clement of Alexandria said so admirably. And similarly the Pseudo-Dionysius, whom St. John of the Cross loved so much to quote: "Of all things divine, the most divine is to cooperate with God for the salvation of souls"; [30] a thing which is done by preaching the Truth and by every true witness given to Love, but above all by the Cross we bear with Christ through all ages and along all the roads of this world.

As the Council said in regard to the mystical Body of Christ: "Still pilgrims on earth, following in his footsteps in tribulation and perse-

[25] Charles Journet, L'Eglise du Verbe Incarné, v. II, p. 57.
[26] Charles Journet, "Le Mystère de l'Eglise selon le IIe Concile du Vatican," Revue Thomiste, 1965–I, p. 11.
[27] L'Eglise du Verbe Incarné, v. II, p. 91.
[28] Cajetan, quoted in L'Eglise du Verbe Incarné, v. II, p. 225.
[29] Stromates, Book VII, Ch. II, quoted in L'Eglise du Verbe Incarné, v. II, p. 326.
[30] Témoignage d'Elisée des Martyrs, 6e avis, Obras, Silverio, IV, p. 351. In the translation of Lucien-Marie de S.Joseph, p. 1369.

cution, we are associated to his sufferings (*passionibus suis*) [31] as the Body to the Head, united to him in his passion (*Ei compatientes*) to be united to him in his glory." [32]

THE CHURCH, HOLY AND PENITENT

The Church is *without stain or wrinkle*, and she is *penitent*. There, perhaps, we have the most troubling enigma, and the most magnificent. The Church is *sine macula, sine ruga*, she is immaculate, there is no name for her dearer to Him who loves her: *Veni columba mea*, come my dove, my all-beautiful (*Cant.* 2:10), without stain or wrinkle, holy and immaculate, *sancta et immaculata*.[33] And I have always felt with regret, when I think of our dissident brothers who refuse her this title, scandalizing in their eye, and of certain intimidated Catholics who hesitate to give it to her, that Christ pardons more willingly the spits on his face than the least doubt on the holiness of his Beloved.

And yet this same Church accuses herself, often in very harsh terms, she weeps for her failures, she begs to be purified, she pleads unceasingly for forgiveness (she does so every day in the Lord's Prayer), she sometimes cries out to God from the depths of the abyss, as from the depth of his anguish one who fears damnation.

For us to take advantage of that to strike hard on *her* breast, when in reality we are speaking either of the failures of the hierarchy or of the sometimes atrocious miseries of the Christian world, that is a silliness—in which many young clerics of today do not fail to take pleasure, as do also many spouters who want to give themselves an air of freedom of the mind, and to earn the favor of audiences stuffed with prejudices—a bit of courage would have been enough to make them more intelligent.

[31] "Passionibus suis." The Council used the same word which is used in the Vulgate to translate τῶν θλίψεων τοῦ Χριστοῦ, in the text of the Epistle to the Colossians (I:24) quoted on p. 184.

[32] Constitution on the Church, Ch. I, Par. 7.

[33] St. Paul: "Christ loved the Church and gave himself up for her that he might sanctify her, . . . that he might present the Church to himself in splendor, without stain or wrinkle or any such thing, that she might be *holy and without blemish*" (*Eph.* 5:25–27).

The truth is that, in the image of the immaculate Christ, the Church too, is immaculate, but not in the same way as he is. Let us remember the distinction we made above between the personality of the Church, a created personality, and the personality of Christ, which is the very personality of the Word: Christ is "holy, innocent, undefiled," [34] because his personality is that of the Word, to whom his human nature is hypostatically united, and because the members of that human body that walked along the roads of Galilee and sat in the synagogues, and was crucified under Pontius Pilate, those feet that Mary Magdalene covered with kisses, and that were pierced, those hands whose touch cured the sick, and that were pierced, never knew the least contact with sin. In taking upon himself the sins of the world he assumed something which was absolutely alien to him, and which he made his own through pure love, pure will to substitute himself as victim for sinful mankind. It is in this sense that St. Paul says that he was made sin so that we might be saved.[35] He himself never had the experience of sin. It was by *loving union with sinners* that he *put on all sin.*[36]

But the personality of the Church is a created personality, and the members that make up its body are themselves exposed to sin. "She enfolds sinners in her bosom." [37] She herself, therefore, and to what depths, has experience of sin—"She is all mingled with sin" [38] —in the countless multitude of all those poor sinners who are her members (and who always are, as they were when he went down to eat in

[34] Constitution on the Church, Ch. I, Par. 8.

[35] 2 *Cor.* 5:21.

[36] "In the Garden of Olives Jesus fixed his gaze on the subject of his prayer, all the sin he would put on and all the dereliction of men and of God . . .

"Darkness of the contemplation of sin, truly merciless night, mystical and unsoundable night, experience founded in charity and in the loving union of Christ with sinners . . .

"He tastes the infinite bitterness of our sins, as in the darkness of divine contemplation the poor saints taste the essential sweetness of God.

"Here the darkness is full, Jesus sees himself abandoned, all justice is accomplished, all is given . . ." (Raïssa Maritain, *"La Couronne d'épines,"* in *Lettre de Nuit, La Vie donnée,* Paris: Desclée De Brouwer, 1950).

[37] Constitution on the Church, Ch. I, Par. 8. "She is therefore," this paragraph concludes (and this is precisely the mystery that concerns us here), "at the same time *holy and always working toward purification."*

[38] Charles Journet, *Théologie de l'Eglise,* p. 239.

the house of Zacchaeus, "the friends of Jesus").[39] Yet she herself, insofar as she constitutes a unique person—in other terms, in her very personality, into which all who are her members in act and visibly are integrated to receive the seal thereof, but which is not their personality, and transcends it—she herself, in her own personality, in her personality as Bride of Christ, is without any trace of sin. That is why when she does penance and asks forgiveness, and accuses herself, and begs to be purified, she too, in the image of the Lamb of God, takes upon herself that which is not hers, but she does not take it upon herself in the same manner that Jesus did. She takes upon herself something which is in her, in her own members—something however from which she herself as a person is absolutely free, since her personality transcends that of her members. It is a created personality, but one which *spiritually* or *"mystically"*—in other words through love, the love of Christ who willed to unite her to him *perfectly and indissolubly in love* (not hypostatically, which is quite impossible)—makes *but one person* with that of the Lord, Head of the mystical Body. And that is why one cannot refuse to the Church as a person (as a created person making *spiritually* but *truly* only one person with the uncreated personality of the Saviour) the name of holy and immaculate [40] without casting a slur on the love of Christ for the Beloved he has united to himself.

Such is the door through which the old peasant passes to enter the doctrine which Cardinal Journet has brought to light and which is one of the blessings we owe to him. I think that one has often misunderstood this doctrine because one has lost sight of the personality of the Church, which is constantly in the background of such a great teaching.

"All contradictions are solved as soon as one has understood that the members of the Church sin, to be sure, but insofar as they do sin, they betray the Church; the Church, therefore, is not without sinners, but she is without sin." [41]

"The Church as a person takes on the responsibility for penance.

[39] Léon Bloy.
[40] "*Indefectibiliter sancta*," says the Council (Constitution on the Church, Ch. V, Par. 39).
[41] *Théologie de l'Eglise*, p. 239.

She does not bear the responsibility for sin. If she resembles then the woman-sinner of the Gospel, it is only at the moment when that woman pours her perfume over the feet of Jesus. It is the Church's members themselves—laymen, clerics, priests, bishops or popes—who, in disobeying her, bear the responsibility for sin; it is not the Church as a person. One falls into a great illusion when one invites the Church as a person to recognize and proclaim her sins. One is forgetting that the Church as a person is the Bride of Christ, whom he 'acquired with his own blood' (*Acts*, 20:28), whom he purified in order that she might stand before him 'in splendor, without stain or wrinkle or any such thing, but holy and immaculate.' (*Ephes.*, 5:27) for she is the 'house of the living God, the pillar and bulwark of the truth' (1 *Tim.* 3:15)." [42]

"Her true and precise borders circumscribe only that which is good and pure in her members, both the just and the sinners, encompassing within herself all that is holy, even in sinners, and leaving out all that is impure, even in the just; it is in our own behavior, in our own lives, in our own hearts that the Church and the world, Christ and Belial, light and darkness, confront one another." [43]

---

[42] *Op. cit.*, p. 241. As Père J. H. Nicolas said so well, "there is no darkness in her, although, sadly, the sins of her members veil her beauty to the eyes of the world, bring upon her reproach and insult, and make her suffer before God. If she asks for pardon it is because she recognizes as her own before God and men those who commit these sins, but not the sins themselves, which they commit only in swerving from her." "*La Plume et la Pourpre*," in *La Liberté*, Fribourg, February 27–28, 1965, p. 6.

[43] *Op. cit.*, p. 244. "The borderline between the Church and the world, light and darkness, cuts across our own hearts." *Nova et Vetera*, 1963, p. 302 (cf. *Nova et Vetera*, 1958, p. 30.)

That is true first of all of those who, while committing evil acts which they promptly confess or which are only venial sins, live habitually a life of grace. (It is equally true of the just who belong to the Church in only an invisible way—the word "borderline" in that instance applies no longer to the personality proper to the fully formed Church, but to her body and her soul—abnormally deprived of the seal of her personality—to which these just belong invisibly.)

It is also true of the baptized who are in a state of mortal sin. The line of demarcation still cuts across their hearts, dividing the evil that comes from them alone, from the good (supernatural to some degree, although insufficient for salvation: actual graces, and all the holy things that remain in them, of which we spoke above) which continues to come to them from the Church. And similarly, the good of a purely natural order continues also, because they are still members (*re, non voto*) of the Church, to come to them from this great body which encompasses all that is good in the moral life of its parts. They owe this privilege to

"It is in the heart of each of us that Christ and the world confront one another"—in other words, the borderlines of the Church pass through our own hearts. "The Church divides in us the good from the evil. She keeps the good and rejects the evil. Her borderlines pass through our hearts." [44] Many years have passed since the day at Meudon when Abbé Journet first spoke these words, and the impression they made on me has not faded, I still treasure them as particularly precious and profoundly enlightening. Forgive me if I borrow from a book of mine a page in which I tried to comment on those words: "The line of demarcation we must consider passes across the heart of each of us. When a man acts in grace and charity, he lives, he draws his life from the life of the Church—which is a life of grace and charity. He is thus a part of her, since any man who has grace and charity belongs vitally to the Church, whether visibly or invisibly. Consequently, the actions in question are not only his, they also manifest in him the life of that whole of which he is a part. His actions are of the Church precisely inasmuch as they are vivified by the grace of Christ, regardless of any secondary imperfections they might allow of.

"But when men act without grace and charity, even if they are visibly members of the Church, they withdraw from her life, they strip themselves of the life of the Church. And their actions are no stain on the Church, on the kingdom of God, because those actions are not hers.

"The line of water-shed between the waters of the rivers which spring from the Church and the other is concealed in the inner recesses of the heart of men." [45]

THE CHURCH, PEOPLE OF GOD

To bring to a close this first section of a long chapter, I would like to mention still another of the Church's names—the title of *people*

the "character" that baptism imprinted on their souls. (Those who lack this "character" and who live in sin are members of the Church only *potentially*, and the borderlines of the Church do not cut *in act* across their hearts as they do, in a diminished sense, across those of the just who belong only invisibly to the Church.)

[44] *Théologie de l'Eglise*, p. 236.
[45] *Pour une philosophie de l'histoire*, Paris, Seuil, 1960, pp. 150–151.

of God, a name to which the Council attached a great deal of importance.[46] People of God, "messianic people," the name emphasizes the "historical dimension" of the Church and turns our attention toward the greatness of the preparations of the past as well as toward the glory of the future.

When we pronounce it, our hearts remember the ancient covenant and the blessed name of Israel—and that descent from Abraham, that *Israelitica dignitas* into which the Church asks that the fullness of the whole world pass.[47] We remember, too, "that it would have profited us nothing to be born if we had not been redeemed," [48] and are reminded once more of this *beata nox* [49] in which, "breaking the chains of death, Christ rose victorious"; and our hearts turn toward the kingdom in pilgrimage that was inaugurated by the Resurrection, and whose ranks are destined to grow in number until the day the Son of God will come in glory.

As the Council says,[50] "at all times and in every nation, God has given welcome to whoever fears him and does what is right. It has pleased God, however, to make men holy and save them not merely as individuals, without mutual bond; rather has it pleased him to make of them a people that acknowledges him in truth and serves him in holiness. He therefore chose the people of Israel as his people. With it he set up a covenant. Step by step he taught this people, making known in its history both himself and the decree of his will and making it holy unto himself. All these things, however, were done by way of preparation and as a figure of that new and perfect covenant, which was to be ratified in Christ, and of that fuller revelation which was to be given through the Word of God himself made flesh. . . . Christ instituted this new covenant, the new testament, that is to say, in his blood, calling together a People made up of Jew and Gentile, making them one, not according to the flesh but in the Spirit. This was to be the new People of God. For those who believe

---

[46] It is the subject of Ch. II of the Constitution on the Church.

[47] "Praesta, ut in Abrahae filios, et in Israeliticam dignitatem, totius mundi transeat plenitudo." (From the liturgy of Holy Saturday, prayer after the second prophecy.)

[48] Blessing of the Paschal Candle.

[49] *Ibid.*

[50] Constitution on the Church, Ch. II, Par. 9.

in Christ, who are reborn not from a perishable but from an imperishable seed through the Word of the living God—not from the flesh but from water and the Holy Spirit—are finally established as 'a chosen race, a royal priesthood, a holy nation, a people whom God purchased for himself, those who once were no people, but now are God's people' (*Pet.* 2: 9-10)."

"The status of this people is that of the dignity and freedom of the sons of God, in whose hearts the Holy Spirit dwells as in his temple. Its law is the new commandment to love as Christ loved us. Its end is the kingdom of God, which has been begun by God himself on earth, and which is to be further extended until it is brought to perfection by him at the end of time, when Christ, our life, shall appear." [51]

Chosen race, royal priesthood, holy nation, purchased people— these words designate the whole Church and all of her members. The royal priesthood under discussion there, which is also referred to as "the priesthood of the faithful," is common to clerics and laymen.[52] St. Peter, in this great passage, is speaking of all those whom Christ redeemed, of all *the people of God.* [53]

As Père Labourdette phrased it, "Sharing in the supreme grace of Christ, purchased for the redeemed by the sacerdotal act of the cross, which is the great victory of the messianic *King,* Christian grace, in the Church as a whole and in each of her subjects, is a grace at once sacerdotal and royal: *gens sancta, populus acquisitionis, regale sacerdotium. . . .* Every Christian, in this sense, is a 'priest,' priest and king, as is his Head: man or woman, whether coming before

---

[51] Constitution on the Church, Ch. II, Par. 9.

[52] The ministerial or hierarchical priesthood differs from it "in essence and not only in degree," yet they "are nonetheless interrelated; each of them in its own special way is a participation in the one priesthood of Christ." *Ibid.*, Par. 10.

[53] As Cardinal Garrone writes in the introduction to Ch. II of the Constitution on the Church (*Lumen Gentium,* Paris, Centurion, 1965, p. 38): "The people of God, as the term is used in this chapter, applies to the entire Church and not simply to the hierarchy. By the same fundamental right everyone belongs to this Church. All have but one calling and one destiny." It follows from this that "the Hierarchy can only, within the people of God, be entitled to render a service: that of exercising authority." And the laity are the great multitude moving, under this authority, toward the final fulfillment of the kingdom which is not of this world.

Christ from Adam on, or following him in history, every soul redeemed by him has, by reason of his grace, that kind of priesthood." [54] He possesses it "by the same right and to the same degree
that he possesses grace," [55] that priesthood is "inscribed in Christian
grace. In heaven, where the 'royal priesthood' will have fully flowered
in the people of God and all its members, the liturgy of praise and
thanksgiving will no longer be a means of obtaining grace nor a figure
of a plenitude that is to come, but an expression of inner glory. The
sacramental sacrifice will no longer be celebrated, the sacramental
priesthood will no longer be exercised, nor will the faithful have to
participate in it. That the Christian is both priest and king will then
be confirmed, both for the elect who have never received either the
baptismal or the priestly character, and for the others. This 'royal
priesthood' will endure for all eternity as the fruit of the sacrifice of
the cross." [56]

Summing up Chapter IV of the Constitution on the laity, Cardinal
Journet points out that the Council is there repeating "with respect
to laymen what had been affirmed in general of all Christian people.
Laymen belong to the people of God, among whom there is 'no in-
equality on the basis of race or nationality, social condition or sex,' [57]
they are brothers of Christ, who came to serve, not to be served.
They have a part in the Church's mission of salvation, her prophetic
mission, her royal service.[58] What is new here (evident in the Constitution on the Church, as in the general orientation of the Council)
is a realization no longer secret and painful, but urgent throughout
the Church—not, certainly, of any inadequacy, with respect to the
world, of her essential and structural catholicity, but of the immensity of the effort that must be made, two thousand years after the
coming of Christ, to catch up the ever-growing mass of humanity.
. . . The Church turns toward her lay children with a concern, not

[54] R. P. Michel Labourdette, *Le Sacerdoce et la Mission Ouvrière* (Paris: ed.
Bonne Presse, 1959), pp. 14–15. This short work, with a preface by Msgr.
Garrone, is a doctrinal Note approved by the theological commission (presided
over by Msgr. Garrone) that was constituted to study, on the level of principles,
the problems posed by the apostolate of the worker-priests.

[55] *Ibid.*, p. 54.

[56] *Ibid.*, p. 56.

[57] Constitution on the Church, Ch. IV, Par. 32.

[58] *Ibid.*, Par. 34–36.

so much to shield them from evil as to *send* them into the midst of dangers with God in their hearts, in order to give witness to the Gospel." [59]

☆

If we wish to enter into the spirit of the Council, and truly follow its inspiration, it is not only our behavior and our activities, but first of all, as I noted at the beginning of Chapter 5, our ordinary patterns of thought which we must renew: and that demands a serious effort of reason, in order to grasp reality more thoroughly. And the first reality to consider, that which governs all the rest when we are speaking of the new fire brought by the Council, is obviously the Church herself whom we must serve better—but whom *first of all* we must know better. She herself dealt with this subject in her dogmatic Constitution on the Church, *Lumen Gentium*. And she has theologians to explain and comment on this Constitution. Why, then, should an old philosopher get mixed up in it? It is surely not his job to make people know the Church better, and he realizes that better than anyone.

But if the Council stirred the whole world, there are few however, and regrettably, who are sitting down to read its documents (although they have been translated into all languages and widely published); and there are still fewer who are sitting down to read theologians. The least incitation then, from no matter how low a quarter, that might induce someone to go into a bookstore and buy and study these documents, can be of use. I am thinking in particular of the *Constitution on the Church*, whose language is much easier to understand than that of the theologians.

Moreover, a testimony may be no great catch, but it is always worth something, even if only as a mild irritant (which is always good) to disturb habits of thought too comfortable, and often sloppy—it's a not infrequent case with many non-Christians who have no idea of what the Church is, and so many Christians who have only a mediocre and deplorably superficial idea. (It is hardly their fault; no one took great pains to teach them.) Reluctantly, then, since I am not

---

[59] Charles Journet, *"Le Mystère de l'Eglise selon le IIe Concile du Vatican,"* *Revue Thomiste*, 1965, pp. 34–35.

completely unaware of my inadequacy, I felt obliged to offer my own poor testimony.

What vexes me about the venture is that it may possibly make me have the air of taking myself seriously, even of imagining I am capable, with cap on my head, of teaching someone something. I have not taken myself seriously, it is my subject that is serious. On such a subject I have not wished to teach anyone anything, but simply to speak my mind: and that, after all, is not such a bold thing to do. It is true, nonetheless, that one cannot speak of things in which one believes with all his heart without becoming deeply involved. That is what I have done, to be sure, while carefully shielding myself behind the powerful shelter of the teachings of the Council and of those who are the wiser, and have a right to teach on such matters.

I am a little afraid that it will be the same story with the sections that follow. I can't help it, I will take the risk. I am still going to speak of things infinitely beyond me—and of which others have real experience. Let people think what they want of the old peasant; at his age one has nothing to lose.

Contemplation in the World

BY WAY OF INTRODUCTION

Speaking to Martha of her sister Mary, the Lord said: *unum est necessarium*, and the phrase does not mean, as one of those translators who today contribute so much to our edification would have it, "One dish is enough."

One thing only is necessary, it is to be with Jesus, given to his love. And the Church has always, in her pilgrimage, considered the part of Mary the most important one in the life of the mystical Body.

We must add that in no other questions more than in those concerning Martha and Mary, has the tendency of our crawling reason to make the notions it uses paltry, stiff and dull, succeeded in stirring up vain controversies and confusing the issues.

Nowhere is there greater need of distinguishing in order to unite—an effort that, as I already noted, our busy contemporaries resent as supremely incongruous. That is what frightens the old philosopher more than ever: not the fear of his contemporaries, to whom he pays no mind, but fear of carrying out badly a difficult task.

The Carthusians, the Trappists, the Carmelites, all the great contemplative religious Orders that, with a view to belonging more completely to God alone, have adopted a mode of life essentially *cut off from the world*, will always be considered by the Church necessary pillars of her temple, or deeply hidden centers of spiritual revitalization that she cannot do without. In these post-conciliar years they too, as far as I know, feel the urgent need of renewal, in order to make the flame of the Gospel burn more intensely in their own lives, and by the same token, still more take on in their prayers and intercession the sufferings of the world, but not at all, thanks to God, to pull down or crack the sacred walls which shield from the world their solitude and the spirit they have received from their founders and from the Paraclete.

But among those who dedicate themselves to the practice of evangelical counsels in an *essentially contemplative* life, other forms of consecration to this life have arisen in our days, this time no longer in separation from the world, but, on the contrary, in the very midst of the world, and "at the core of the masses." St. Therese of Lisieux and Père de Foucauld have been providential precursors of this great new movement, which assigns to those consecrated people *in the world*, as well as to the Orders at their side who live apart from the world, the part of Mary in the mystical Body.

I have for long years had the privilege of knowing some of these new religious brotherhoods. I attended in the Basilica of Sacré-Coeur the mass of foundation of the Little Brothers of Jesus, who have now welcomed me in their midst as a kind of old hermit who has always loved them. For many years I have also known and admired the Little Sisters of Jesus, as I have known a Dominican community that —like my friends the Little Brothers, spread out over this thankless planet or reunited for some years in their huts of studies at Toulouse —is very close to my heart: the Regular Third Order of Catherine de Ricci—uncloistered, contemplative women whose form of poverty similarly consists in living from the work of their hands (but within their convent). Before settling in Crépieux, they first lived in Bellevue, next to Meudon, where Raïssa, Véra and I passed the best part of our poor existence; and now they have a house at Toulouse: so that by a singular gift of Providence I can enjoy at the same time the blessings of common life with my dear Little Brothers, and the fraternal help that these Dominican sisters generously lavish upon me. This is a good occasion for me to thank God for having kept alive the great souls whom he inspired to found these Orders, and to affectionately greet Soeur Magdalene, the foundress of the Little Sisters, as well as to ask Père Voillaume, founder of the Little Brothers of Jesus, and Mère Marie-Madeleine, foundress of the Dominican Sisters of Crépieux, to allow the old peasant publicly to express here the deep gratitude and the deep friendship that binds him to them forever.

I have been speaking of the religious orders I know personally among those which lead a life essentially dedicated to contemplation in the world. There are certainly other institutions that, whether taking the vows in a traditionally religious framework or under some other form, particularly that of secular Institutes, set themselves the goal of living a contemplative life in the world. I think that they all are a blessing for our times.

But since I have spoken of the undeserved gifts I have received from God, I want to mention the greatest of them: that of having shared, for nearly fifty-five years, since the date (June 11, 1906) when the three of us were baptized, the life of two blessed ones, Raïssa and her sister, who in the midst of the trials of a very agitated existence, remained faithful to contemplative prayer without faltering an instant, all given to union of love with Jesus and love of his Cross, and to the work that, through such souls, he pursues invisibly among men. They taught me what contemplation in the world is. I myself was a laggard, a laborer of the intellect, risking by the very fact to think I was really living certain things because my head understood them a little and my philosophy could dissert upon them. But I have been taught, and taught well, by the experience, the sorrows and the insights of these two faithful souls. That is what gives me the courage to try to give witness to them, in speaking here of things that are above me, knowing well that to have been instructed by example and on the job does not make it easy, far from it, to translate what one has learned into ideas and words.

Be that as it may, and passing on to more general considerations, I see one truth clearly: what matters in a very special way, and perhaps more than anything else, for our age, is the life of prayer and of union with God lived *in the world,* not only by new brotherhoods such as those I spoke of above, but also by those who are called to this life in the common condition of lay people with all its turmoil, its risks and its temporal burdens. And such people are not as rare as one might think, and they would become more numerous if their spiritual guides did not dissuade them from the purpose in question, whether because they suppose them incapable of achieving it, or because they indulge, as regards contemplation, in a deep and equally inexcusable ignorance or dis-esteem, or because they consider it more urgent to organize all laymen of good will in the fascinating efficacy of collective action, as far as possible technically organized.

There was a time (the "baroque age") when apparently among some theologians, and in any case in the mass of good Catholics who were reasonably well-provided with the good things of the earth, the religious state—that is to say, the state of those who vow themselves to the search for perfection—was regarded as the state of the perfect ones, and consequently the secular state was looked upon as the state of the imperfect ones: in such a way that the duty and function providentially assigned to the imperfect ones was to be imperfect and to stay that way; to live a good worldly life, not over-pious, and solidly planted in social naturalism (above all, in that of family ambitions).[60] One would have been scandalized had laymen tried to live in any other way; they had only to make prosper on earth, through pious foundations, monasteries which were, in exchange, to win heaven for them; and thus the providential order would be satisfied.

"This manner of conceiving the humility of laymen seems to have been widespread enough in the sixteenth and sevententh centuries. That is why the catechism with explanations for the faithful written by the Dominican Carranza, then Archbishop of Toledo, was condemned by the Spanish Inquisition on evidence proffered by the famous theologian Melchior Cano."[61] Cano declared "completely worthy of condemnation the temerity of giving to the faithful a religious instruction that was only proper for priests. . . . He spoke out vigorously against the reading of the Holy Scriptures in the vernacular, and against those who make it their business to hear confessions

[60] One finds startling evidence of this point of view in the great work of Louis Ponnelle and Louis Bordet on the life of St. Philip Neri and the Roman society of his times (Paris, 1929).
[61] *Humanisme Intégral,* p. 129.

all day long. He held highly suspect the zeal displayed by the
'spiritual' in inciting the faithful to go to confession and communion
frequently, and he is reported to have said in a sermon that frequent
and widespread reception of the sacraments was one of the signs of
the coming of the Antichrist." [62]

We are far from Melchior Cano and his times—but perhaps not so
far as it might seem. The prejudice must have been a strong one, for
today a Council of the Holy Church had to take care, if I may say so,
to raise laity on the shield, to highlight explicitly its essential role in
the mystical Body, and to remind the world that, according to the
teaching of the prince of the apostles, all members of the people of
God, insofar as they live from the grace of Christ, participate in his
royal priesthood.

And what I want above all to stress here is the force with which
the Council has insisted on the universal range of the Lord's great
words: "You therefore be perfect, as your heavenly Father is perfect." [63] From which one can conclude that the precept to tend
toward the perfection of charity applies to all.[64] "It is clear that the
call to the fullness of the Christian life and the perfection of charity is
addressed to all those who believe in Christ, whatever their state or
way of life." [65] The laity, contrary to what Melchior Cano thought
(and well before him, Conrad de Megenburg) [66] "must strive to
acquire a more profound grasp of revealed truth, and insistently beg
of God the gift of wisdom." [67]

A DIGRESSION

(ON THE TEMPORAL MISSION OF THE CHRISTIAN)

The gift of wisdom does not seem to be especially coveted by
those who hold that the vocation of the laity is purely temporal, and

---

[62] Saudreau, "Le mouvement antimystique en Espagne au XVIe siècle," Revue
du Clergé français, August 1, 1917.

[63] Matt. 5:48. Constitution on the Church, Ch. V, Par. 40.

[64] This was the central theme of Père Garrigou-Lagrange's book, Christian
Perfection and Contemplation (St. Louis, Mo.: Herder & Co., 1946).

[65] Constitution on the Church, Ch. V, Par. 40.

[66] See p. 166 note 36.

[67] Constitution on the Church, Ch. IV, Par. 35.

entirely directed to the good of the world. In their eyes lay Christians would have for their only vocation to work to transform the world, a sacred vocation that should carry the world, thanks above all to the messianic mission of the proletariat, to the supreme term where it would be fully humanized in Christ, and installed in a final reign of justice, peace, and human *épanouissement*, which they confuse with the kingdom of God decidedly arrived.

It is clear that prophets who muddle the things of Caesar and those of God to such a point, are false prophets. Yet they have the merit of obliging us to ask ourselves in what sense we ought to understand this "mission to transform the world," which enfolds in the same formula a basic truth and equally basic errors.

To transform the world *spiritually* by means of the Gospel, with a view to attaining the ultimate end, parousia and the kingdom of God in the glory of the risen—Christians have known since Pentecost that they are called to that. But the point in question with what is called in our day the mission to "transform the world," is something quite different. The phrase is now used to mean a *temporal* transformation of the world with a view to an end which (far from what a Christian holds to be the absolutely final end)—*is the good of the world itself in development*. Further, one then acknowledges for oneself *consciously and explicitly* the obligation or the mission to work toward such a transformation.

It might be said that from the time of primitive man until that which we call the modern age, this explicit notion, which is now so brightly in the forefront, of such a duty of such a mission, remained absent from the mind of men and played no role in their history. It is after a tremendously long period of pre-modern history (or, if you prefer, of modern pre-history) that it began to take form—since about three centuries, let us say, somewhat allegorically, since Descartes declared that man must become *master and possessor of nature*. Have we to say, too, that Christians should long ago have perceived that, along with their spiritual vocation, the ultimate end of which is eternity, they also had a *temporal* task with respect to the world, its well-being and its transformation? That would be to speak idealistic nonsense, because (without, moreover, losing sight of the extraordinary effort—quite new in history for its breadth and continuity—of the works of mercy that have occupied all Christian centuries, at once

a substitute and a real preparation for the awareness of a "transformation of the world" to be accomplished) historical conditions, speaking
concretely, were, neither socially and culturally, nor spiritually ripe
for such an awareness. To tell the truth, that awareness appeared first,
not among Christians, but in a messianic atheism that was at one and
the same time a fruit of modern philosophy and "the last Christian
heresy." Hence the serious ambiguities from which we suffer today.

Man's mission to transform the world temporally, it is Marx who
brought it to light; but in the wrong way, because of his atheism, and
of his philosophy (Hegelianism turned upside down) where all
"nature" is absorbed in the becoming and the dialectic process, and
because of his faustianism (to exist is to create, existence precedes
essence, man creates himself by his work). Man, then, is called to a
titanic labor ("arise, titans of the earth," as is sung in the *Inter-
nationale*) that will give him full and complete mastery of the world
and will make him, so to speak, the god of the world.

It seems to me that one of the aspects of Teilhard de Chardin's
work was (without his having deliberately set himself such an objective) an attempt to correct this notion; but he corrected it in the
wrong way, because of his evolutionism, very different from that of
Marx, but as radical or even more so, and because of his cosmization
of Christ and Christianity, a sort of reply to "dialectic materialism"
made by means of a cosmo-christic messianism. Man, then, is called
to a divinizing work by means of which he will fully accomplish the
destiny of the world, in the glory of the Risen One, and which will
make him something like the spirit of the world, in the finally
triumphant Christ.

I think that the task of Christian philosophy and theology today is
to give its true meaning to this mission to transform the world temporally, which up to now has been presented in such mistaken perspectives. All that I can do as an old philosopher who has already
cleared the land a bit and is now at the end of his life, is only to
sketch out some ideas that I believe to be true (and, of course, some
distinctions that I believe to be well-founded, and terribly necessary).

First of all, we must, it seems to me, distinguish two fundamentally
different ways in which men engaged in the life of the world may work
in the world *for the good of the world*. From earliest times men have

worked there, in their ordinary affairs, poor daily labors or great imperial enterprises, *unconsciously* (like moss or lichen in the process of invading a piece of land little by little); and they will continue to do so forever, pulled along without their knowing it in the movement of history. This is a first level of action, that of ordinary day-to-day tasks of temporal life.

The second level is that of a *special* task in temporal life; the mission to transform the world temporally, this time assumed *consciously*, with awakened understanding, as free agents capable of universal purposes.

Christians, like everyone else, have worked and will always work on the first level of action. And today (in our age of civilization and our regimes either of free democracy or of constraint) they have to work also on the second, and, to tell the truth, they alone are in a position to work well there (supposing, naturally, that they do not lose their head). To that end it is essential that those who take charge of guiding such a work in movements or parties of Christian inspiration, and who have a heavy responsibility with regard to the masses which follow them, have a particularly rich doctrinal formation and practical wisdom, enlightening them both about the things of the kingdom of God and those of the earth, and resting on a theology and a philosophy founded in truth.

But what does it consist in, this transformation of the world which is the goal of the temporal mission of the Christian? [68] Man will never be *Master and Possessor* of nature and history, titan of the world or divinizator of the world; it is a lie to try to convince him of such a thing. What is demanded of the Christian is to *intervene* in the destiny of the world, winning at great pains and at the risk of a thousand dangers—through science and through social and political action—a power over nature and a power over history, but remaining, whatever he does, more than ever a *subordinate* agent: servant of divine Providence and activator or "free associate" of an

[68] To define the vocabulary and avoid all ambiguity, we will reserve the term *"the temporal mission of the Christian"* to describe this task of *working for the transformation of the world;* whereas the expression *"the temporal vocation of the Christian"* will be used in a much wider sense, which I will stress later. It is unfortunate that I have to use terms so similar to one another: their meaning is completely different.

evolution he does not direct as a master, and which he also serves,[69] insofar as it develops according to the laws of nature and the laws of history (themselves founded on the dynamism of "natures").

One must understand, moreover, that the Christian can, and must, ask for the coming of the kingdom of God in glory, but is not entitled to ask for—nor to propose as the end of his temporal activity— a definite advent of justice and peace, and of human happiness, as the term of the progress of temporal history: for this progress is not capable of any final term.

Some philosophical considerations are necessary here. Temporal history, true, tends toward an end, since it implies progress. But the end to which temporal history tends cannot be the final end; it can only be an "infravalent" end: that to which a world *in becoming* tends, and the becoming of which, both in the cosmic (astrophysical) order and in the human order, is an evolution, a genesis, a growth that has no final term here on earth. Two, and only two hypotheses, in effect, are possible here (I am inclined to the second). One can think that the becoming of the physical world is indefinite, or, putting it a different way, that it takes place through successive cosmic phases of expansion and retraction, progress and regression. In that case, human history would have to start each time from a new level in recession with respect to the term attained in the progressive phase (though probably higher than the starting point of said phase; and this would go on endlessly). There would be a term for each phase, but no final term. In this hypothesis the absolutely final end in which the Christian believes (the advent of the kingdom of God) would come as an *interruption* of a becoming (both cosmic and human) that by itself would have continued indefinitely.

In the other hypothesis (where the cosmic future would not imply such phases), human history would tend toward a final term which could only be the *perfect natural happiness* of mankind, the end of all the groanings of the creature, and which precisely for that reason is *unattainable*. Because while the living conditions of the human

---

[69] I would love to find a comparison drawn from our human affairs, but I cannot find a good one. For want of a better one, let us think of the staffs of social assistants and planners that might have been sent from a more developed country to the Queen of Babylon and her empire (and who, naturally, would have been subject to the laws of the latter).

community would improve, death and corruption would always be there—along with the aspirations of the human person which transcend the earthly well-being of the community, and to which, supposing that the person is growing more and more in consciousness, death and corruption will become more and more repugnant. And human freedom would always be there, capable of using, either for good or for evil, more and more powerful means placed at its disposal, so that progress in good and progress in evil would move ahead side by side along the road—all that we can hope is that the first will take precedence over the second.

Hope and anguish would grow together, the groaning of all of creation "in the pain of childbirth" [70] would still be there, and the expectation that it expresses would become more and more impatient: the child with whom the world is pregnant would not come out from the womb of the creature. And the upward curve of the progress of the world would still continue indefinitely, but in another sense than in the first hypothesis. It would be an asymptotic curve, human history tending unknowingly toward the kingdom of God, but incapable in itself of reaching this final term. The coming of the kingdom would not, in that case, be a simple interruption of a becoming with no final term, it would be rather an *eruption* by which the divine glory would interrupt the earthly becoming, but in order to lead it, through a miraculous begetting, to that final term toward which it is tending with no power to reach it: no longer natural happiness, but supernatural beatitude.

If you are not satisfied with this interlude of Christian philosophy, you can at least, assuming that you have the faith, listen to the revelation of which the Church is the custodian, and which forbids us to mix up the orders of finality by imagining that the goal of the temporal mission of the Christian is the coming of the kingdom of God on earth. This coming will need a new earth and a new heaven, and the resurrection of the dead. We must be ready to suffer anything for justice's sake in the temporal struggle, but this struggle does not claim to eliminate definitively evil, nor to assure definitively the

[70] Cf. St. Paul, *Rom.* 8:22–23: "For we know that the whole creation has been groaning in the pain of childbirth together until now; and not only the creation, but we ourselves, who have the first fruits of the Spirit, groan inwardly as we wait for . . . the redemption of our bodies." See Appendix 1 at the back of the book.

triumph of good. It is fought to oppose as much as possible the progress of evil, and to accelerate as much as possible the progress of good in the world; here is the proper business of Christians fighting as Christians for the good of the world in a world subject to the law of time and of becoming.

The temporal mission of the Christian, his mission to transform the world, has more modest ends than those a Marx or a Teilhard assign to man, but much more important ends for man, by virtue of the simple fact that they are not illusory (this counts, all the same): to make the earthly city more just and less inhuman, to assure to every one the goods basically needed for the life of the body and the spirit, as well as the respect, in each one, of the rights of the human person; to lead peoples to a supra-national political organization capable of guaranteeing peace in the world—in short, to cooperate with the evolution of the world in such a way that the earthly hope of men in the Gospel should not be frustrated, and the spirit of Christ and of his kingdom would in some fashion vivify worldly things themselves. Such a work needs to be thus vivified, for without the strengthening assistance of Christ's grace our nature is too weak to carry it out. Justice without love is inhuman, and love for men and for peoples, "which goes well beyond that which justice can accomplish," [71] is itself fragile without theological charity. Without the love of charity, work as we might, we will work *nothing*.

And these very ends of the temporal mission of the Christian—not to be confused with either the absolutely final end which is the full coming of the kingdom of God, or with a final term, supposedly attainable, of the earthly becoming—we well know that, if they are possible of themselves (not illusory), they will still never, as a matter of fact, be attained in a fully complete and fully satisfying way here on earth. Those who fight for such a purpose know that they will always be resisted, will win only contested successes, and that they will often fail. But what they do they will do well, if they do it truly as Christians.

Let us add finally that the struggle they are conducting in the temporal order in full faithfulness to the spirit and the teachings of Christ, is the proper task (to very different degrees, because some

---

[71] Constitution on the Church in the Modern World, Ch. V, No. 79, Par. 2.

guide and others follow) of Christians who live in the world: they conduct the struggle at their risk and peril. They are *helped* in this battle by the counsels they receive from the Church, and without which they could do no good; and they can even be *helped* in that respect by the Church in another fashion, in particular cases, when her ministers, facing an especially serious situation, judge it their duty to raise their voices and to intervene in the temporal order by a word of truth, giving witness to divine precepts. In any case, for the Church it is always only a question of helping the world to resolve its problems, not resolving them for it.

ANOTHER DIGRESSION
(ON THE CONDITION OF THE LAYMAN)
AND END OF THE INTRODUCTION

I apologize for this long digression. To tell the truth it was announcing another. Because the temporal mission of which I was speaking, a concept that has only appeared in our modern age, is far from constituting all the temporal activity of the Christian working in the world. We must go on, then, to a completely different order of questions, more general and more fundamental, which no longer concern the temporal mission (of transforming the world) that lay Christians of today, at least those who feel a "calling" to it, acknowledge as pertaining to them (I'm finished with that, I won't come back to it any more), but which concern the layman himself.

As soon as one reflects a bit seriously on the condition of the layman, one perceives that it is not as easy as it seems to understand it exactly, and moreover that it involves a rather troubling problem which we must try to clarify. The Christian layman, in effect, has two different vocations; one spiritual, the other temporal, to each of which nevertheless, he must respond fully, and even while doing his daily task. And in addition he himself is the subject of a deplorable ambiguity of vocabulary, at least in a language like French: in his quality of layman, the layman is *of the world*, is he not, as he is of the human city (this is expressed in Latin by the genitive: "est aliquid *mundi*"), and he works (even without the least deliberate purpose) for an end which is not the ultimate end, but the well-being of the world, its beauty, its progress. And in his quality as a member of the Church he works for the final end which is the kingdom of God fully consummated, and he is not *of this world;* he is in the world without being *of the world* (this is distinguished in Latin by the ablative: "non est *de hoc mundo,* non est *de mundo*"). He is of the world without being of this world? We ought to look at this closely.

Let us note first of all that the word "layman" belongs originally to the language of the Church. "The notion of the layman includes all the positive values and the richness of membership in the Church, all the fullness that the name Christian implies. The word 'layman' designates a member of Christ, a member who may be a sinner and therefore at present dead, but who normally lives with the activities of the royal and sacerdotal grace received from Christ. Through the sacraments of Christian initiation—Baptism and Confirmation—he entered fully into the ecclesial society, the mystical Body of Christ; besides grace he received certain 'characters' which integrate him into the sacramental organization of the militant Church and depute him in a permanent manner to taking part in the celebration of the holy cult, not to administer the sacraments but to receive their effects—which is also a power, a supernatural capacity derived from the priesthood of Christ, but this time in terms of the sacramental economy. . . . In the proper sense, the layman is no less of the Church than the priest; as baptized and confirmed, it is to the Church that he belongs, it is toward her and her grace-giving activities that he is turned, it is in those terms that he is defined. He is part of an eschatological kingdom whose life he must endeavor to lead, and to which the Christian community all together must give witness in the eyes of the world." [72]

Thus the layman—let us say, to adapt ourselves to the current idiom, the Christian layman—is in the full sense of the word a member of the Church. Hence it follows that he is not of this world (*de hoc mundo*) as the Church is not of this world; *Regnum meum non est de hoc mundo* (*John* 18:36). *Ego non sum de hoc mundo* (*John* 8:23). "They are in the world" (*John* 17:11), but "they are not of the world, even as I myself am not of the world (*John* 17:16)." Hence it follows too, that the layman has a spiritual vocation, and that he has been appointed to work for the kingdom of God (a kingdom that

[72] Michel Labourdette, O.P. *Le Sacerdoce et la Mission ouvrière*, Paris, éd. Bonne Presse, 1959.

has already come in a state of pilgrimage and crucifixion, but is still to come in its plenitude).

What, then, of his relationship to the world? And how can he be something of the world, and appointed to work for the good of the world? The answer, in my opinion, is to be found in the fact of his double birth: he was born twice, as is every Christian. He was *born of the world*, and in original sin, as all men are when they come from their mothers' wombs. And by baptism he was born again, he was *born of God*. (One can say as much also, though in a much less complete sense, of those who are invisibly members of the visible Church, and who, without having the character and grace of baptism, are nonetheless born anew, they too, with the life of the grace of Christ and of charity; but it is not of them I am speaking here.) It is by virtue of this new birth that, from the day of his baptism, he is a member of the Church and not *of this world*.

And of his first birth he retains nothing as concerns the sin of Adam (except the weaknesses and inner disorder our nature has inherited from it)—he is delivered from this sin insofar as it prevents him from entering into beatitude and the vision of God. He is washed, rescued, redeemed by the grace of Christ. But he keeps, like everyone else, being a man in the world; and further—if he does not decide to dedicate himself either to the cult of God and the power of giving the sacraments by becoming a priest, or to the search for perfection by embracing the religious state (being, in either case, even more deeply in the second instance than in the first,[73] separated from the world and from the ordinary human vocation)—he also keeps the

---

[73] Members of religious communities who live in the very midst of the world (not separated or shielded from it in as externally visible a sense as those who have chosen cloistered life) are nonetheless, by virtue of their vows and their consecrated state, and the duties which that state imposes on them, *intrinsically separated from the world*.

And to a certain degree the priest also (a good many of them, today, do not like this, but that's the way it is) is separated from the world by virtue of his dedication to the cult and to the administration of the sacraments. He is no longer a laborer of the world, nor assigned to a temporal mission aiming at the good of the world. He is no longer answerable to the temporal order except, if I may say so, by lending himself to it, and in order "not to scandalize them," as Jesus said to Peter with respect to the tax collectors, *ut non scandalizemus eos:* "But that we may not scandalize them, go to the sea and cast a hook, and take the first fish that comes up. And opening its mouth you wilt find a stater; take that and give it to them for me and for you." (Matt. 17:27)

ordinary human condition and vocation that come to us by virtue of our first or natural birth (washed of sin by the second). A member of Christ and of the Church, he is no longer *born of the world,* he is no longer *de hoc mundo;* but finding himself in the ordinary state of life in which men are placed by virtue of their being born here below, he has to work for the good of the world and is something of the world (in the genitive, *aliquid mundi*): what word may I use? He is a laborer of the world: (I do not say a "member" of the world, because the world does not have organic unity.) The layman is a *member* of only one universal body—the Church, which embraces heaven and earth. And as a laborer of the world he is also *of the world,* a fact which prevents him in no way from being no longer *of the world,* no longer *de hoc mundo,* by virtue of his second birth.

That is, if I have reasoned correctly, how the ambiguity implicit in the word layman is resolved.

And that, too, is how the layman does have two distinct vocations: a spiritual vocation as member of the Church; and a temporal vocation as a laborer of the world, as a *member of the Church who is a laborer of the world.* The two vocations are distinct, they are not separate. He is not a laborer of the world with a certain portion of his being, and a member of the Church with another portion: it is the member of the Church who *is* the laborer of the world, sent to the land of the things which are Caesar's.

His temporal vocation, his vocation as a laborer of the world (which covers only a part of his life and his activity—obviously the larger part and the part which demands more of his time), is to assume the ordinary tasks of the secular condition. His spiritual vocation, his vocation as a member of the Church—which is distinct from his temporal vocation but which must inspire it, because it covers his whole life and all his activities—is to live more and more profoundly the life of the mystical Body, and therefore first of all to watch over his own soul and to respond as well as possible to the precept (addressed to all within the Church) of tending to the perfection of charity; to participate in the sacraments of the Church and her worship; and to participate also (a point that the Council particularly emphasized) in her apostolate.

What form should this participation in the Church's apostolate take? Many different forms (of which one only, as I will emphasize

in a few minutes, is absolutely fundamental and required of all).
More distinctions? It can't be helped; what is at stake is worth the
trouble.

There are many different cases to consider: that, for example, of
Catholic Action properly so called, where certain laymen participate
in the apostolate of the Church, with a special mandate from her, in
organizations whose activities involve, by reason of this mandate, the
Church herself and the hierarchy. These organizations, which were
born of the initiative of Pius XI, undoubtedly play an important role,
but in a restricted sphere.

Next are a great variety of cases, and I can only speak of them in
general terms: from the case of certain laymen (still laymen and
laborers of the world, sometimes even in positions of power) who
participate in the apostolate of the Church in groups that partake
more or less of the nature of the religious state (of itself, separated
from the world), to the much more common case where laymen like
others participate in this apostolate by cooperating with movements
or works dedicated either to the development of spirituality (retreats,
for example) or to a missionary task. These varied forms of participation in the apostolate of the Church have two things in common:
they are, to a greater or lesser degree, under the direction of the
clergy, and they are, on the other hand, for those laymen who devote
part of their time to them, extra activities. Good, useful, excellent,
let us not lose sight of the fact that we are running the risk—by the
very fact that they are special and particularly remarkable forms of
participation in the apostolate of the Church, whose usefulness is self-
evident—of being mistaken about them. How? By somewhat heed-
lessly limiting the participation of laymen in the apostolate of the
Church to these forms, and by believing that this participation consists only in them.

That is not the case. All these diverse forms of the lay apostolate
are optional. But there is one that is absolutely basic and *necessary
for all*, and this one has a properly fundamental importance: I mean
the apostolate that laymen exercise *in their daily tasks themselves* (in
the *ordinary* labors of the life of the world),[74] and in all their activi-

---

[74] There we have the first temporal level of action that I alluded to (p. 201)—
that which is absolutely universal, and in which every (Christian) layman has been
involved ever since there have been Christians.

ties, if they acquit themselves *as Christians* in these labors and
activities. Their spiritual vocation and their temporal vocation, then,
have to do with *the same work*: the temporal vocation having to do
with the object of this work, the spiritual vocation having to do with
the mode or the manner in which it is accomplished, *the spirit* in
which it is done.[75]

As soon as a layman lives from the life of Christ and of the mystical
Body in the depths of his soul, and does not imagine that when he
does his ordinary task as a layman he should, under the pretext that
he is a layman, seal in those depths of his soul faith, fraternal charity,
and the love of Jesus which inhabits his heart; as soon as he grants the
Good News that he carries within himself its freedom of movement;
in short, when he *never forgets*, whatever he does, that he is a Christian; in other words, when he does *as a Christian* everything that he
does: [76] then the spirit which animates him will radiate from him,
and he will give witness to the Gospel, not by preaching it, but by
living it, and by the *manner* in which he carries out the most banal
tasks. And that will happen without his having to think of *exercising
an apostolate*: the less he thinks of it, the more it will be worth! It is
from itself and as if instinctively, that the testimony of the Church
will pass through him; it is enough for this that this Christian should
never hide—either from himself or from others—that he is a Christian; it is enough that he should never have before others, through
fear of offending what they think to be proper, any kind of shame in
being a Christian.

Obviously, to act as a Christian one must be as instructed in the
Christian verities as is possible, according to one's state and the role

[75] "They live in the world, that is, in each and in the all of the secular professions
and occupations they live in the ordinary circumstances of family and social life, from
which the very web of their existence is woven. At this place they are called by God,
so that, by exercising their proper function as led by the spirit of the Gospel, they
may work for the sanctification of the world from within as a leaven. In this way
they may make Christ known to others, especially by the testimony of a life re-
splendent in faith, hope and charity." (Constitution on the Church, Ch. IV,
Par. 31)

[76] That is what the apostles' teaching tells us: "Whether you eat or drink, or
whatever you do, do all to the glory of God" (1 *Cor.* 10:31). (Cf. *Col.* 3:17 and
1 *Pet.* 4:11)

one may have to play in cultural and political life.[77] Obviously also, some laymen animated by the spirit of the Gospel may be led to form more or less short-lived groupings born spontaneously out of *friendship*, and which are neither denominational nor under the direction of the clergy, but which will still demand from those who animate them a more extensive doctrinal preparation. These, however, are particular cases and I am now speaking, on the contrary, of that which is *common to all*, the radiance of the Gospel shining through the daily task itself. The medium through which this radiance passes may be sometimes a simple brotherly word, a look, a gesture, the spontaneous manner of reacting to an event, one of the almost imperceptible signs (so much more important than is usually thought), one of these microsigns of the physics of the soul that are registered in the unconscious and that our fellow-beings perceive with such redoubtable infallibility. Or else it may be more tangible evidence—a word of truth, a concrete engagement, a pardon granted, a sacrifice, a perhaps grave risk taken for the good of someone else or for justice's sake. That truth is always there, that whatever task he performs, a Christian can, and must, perform it *as a Christian*. I have said often enough in this book that one can philosophize *as a Christian*. One can also teach history, literature, even mathematics as a Christian—not by trying to make mathematics say something Christian, but in praying for one's students and loving them, and by the very manner in which one treats them, and the very manner in which one teaches, for teaching is something concrete that betrays, without our noticing it, many things that we have within us, and through which we are in a human relationship with others, while speaking to their minds. One can practice medicine as a Christian, direct a business as a Christian, be a carpenter, a potter, an automobile mechanic as a Christian; one can be a factory hand as a Christian (not, no doubt, while working on the production line, but there are always one's "buddies" and the pub where one goes to have a drink with them). Human relationships extend everywhere. And wherever there

[77] We have already discussed (pp. 198–205) the *temporal mission of the Christian* (which has for its goal the "transformation of the world," and which is on another level of temporal activity, where the layman is not merely a laborer of the world but an activator of the world). To act *as Christians*, those who guide others need then a particularly complete doctrinal formation. I am not speaking of that here because it is a *special* task of the secular life.

are human relationships, the Gospel, if we live it, introduces of itself its testimony, through the manner in which we act.

I am dwelling on all this because it is the very consequence of the all important truth discussed above on the subject of the lay Christian, a member of the Church who *is* a laborer of the world, and whose spiritual vocation covers his whole life.

For many centuries our Western civilization has suffered from a fatal separatism, an unnatural gash or cleavage—everywhere, on all levels of activity—between the temporal work of the lay Christian and the spiritual vocation he owes to what he is: a member of the People of God. It is this evil that one must remedy first of all.

☆

So much for my two digressions. They help us, perhaps, to see more clearly the implications and the practical consequences of that call to holiness, and to a real and personal participation in the life of the mystical Body, of which the Council so vigorously reminded all members of the People of God, laymen as well as others.

"The Lord Jesus, the divine teacher and model of all perfection, preached holiness of life to each and every one of his disciples of every condition. He himself stands as the author and consummator of this holiness of life: 'You therefore are to be perfect, even as your heavenly Father is perfect' . . .

"Thus it is evident to everyone that all the faithful of Christ of whatever rank or status, are called to the fullness of the Christian life and to the perfection of charity." [78]

All are called to holiness—I am thinking of my old godfather Léon Bloy and of that great phrase of his which echoed so powerfully in many hearts: *"Il n'y a qu'une tristesse, c'est de n'être pas des saints."* ("There is only one sadness; it is not to *be a saint.*")

I am also thinking that in order to answer this call addressed to all, the important thing is to start out, wherever one happens to be, in relying entirely on the grace of God; yet to advance along this road, where, with respect to that which comes from man, everything is so difficult, and so marvelously disposed with respect to that which comes from God, there are certain normally indispensable aids that

[78] Constitution on the Church, Ch. V, Par. 40.

we receive, on the one hand, from the liturgical life of the Church (above all, the sacrifice of Mass); on the other hand, from the communion of the soul with its God in *oraison* (I am using the French word because *orison* has become obsolescent)—let us say, in wordless prayer of love, and in that union of love that we call contemplation. (To translate *oraison*, I shall henceforth say "love-prayer" or "contemplative prayer.")

There are some questions to be cleared up here, and which are not easy. I shall try to say a few words about them in the following section.

THE TWO NECESSARY AIDS
ON THE NEVER-ENDING ROAD

I would like to submit here only a few reflections of a very general nature on the two normally necessary aids for men who have heard the call addressed to all, and who are stumbling ahead along a road whose final end is not of this world. (The road is not of this world either, although we move along it in the world, and it is precisely because of that that we cannot see the end.) The first aid is the common prayer of the Church ("common" is the right word; "communitarian" is, in the present instance, a bastard word in which one finds delight only because it sounds social-minded). The second aid is what is called "private" prayer (a bad word, because when one is with Jesus, Mary, and all our friends in heaven, right in the midst of the invisible communion of saints, one certainly doesn't lack company) —let us rather call it contemplative *oraison* which comes about *clauso ostio* (or in the desert where there are no doors, or even in interior solitude when the doors have been broken open).

On one hand, therefore, we have liturgical prayer, which has the unparalleled privilege of being centered on the Mass; on the other hand, contemplation, which has the wonderful privilege of making the heart, in a union of person to person, listen to Jesus present within it. These two privileges are eminent signs of the essential distinction that we must make between the liturgy of the Catholic Church (and of her separated sister-Churches in the East) and the ritual services of other religious families, however venerable they may sometimes be; as well as between the supernatural and the natural mystique, no matter how far the latter may sometimes advance in interior concentration. These two distinctions, moreover, do not overlap: the first having to do with the cult, which is visible, the second having to do with a spiritual experience that, when it is supernatural, presupposes the habitual regime of the gifts of the Spirit—which is not the case with the natural mystique, even in souls inhabited by grace.

LITURGY

Raïssa and I published, some years ago, a little book entitled *Liturgy and Contemplation*.[79] I shall not retrace here the positions that we advanced, except to state that I adhere to them more firmly than ever. But I would like to dwell on one point that, with respect to the liturgy, seems to me of primary importance.

In the public worship that the Church offers to God, the holy work in which we participate is accomplished at one and the same time by the mystical Body and by its Head, by the Church and by Christ himself. "The sacred liturgy is . . . the public worship which our Redeemer as Head of the Church renders to the Father as well as the worship which the community of the faithful renders to its Founder, and through him to the Heavenly Father. It is, in short, the *worship rendered by the mystical Body of Christ, in the entirety of its Head and members*. . . ."[80]

That is true of all liturgical functions—the liturgy of the sacraments or the common recitation of the canonical hours: Christ is always there, either to act through the agency of the one who administers the sacrament, or to be in the midst of those who are gathered together in his name. But this is true of the Mass in an absolutely eminent sense, because the Mass is the act or the sacramental mystery by means of which Christ perpetuates on earth and in time, until the end of centuries, the sacrifice from which the Church draws her life. That is why, even if we imagine the most dire prospects of

[79] New York, P. J. Kenedy and Sons, 1960.
[80] Pius XII, Encyclical *Mediator Dei et hominum*, November 20, 1947. Official English version (The Sacred Liturgy), Vatican Polyglot Press.

universal persecution, I do not believe that God will ever permit that a single day pass without at least one Mass being celebrated in the world. The Mass is thus the center, uniting heaven and earth, of the life of the kingdom of God in its earthly pilgrimage. It is also the center of the worship that the Church offers to Christ and to his Father. The sacrifice of the Mass is the center to which all other elements of the liturgy relate.[81]

At a certain moment during the Mass (and that is why the "sacred silence" [82] is then demanded), there is a kind of divine flash of lightning; at the words of the double consecration (which, from the fact that it sacramentally separates the Body of the Lord from his Blood, is an efficient sign of his death on the cross), Jesus makes himself present on the altar in the state of a victim: suddenly and mysteriously, during a few minutes of our lives, the sacrifice in which he gave himself for us is there before us, his supreme offering of himself to the Father, the act by which he won for all men the grace of redemption. At the Mass the faithful do not sacrifice with the priest; the priest alone, by virtue of the sacrament of Holy Orders, has the power to sacrifice. The faithful possess by virtue of their Baptism another sort of power, the power to unite themselves to the priest in the offering of the sacrificial victim (and also, like the priest, to be nourished by the Body of Christ after he has been nourished by it in the sacramental communion in which he consumes the sacrifice). They act, then, in their very title as visible or sacramentally *marked* members of the Church who, in union with her Head, and in a sacred rite performed in common with him, offer to God the Lamb that takes away the sins of the world. If in the same sanctuary there are present unbaptized souls who seek God, it is possible that during the Mass they receive greater graces than some of the baptized present, yet, having not the mark of Baptism, they are not included in the sovereign act of adoration and thanksgiving that the Church is accomplishing.

[81] Everything in the liturgy relates to the Mass, either directly and explicitly, as is the case with all that is done during the Mass itself, before the sacrifice (the readings and the sermon) and after it—or else indirectly and implicitly, as is the case in the liturgy of the sacraments and the sacramentals, or in the recitation of the canonical hours, or in the cycle of the liturgical year. That is why I speak here especially of the Mass.

[82] Constitution on the Sacred Liturgy, Par. 30.

When we meditate on all this a bit, it seems to me that we see several things a little better. In the first place we see more clearly the essentially collective or common aspect of the liturgical celebration. It is a single Body that acts, in union with its Head, and it is precisely as a member of this Body, taken into the action of the Body and participating in it, that each of the faithful gathered in the common celebration offers to God the worship that is due to him.

In the second place, one sees a bit better why it is necessary to say that the celebration of the Mass is the most exalted act that can take place on earth, and that "the liturgy is the summit toward which the activity of the Church is directed; at the same time it is the fount from which all her power flows." [83] That is obvious, since in the Mass, the center of the whole liturgy, it is the Head of the mystical Body himself, the Incarnate Word, who, while still remaining in heaven, makes himself, as well as the supreme act that he accomplished on the cross, invisibly present on earth; and it is to his action, an action of *God made man* that the priest and the community of the faithful are united, the latter as well as the former by virtue of the sacrament whose character he bears (Holy Orders for one, Baptism for all).

In the third place, one sees a bit better how the end that Christ himself (with the entire Church) intends and attains in the celebration of the Mass, wherever held, let us say the *divinely attained* aim of this celebration, is the common act of offering and adoration that Christ himself and the Church accomplish through the medium of a tiny part of the Church—a local assembly offering its worship to God on such and such a day and in such and such a church or chapel. The priest may have all the human weaknesses possible, the faithful may be as distracted and inattentive as can be (as is the case in many funeral masses, which are nevertheless very moving when accompanied by the old traditions of the poor people, and in many masses to celebrate the annual reopening of civil institutions): if one does what he has to do, in performing the sacrifice that sanctifies the Church, whatever may be the case with others, who should be uniting themselves at the same moment to the offering of the sacrificial Lamb, the *divinely attained* aim will certainly have been attained, the

83 Constitution on the Sacred Liturgy, Ch. I, Par. 10.

act of offering and of adoration that the Church wanted to perform will have been performed, the Mass will have been celebrated.

Undoubtedly; but assuming the conditions that I have mentioned, the aim *divinely attained* by means of men will have been attained, but *badly attained* as far as men are concerned; the work that the Church wanted to accomplish will have been accomplished, but *badly accomplished* as far as men are concerned; the Mass will have been celebrated, but *badly celebrated* on the part of men. For what is involved is a holy work, and therefore the celebrant as well as the faithful should there be recollected in God as far as possible; the celebrant himself should lead as saintly a life as possible, and the faithful, too, should strive toward such a life. That is why the liturgical reform, so necessary and so long awaited, insists so earnestly that the faithful *"should participate consciously, devoutly and actively in the sacred action":* [84] this is done by speaking and singing as public worship de-

[84] "They should learn *to offer themselves; through Christ their Mediator, they should be drawn into ever more perfect union with God and with each other,* so that finally God may be all in all." Constitution on the Sacred Liturgy, Par. 48. Let me observe that, as regards the application of this precept, many commentators, when they come to the formula quoted here in my text (all in italics in the Constitution itself) put strong emphasis on the word *actively*, without giving the same attention to the word *devoutly*, which receives the same emphasis in the Constitution. Let me point out also that the word *actively* itself refers to the inner movement of the soul as much as (and even much more, according to the teachings of the Encyclical *Mediator Dei*) to the external activity of the voice.

Finally, I would like to make one last remark. (I know that this will displease many people, but I can't help it, truth obliges me to speak.) If, among those who assist at Mass, there are prayerful souls who find themselves so drawn to inner recollection that they can neither speak nor sing, nor participate actively in the liturgy except on the highest level, one should leave them to their silence and respect in them the liberty of the Spirit of God.

I read in a pamphlet published in 1957 by Mlle. Madeleine Basset on the little servant of God, Anne de Guigné, who died at ten and one-half years of age, that toward the age of eight or nine she asked her mother one day: "Mama, would you let me pray without a prayerbook during Mass, because I know the prayers by heart and I am often distracted when I read them, but when I speak to Jesus I am not distracted at all. It is like talking with someone, Mama, one knows well what one is saying."—"And what do you say to Jesus?"—"That I love him, then I talk to him about you, about the others [her brothers and sisters, her relatives], that Jesus might make them good. I talk to him most of all about sinners. And then, I tell him that I would like to see him. . . ." This little girl did not have a special duty like the priest or the altar boy, to pronounce the words required for the sacred function. The silence in which she spoke to Jesus had without a doubt much more value than if she had sung, under duress, even the Gloria or the Credo.

mands; but words and song alone do not suffice, the inner attention of the soul is needed, and a desire for God.[85] Indeed, the faithful do not assist *well* at Mass, and do not participate *well*, unless, according to the vast diversity of the conditions of each one, there is in them, be it in the most implicit and unapparent manner, by a mere sigh of the soul, a response to that universal call to sanctity on which the Council has also insisted.

Finally, in the fourth place, and this is the point I was coming to, one understands a bit better why the liturgical life is a *normally neces- sary* aid for those who set out toward the perfection of charity. Be- cause in the Church, and in an infinitely more real sense than in all other "societies" worthy of the name, is verified the principle that the common good is a good common *to the whole and to the parts;* or in other words, the common good flows back finally on to the parts, who are human persons. It is *by virtue of the work accomplished in com- mon* in the liturgical celebration, and the sanctification that flows back from it to each of those who have truly participated, that Chris- tians who endeavor to advance toward sanctity are made better able

[85] After having reminded us that the liturgy is at the same time an interior and an exterior worship, Pius XII, in the Encyclical *Mediator Dei*, strongly emphasizes that "the chief element of divine worship must be interior. For we must always live in Christ and give ourselves to Him completely, so that in Him, with Him and through Him the Heavenly Father may be duly glorified. The sacred Liturgy re- quires, however, that both of these elements be intimately linked with each other. This recommendation the Liturgy itself is careful to repeat, as often as it pre- scribes an exterior act of worship . . .

"Very truly, the Sacraments and the Sacrifice of the altar, being Christ's own actions, must be held to be capable in themselves of conveying and dispensing grace from the divine Head to the members of the mystical Body. But if they are to produce their proper effect, it is absolutely necessary that our hearts be rightly disposed to receive them. . . . These members are alive, endowed and equipped with an intelligence and will of their own. It follows that they are strictly required to put their own lips to the fountain, imbibe and absorb for themselves the life- giving water, and rid themselves personally of anything that might hinder its nutritive effect in their souls."

The Constitution on the Sacred Liturgy presupposes the teachings of *Mediator Dei;* it did not have to repeat them, because its object is first of all to reorganize the liturgy in practice. The Constitution does not, however, fail to note that "in order that the liturgy may be able to produce its full effects, it is necessary *that the faithful come to it with proper dispositions,* that *their minds be attuned to their voices,* and that they *cooperate with divine grace lest they receive it in vain.*" (Constitution on the Sacred Liturgy, Par. 11.) Concise formulas that, if we read them with the proper attention, go extremely far (as do those quoted above, at the beginning of the preceding note), and that confirm what I have tried to say here.

to move forward. What they *have done* during the celebration, they have done as *members* of the whole. What they *receive*, they receive ultimately as *persons*.

And I am not speaking of the special graces of light and love that one or another may receive from a single word of the liturgy that strikes the heart by surprise (and seems sometimes to have been said *for you*), nor am I speaking of the sort of release and liberation [86] that sacred song (availing itself of the natural grace of music) often has the power to produce through the native tenuousness of the human voice. (This is not the case with loud-speakers.)

The conclusion of these reflections can, it seems to me, be formulated thus: it is essential to the Christian to be at one and the same time *person* and *member;* and he is always both, since these two aspects of him are distinct but cannot be separated. I observed a moment ago that in the liturgical celebration Christians are sanctified first of all through the flowing back on each one of the good accomplished through their common work. It is not above all, therefore, *by* what he *does* as a *member* of the whole, in doing his part of the work of the whole, it is above all *by* what he finally *receives* as a *person* on whom the good of the whole is flowing back, that the Christian is then sanctified, and that the liturgy is for him an indispensable aid in his progress toward God.

I have just said that this aid is indispensable, that it is *normally necessary*. It should be added that God's ways are infinitely gentle,[87] and take into account the conditions and possibilities of each, in their limitless variety. So much the better if we have the possibility of assisting at daily Mass. Most laymen do not. And the sick (and sometimes even those in good health, because of some insurmountable obstacle) are deprived even of Sunday Mass. God will certainly find a way to send them a crumb of the great common meal. We have the sacrament of the sick, and a priest can bring them the Body of Christ.

---

[86] "Letting singing and music act in oneself, letting the soul 'open itself to divine things' (St. Thomas). When music produces this liberating effect, one is suddenly delivered from the constraint of effort and from distractions, from irrelevant images, and, as it were, from the distance between time and eternity. Burning love invades the soul. The conquered heart gives us the sweetness of tears." *Journal de Raïssa*, n. 161, p. 304. From the English translation by Antonia White (to be published).

[87] Cf. the tract, *Des Moeurs divines*, quoted farther on, p. 239.

And even if that is impossible, and if a man lacks the strength to utter a word, or to join himself in spirit with what the Church is doing, or even to sigh for God, charity is enough, if it is in his heart.

CONTEMPLATION

Pati divina, to suffer things divine, in an inner experience in which the soul does not act but is rather acted upon, acted upon by God under the regime of the gifts of the Holy Spirit; *pati divina*—these are the words that come to me the instant I try, as poorly qualified as I might be, to speak of contemplation. This word "contemplation," like all words when one uses them to describe things of a very high order, is apt to betray those exalted things. There is a natural or philosophical contemplation [88] which is only of an intellectual and speculative order. Christian contemplation, because it comes from love and tends to love, and is a work of love, has nothing to do with that. *Per amorem agnoscimus*, there "we know through love," said St. Gregory the Great.[89] It is only out of respect for this mysterious knowledge, given by love, that Christian tradition has preserved the word "contemplation."

But with the word "contemplation" vocabulary plays many other tricks on us, and I would like to say a few words about this right at the start. Suppose you were trying to find out what poetry is: you would go immediately to poets; in reading them you would learn, let's hope, what poetry consists of, or what it is by nature, and you could then speak of poetry as a thing known or grasped *in itself* or *in its typical traits*. At the same time and by the same token you would be speaking of the poetry *of poets*.

After that you will become aware that poetry is not confined to poets. There is an admirable poetry in the life of a Christopher Columbus or a Benedict Labre, in the thought of a Plato or an Einstein, in the movement of the galaxies. Are you going to look there to find out what poetry is *in itself* or *in its typical trait*? That would be im-

---

[88] There is also a "theological contemplation," in which the theologian, at the end of his labor of reason, contemplates intellectually, but with the savor of grace, the truth that he has attained as a summit of the *opus theologicum*. The infused contemplation of which I am speaking here is not at all like that either.

[89] *Moralia*, X, 8, 13.

possible, because it is found there in an *atypical, hidden* or *masked* mode. It is the poetry of great discoverers and great saints, of philosophical or scientific geniuses, of the world of the stars. You ought to recognize the existence of this poetry, which is not that of the poets (nor of the musicians or other servants of art).

But in fixing your attention and that of others on the poetry of the poets, as you must do when you describe what poetry is *in itself* or *in its typical traits,* you risk making yourself and others believe that poetry is confined to the poets (or the other servants of art). And the poetry which *does exist* elsewhere is thus in danger of being disregarded.

Something a bit like that happens with contemplation, but there it poses much greater problems. We have the contemplation *of contemplatives* in the strict sense of the word, of souls wholly dedicated to contemplation: it is to that type we are referring when we speak (as I would like to do now) of what contemplation is *in itself* or *in its typical traits.* But we must not forget that there is also the contemplation of those who are not contemplatives in the strict sense of the word, souls wholly dedicated to contemplation, but who have nevertheless crossed a certain threshold in the life of the spirit that the contemplatives also cross. We love to contrast Martha and Mary, but we must not forget that Martha was not some directress of the works of proselytism in the Temple praying only with her lips, as may be the case occasionally (that sometimes happens). Martha prayed in her heart, like Mary; she was concerned with many things, but she devoted herself to *oraison* and contemplated in secret, perhaps pleasing God as much as Mary, while cooking and busying herself with all those things of which her sister left her the burden. Was she too perhaps one of those faithful souls in whom contemplation remains atypical and masked? In her particular case this seems highly improbable. In any case, like all souls that advance toward God (and like all saints—we venerate her as such) she answered, and answered well, the call to contemplation addressed to all. I shall come back a little later to these questions of major importance. I have alluded to them here parenthetically, as a preliminary to what I will say later. The parenthesis is closed.

I recalled a moment ago the words of St. Gregory the Great: in contemplation "we know through love." In Christian contemplation intelligence is there supremely alive, in a nocturnal darkness more instructive than any concept: blind as to its natural mode of operation, intelligence knows only by virtue of the *connaturality* that love creates between the soul who loves and the God it loves, a God who loves it first.

"Contemplation," said Père Lallemant, "is a simple, free, penetrating view of God or of things divine, which proceeds from love and tends toward love. . . . It is the exercise of the purest and most perfect charity. Love is its beginning, its exercise and its end." [90]

We could also say, more briefly, that "contemplation is a silent prayer which takes place in recollection in the secret of the heart, and is directly ordered to union with God." [91]

According to the common doctrine of the theologians, contemplation is dependent at one and the same time on the theological virtues, supernatural in their essence, and on the gifts of the Holy Spirit, "doubly supernatural, not only in their essence like the theological virtues, but also in their mode of action." [92] This mode of action exceeds human measure because "the soul is guided and immediately moved by divine inspiration." [93]

☆

I have noted before that the Christian is at one and the same time inseparably *person and member*.

In the case of the liturgy (and, *par excellence*, of the Mass) it is not primarily *by* what the Christian *does*, as *member* of the mystical Body, in participating at the celebration (in speaking, singing, and above all in uniting himself wholeheartedly to the work of offering and of adoration accomplished by the mystical Body and by its Head), it is primarily *by* what he *receives*, by that which flows back on him, as *person*, from that common work, that he is helped in his progress toward the perfection of charity.

With contemplation, the terms are inverted: it is first of all *by*

---

[90] *La Doctrine spirituelle*, ed. Pottier (Paris: Téqui, 1936), pp. 430–432.

[91] Raïssa, in *Liturgy and Contemplation*, p. 31.

[92] R. P. Garrigou-Lagrange, *Perfection chrétienne et Contemplation*, Paris, Desclée De Brouwer, 5th ed., v. I, p. 34. He treats of the contemplation that the theologians call "infused" (that which is under discussion here).

[93] *Ibid.*

what the Christian does, or rather receives himself as *person* "immediately moved by divine inspiration," that he is helped in his progress toward the perfection of charity. And by the same token, since this person is, inseparably, a *member* of the mystical Body, all the communicable goods, all the treasures of redeeming grace that overflow from his contemplation are made part of the common good of the mystical Body, and come to enrich the common treasury of the communion of saints.

And the contemplative, by his testimony and his presence among men, is useful and necessary to their spiritual life in yet another way, more apparent but less essential, if I may say so, though certainly needed of itself. "If they lapse, is it not because they no longer remember the relish of God and of his Light? To make them know them, such is the outward function of the contemplative: the uncreated Light, the eternal Wisdom which is Christ; the substantial Saviour which is the Holy Ghost. External works themselves, works of mercy, owe their excellence to the power they have of revealing the benevolence of God. There have to be souls solely occupied in drinking at this heavenly spring. Through them, afterwards, the living water of love and its divine taste reach those whose vocation comprises more activity. Contemplation is like a water wheel which draws up the water and makes it flow into channels. If contemplation ceased entirely, hearts would soon be dried up. . . . Love of one's neighbor, as well as love of God, obliges the contemplative to remain close to the divine source." [94] All that, which is so true, is like the sign which makes manifest among us the completely invisible function of which I have just spoken, and which is essentially, in the mystical Body, the function ("mystical" itself, in the same sense of the word) of the contemplative as *member* of that Body.

Member and person at the same time, the member who participates in the liturgy receives its fruits as person, because the good of the whole flows back on the part. At the same time person and member, the human person who contemplates God in love gives his fruit as member by virtue of the integration of the good of the part into the good of the whole.

We can see that two different and complementary perspectives are involved here. And by the same token we can see how absurd it is to

[94] *Journal de Raïssa, op. cit.,* p. 67.

oppose liturgy and contemplation to one another. They demand one
another, and one implies the other. The liturgy, because it is worship
in spirit and in truth, requires, in order that one truly participate in
it, that the participants harbor in their souls the love of God and the
desire to unite themselves to him. It does not require that they all be
contemplatives, which would be to ask the impossible, nor that they
all habitually live the life of love-prayer (so much the better, however, if they could!). But it demands that there be among them some
who habitually live the life of love-prayer, and it demands that the
others have at least the first seed of this life within them without their
knowing it, thanks to the attention of their heart to the words that
their lips pronounce. And the fruit of the liturgy is to help all those
who participate in it to advance, from as distant a point as it may be
for some, toward the perfection of charity; and to help those who aspire to contemplative prayer to advance along that road.

And contemplation develops in the soul of the contemplative the
desire to unite himself to the worship offered by the Church he loves
to the One whom she loves and whom he loves; and it develops first
of all the desire to participate in the celebration of the Mass, in which
the sacrifice of the Lamb is perpetuated among us, and in which his
Body is given to us as food. And contemplation has for its fruit an increase in the common treasury of the goods of the communion of
saints.

We also see that, far from being opposed, the two great declarations
of the Council and of Pope Paul VI complement and confirm one another: the Council's assertion that "the liturgy is the summit toward
which the activity of the Church is directed; at the same time, it is the
fount from which all her power flows"; [95] and that of Paul VI, that
"contemplation is the most noble and the most perfect form of human activity, against which one measures, in the pyramid of human
acts, the proper value of these acts, each according to its kind." [96]

And this is so because the first statement is made in the perspec-

---

[95] Cf. p. 216.

[96] Discourse of December 7, 1965, delivered by the Pope at the closing of the
Council. ". . . Adeo ut homo, cum mentem et cor suum in Deo defigere nititur,
contemplationi vacando, actum animi sui eliciat qui omnium nobilissimus ac
perfectissimus est habendus; actum dicimus a quo nostris etiam temporibus
innumeri humanae navitatis campi suae dignitatis gradum sumere possunt ac
debent." A.A.S. of January 31, 1966, p. 53.

tive of the common work accomplished by the Church, which ultimately flows back on the individual person, and the second is made in
the perspective of the highest act of which the individual person is
capable, and which ultimately flows back on the Church.

The fact remains that in the equal pre-eminence of the common
work accomplished by the Body and its Head, and of the act by which
the contemplative becomes one with his God, the liturgy retains an
inalienable privilege: in the Mass heaven comes down to earth; Jesus,
at the words of the priest, is suddenly there, under veils, to perpetu-
ate mysteriously his unique Sacrifice, and his presence among us in
the Holy Sacrament. But contemplation also retains an inalienable
privilege: in contemplation a man who is a *self*, a universe to himself, is united to Jesus in a union of person to Person, a union of love,
and he joins in the night of faith the End for which he himself and all
the universe were created. In contemplation heaven begins on earth
(for contemplation will continue in heaven, whereas the Mass will
not). The mystical Body is composed of human persons each of
whom was made for this purpose of seeing God in eternity, and being
united with him through love on earth, and for each of whom Christ
gave his life in his supreme act of love. He gave it for the entire
Church and for all the People of God, but that was possible only by
giving it *for each one* as if he were alone in the world. And it is the
duty of each, to the extent that he knows what God did for him, to
answer such love by a total gift of himself in love.

"The love of God is always from Person to person, and our love for
God is always from our heart to His heart, which has loved us first, in
our very singularity." [97] "As a member of a Body whose common
good is identical with the ultimate good itself of each person," each
is helped by this Body to love God, but "each one is alone before
God to love him, to contemplate him here below and to see him in
heaven, as also to be judged by Him—each one according to his
love." [98]

☆

From that one understands a bit better the importance of the
Psalmist's injunction: "Be still and know that I am God" (*Ps.* 46.

[97] *Liturgy and Contemplation*, pp. 83–84.
[98] *Ibid.*, p. 83.

[45]). "Taste and see how much the Lord is good!" (*Ps.* 34 [33]). And one understands a bit better why the saints have never tired of asserting that wordless prayer (which of itself tends to contemplation) is a normally necessary way of approach for anyone who has a firm resolve to advance toward the perfection of charity. That is what the Constitution on the Liturgy reminds us: "The Christian is indeed called to pray with his brethren, but he must also enter into his chamber to pray to the Father in secret; yet more, according to the teaching of the apostle, he should pray without ceasing." [99] This was the teaching of St. Irenaeus in the second century, St. Ambrose and St. Augustine in the fourth and fifth centuries, Cassian in the fifth, and then St. Gregory the Great, St. John Climaque, St. Bernard, St. Hildegarde, St. Albert the Great, St. Bonaventure and St. Thomas (he tells us that contemplation "aims directly and immediately at the love of God himself" and that it "is not directed to whatever a kind of love of God, but to perfect love"),[100] St. Gertrude, St. Catherine of Sienna, and later, in an age when a strong impulse toward self-reflection had its drawbacks but of itself, like every *prise de conscience*, marked an undeniable progress, St. Teresa of Avila ("there is only one road that leads to God, and that is *oraison*") and St. John of the Cross (the same saint who said "in the evening of this life you will be judged on love," said also: "contemplative prayer must take precedence over all other occupations, it is the strength of the soul"); and after them, the great Jesuit spirituals, Lallemant, Surin, Grou, Caussade, and then St. Therese of Lisieux.

Père Lallemant wrote: "Without contemplation we will never advance far toward virtue . . . we will never break free of our weaknesses and our imperfections. We will always be attached to the earth, and will never raise ourselves much above the sentiments of nature. We will never be able to offer a perfect service to God. But with contemplation we will do more in a month, for ourselves and for others, than we would have been able to do without it in ten years. It produces . . . acts of sublime love of God such as one can hardly ever accomplish without this gift . . . , and finally, it perfects faith and all the virtues. . . ."[101]

---

[99] Constitution on the Sacred Liturgy, Par. 12.
[100] *Sum. theol.*, II–II, 182, 2; 182, 2, ad 1.
[101] *La Doctrine Spirituelle*, pp. 429–430.

This whole long tradition remained faithful to the teaching of St. Paul, for whom, as Father Lebreton wrote, charity, which "when we die will flower into eternal life," is "the means and the end of contemplation." [102]

And there is one greater than St. Paul. Christ himself, as St. Bonaventure repeats again and again, promises to those who love him this experience of things divine when he says, in St. John: "He who loves me will be loved by my Father, and I will love him and manifest myself to him" (*John* 14:21). And it is he who tells us: "When you pray, go into your room, and shut the door, and pray to your Father in secret; and your Father who sees in the secret will reward you" (*Matt.* 6:6). *Clauso ostio!* It is the door of the room and it is the door of the soul. And it is also He who is the Door (*John* 10:9), and who encloses us in him when we are recollected in *oraison*.

And it is Christ who said: "You must pray constantly" (*Luke* 18:1). *Sine intermissione orate* "pray ceaselessly" (1 *Thess.* 5:17), St. Paul will say, following his master. The Church applies this precept in her liturgy. But it is addressed to all; and this is not impossible.

How can one manage to pray constantly? By repeating a short formula so unremittingly that it becomes rooted in the soul? This is the means that Christians of the Eastern Churches have employed for centuries with the "Jesus prayer" (Lord Jesus Christ, Son of God, have pity on me a sinner) repeated incessantly. Such a method—in which, in the last analysis, a sort of psychological technique utilizes a practice ("ejaculatory prayer") that is holy in itself (when it springs from the heart)—might in the course of time result in a habit no doubt rooted in the soul, but one in which a verbal formula made incessantly present by a natural automatism plays much more of a part than does that vital (and supernaturally vital) act that is prayer.

The true answer is to be sought in this vital act itself. With a St. Theresa when she was busy with her foundations or a St. Vincent de Paul when he was busy with his poor, it went on *virtually*, always ready to spring up, by very reason of the profundity and intensity with which it filled their souls in the hours of meditation reserved for wordless prayer.

And this true answer is, no doubt, given us in the most decisive

[102] *Dict. de Spiritualité*, col. 1715 and 1711.

fashion by what Father Osende, in a remarkable page of his book
Contemplata,[103] calls *l'oraison du coeur,* "the prayer of the heart." It
is, I think, through this sort of prayer or contemplation, so silent and
so rooted in the depths of the spirit that he describes it as "unconscious," that we can best and most truly put into practice the precept
to pray constantly.[104] And was it not to it that St. Anthony the Hermit alluded when he said that "there is no perfect prayer if the religious is himself aware that he is praying?" [105]

The prayer that Father Osende calls the prayer of the heart and that
he describes as unconscious (it pertains to that "supra-conscious of
the spirit" of which I have said a great deal elsewhere) can and must,
he says, be continuous in the contemplative soul. "For we cannot
fix our mind on two objects at the same time nor continue to think
always, whereas we can love always" (at least in the supra-conscious
of the spirit—only there, in effect, can love be *in act* continuously).
We are then no longer dealing simply with the vital impulse of prayer
always present *virtually* in consciousness; the prayer of the heart itself
remains in act—in the supra-conscious of the spirit. It is an unformulated act of love that can be constantly present, like that of a mother
—an example dear to Bergson—who while she sleeps, still watches
over the infant in the cradle. "Who does not see that this is possible,
and very possible? Do we not see that, even in the natural order,
when the heart is dominated by a great love, no matter what the person does, his entire soul and life are on what he loves and not on

---

[103] Translated into English under the title *Fruits of Contemplation* (St. Louis,
Mo.: Herder, 1953). I would like to point out here that the pages in *Liturgy and
Contemplation* that deal with the prayer of the heart and with Father Osende
stand in need of correction. In writing these pages I inadvertently spoke (probably
because of the "unconscious" character of this prayer) of "atypical" or "masked"
contemplation, which we will discuss later. This was a serious error. The prayer of
the heart springs from the supra-conscious of the spirit, but it is not at all
"masked" contemplation; it is a typical *form* of contemplation, and one of the
most precious.

[104] The idea of perpetual or uninterrupted prayer which is carried on even in
sleep by a mental activity inaccessible to the consciousness, plays a central role with
Cassian. (Cf. *Dict. de Spiritualité,* art. Contemplation, col. 1924 and 1926.)
Père Grou in the eighteenth century also notes (*Manuel,* p. 224 ff.) that uninterrupted prayer is a prayer that escapes the consciousness. Cf. Arintero, *The Mystical
Evolution in the Development and Vitality of the Church* (St. Louis, Mo.: Herder,
1951), p. 45.

[105] "Non est perfecta oratio in qua se monachus vel hoc ipsum quod orat
intelligit." Cassian, IX, 31.

what he does, though he may apply to his work all his attention? If natural love does this, how much more should divine love. . . ." [106] He who has reached the stage of the prayer of the heart, therefore, fulfills in the best way possible the precept to pray *constantly*.

THE DIVERSITY OF THE GIFTS OF THE HOLY SPIRIT

It is with contemplation considered in itself and in its typical traits, in other words, with those who are wholly dedicated to contemplation, that the previous considerations dealt. Here we must note that serious errors are possible if we misread the doctrine of the saints, I mean if we understand it in the manner of a "univocal" assertion, a mathematical proposition or an article of law, without taking into account the freedom, the breadth and the variety of the ways of God.

The word "contemplation" makes many people afraid, and I have noted earlier that, like every human word that designates exalted things, it is not without risk of deceiving honest readers. In addition, the very sublimity of those who teach us about it is enough to frighten one. To advance as one must toward God, is it prescribed to me, a businessman or a factory worker, or a doctor overwhelmed by his practice, or a family father bent under his burden—to talk with God like St. Gertrude or St. Catherine of Sienna, and to aspire to the transforming union and the spiritual marriage like St. Teresa and St. John of the Cross? Not really; that is not what is involved.

Contemplation is a winged and supernatural thing, free with the freedom of the Spirit of God, more burning than the African sun and more refreshing than the waters of a rushing stream, lighter than birds' down, unseizable, escaping any human measure and disconcerting every human notion, happy to depose the mighty and exalt the lowly, capable of all disguises, of all daring and all timidity, chaste, fearless, luminous and nocturnal, sweeter than honey and more barren than rock, crucifying and beatifying (crucifying above all), and sometimes all the more exalted the less conspicuous it is.

When the theologians, after having shown us the sublimity of the goal and having a little frightened us with it, speak to us of the call of all to contemplation, they soften their language, but not less energet-

[106] V. Osende, *Fruits of Contemplation*, pp. 157–159.

ically. They explain that this call (it is a call, not a precept, because contemplation, with respect to the only End, which is the perfection of love—and in the same way, participation in the liturgy—are only means, as normally necessary as they are), they explain to us that this call is similar to another call (this one a precept)—the call to the perfection of love. It is, at first, a "distant" call which some day perhaps will become "immediate." [107] And it is the distant call that is addressed to all; and in order not to be in fault at this point it is enough only to set out, even without knowing it.[108]

But what is still more important, it seems to me, what it is, first of all, important to observe, is that the response to the immediate call, or, in other words, the entry into the path of contemplation, coincides with something of a much more profound and much more hidden order, which may be called *the entry into the life of the spirit:* I mean that it takes place at the end of a transitional phase during which—in a manner inaccessible to consciousness (in the depths of the supra-conscious of the spirit)—the soul has been gradually introduced to a new regime of life; then, once arrived at this new stage of its spiritual progress, the soul no longer receives only from time to time, in order to extricate itself from some exceptional difficulty or

[107] St. Bonaventure and St. Thomas each, in conformity with the tradition of the saints, that all souls are called in a distant way to contemplation, considered as the normal flowering of the grace of the virtues and the gifts of the Holy Spirit. The immediate call "exists only when the presence of the three signs mentioned by St. John of the Cross, and before him by Tauler, is ascertained: first, meditation becomes unfeasible; second, the soul has no desire to fix the imagination on any particular object, interior or exterior; third, the soul is pleased to find itself alone with God, fixing its affectionate attention on him." R. P. Garrigou-Lagrange, *Perfection chrétienne et Contemplation*, II, pp. 421–422.

[108] "One does not sin against the precept," writes St. Thomas with respect to the precept concerning the perfection of charity, "simply because one does not accomplish it in the best manner; it suffices, in order that the precept not be transgressed, that it be accomplished in one way or another" (*Sum. theol.*, II–II, 184, 3, ad 2). And Cajetan comments: "The perfection of charity is commanded as an end, one must will to attain the end, the whole end; but precisely because it is an end, to obey the precept it is enough to be in a state of someday reaching this perfection, even if only in heaven. Whoever possesses charity, even to the most tenuous degree, and advances thus toward heaven, is on the way to perfect charity, and thereby avoids transgression of the precept."

Similarly, we are not deaf to the call of contemplation if we do not answer it in the best manner. Whoever has within him, even to the feeblest degree, the will to pray to God, whether by mumbling paternosters or by crying out to God, is without knowing it on the way to contemplation.

some temptation, the help of the gifts of the Holy Spirit (which are necessary to salvation, as I recalled above). When the soul has arrived at this new stage, when it has crossed this threshold, it begins to be *habitually* aided by the gifts of the Holy Spirit, and that is what the theologians call entering under the habitual regime of these gifts.

Now the gifts of the Holy Spirit, the enumeration of which Catholic theology takes from Isaiah,[109] have different objects. Certain, like the gifts of Counsel, Fortitude, Fear of the Lord, and Piety, are related above all to action; the others, like the gifts of Wisdom, Understanding and Knowledge, are related above all to contemplation.

From this it follows that there are very diverse ways and extremely different styles in which souls who have set out on the path of the spirit can advance along it. In some it is the highest gifts, the gifts of Wisdom, Understanding and Knowledge, which are at work in an eminent way—these souls represent the mysterious life of the spirit in its normal plentitude; and they will have the grace of contemplation in its typical forms, whether arid or consoling. In the others, it is the other gifts which are at work above all—they will live the life of the spirit but above all with respect to their activities and their works, and they will not have the typical and normal forms of contemplation.

"It is not, however, that they are deprived of contemplation, of the loving experience of things divine; for according to the teaching of St. Thomas, all the gifts of the Holy Spirit are linked to one another; [110] they cannot, therefore, exist in the soul without the gift of Wisdom, which, in the case we are discussing, is at work, though in a less apparent way. These souls whose style of life is an active one will have the grace of contemplation, but of a *masked*, not apparent contemplation. Perhaps they will only be able to recite rosaries, and wordless *oraison* will give them a headache or make them sleepy. Mysterious contemplation will not be in their conscious prayer, but perhaps in the glance with which they will look at a poor man, or will look at suffering." [111]

We can understand nothing about the things we are discussing at this moment if we do not carefully take into account these atypical,

---

[109] Is., 11:2. Cf. *Sum. theol.*, I–II, 68, 4 to 8.
[110] *Sum. theol.*, I–II, 68, 5.
[111] *Action and Contemplation*, in *Questions de conscience* (Paris, Desclée De Brouwer, 1938), p. 146.

diffused or disguised forms of contemplation. If I put this much emphasis on them, it is because I am a bit hopeful, after all these explanations, that a reader, even one trained by the clergy of today, will be less scandalized by the idea that contemplation (open or masked) lies in the normal path of Christian perfection. But I also think that, all things considered (it is only a question of vocabulary, and in order to spare the "modern mentality" misunderstandings for which it has, moreover, a singular avidity), it would perhaps be better—instead of saying "the call of all the baptized to contemplation"—to say, what is the same thing, "the call of all the baptized to the loving experience of the things of God."

Be that as it may, if the call is addressed to all, we must recognize also that in fact, given our dear nature, so dear to our Christians renewed by Evolution, and given the general conditions of human life, those among the baptized who answer the call in question, but badly, like idlers and laggards, and who soon sit down at the edge of the road, will always be the most numerous. It is a pity, but it is true. And this fact shows how important a part, for the life of the kingdom of God in pilgrimage here below, is played by these (not so rare, however, as one might think) who have crossed the threshold of which I spoke above, and who make up for the great deficiency as to the common good of the Church—and the cruel privation each of the laggards inflicts on himself—which the mysterious patience of Jesus tolerates in the greater part of his flock.

CONTEMPLATION ON THE ROADS

I shall still be speaking here, and at some length, of things that refer to the inner life and the search for the perfection of charity. Is this to forget that *The Peasant of the Garonne* is written by "an old layman who questions himself about the present time"? Certainly not—I am not forgetting my subtitle; and my reflections always concern—and more so than ever—our times. For if our age scarcely thinks of these things (has there ever been an age in history that has thought a great deal about them?), there is still—precisely because it feeds on a heap of flattering illusions—nothing of which it stands in greater need than attention to these things by a certain number of human beings: a relatively small number, no doubt, but which certainly could, and should be much larger. To tell the truth, it is in having this small number in mind that this whole book was written, I mean in order to offer known or unknown friends an opportunity to heave for a moment a sigh of relief (it is always a pleasure to hear some imprudent talker stammer out truths which are not welcome).

As far as this last section is concerned, the fact is that it is hardly mine. It is more Raïssa's than mine. My task was above all to weave together in an order that seemed appropriate to my sketch many texts written by her and that stand on their own, because a breath passes in them of an experience of that deep Christian life whose mystery they enlighten for us a little.

☆

La contemplation sur les chemins—contemplation on the roads—that is the title of a book that Raïssa wanted to write (our friends had encouraged her to do so), and which in her mind was addressed to those—much less rare than one thinks—who, while living what we call the ordinary life of the good Christian in the world (family duties and vocational duties, Mass on Sundays, cooperation in some apostolic work, the desire to help one's neighbor as much as possible, and a few moments of vocal prayer at home), are ready to go further, and whose hearts are burning to go further, but who find themselves prevented by many fears and obstacles, more or less illusory—or sometimes dissuaded by the very persons who have the charge of guiding them.

I have a notion that the widespread infatuation that today prevails for action, technique, organization, inquiries, committees, mass movements, and the new possibilities that sociology and psychology are discovering—all things that are far from being contemptible, but which, if one confided only in them, would lead to a strange naturalism in the service (so one hopes) of the supernatural—will some day give rise to a great deal of strong disappointments.

In order to make the teachings of the Council pass into their lives, were not Christian people going to try first of all to be attentive to the wishes of that Spirit, without whose assistance "there is nothing innocent in man"? Such a wish would be a little too much oblivious of the historical conditioning to which the world is subject. In any case, the fact remains that at this moment many souls are dying of thirst, and receive hardly any help except from the few hidden but nevertheless radiant centers that, in consecrated or lay persons, contemplation has reserved for itself on this poor earth, and through which the Spirit of God comes to touch them. As I have previously noted, the titanism of human effort is the great idol of our times. And consequently it is clear that an invisible galaxy of souls dedicated to the contemplative life—in the world itself, I mean, in the very heart of the world—is our ultimate reason for hoping.

Unlike souls dedicated to action, who, if they advance in the ways of God as is demanded of them, partake in the "masked" contemplation I discussed earlier, the souls I am now referring to partake in "open" contemplation. But their path is a very humble one; it demands nothing but charity and humility, and contemplative prayer without apparent graces. This is the path of simple people, it is the "little way" (La *petite voie*) that St. Therese of Lisieux was in charge of teaching us: a kind of short-cut—singularly abrupt, to tell the truth—where all the great things described by St. John of the Cross can be found divinely simplified and reduced to the pure essentials, but without losing any of their exigence.

The soul is laid bare, and its very love-prayer as well—so arid at times that it seems to fly into distractions and emptiness. It is a path that demands great courage. Complete surrender to Him whom we love accepts every burden, will make the soul pass through all the stages willed by Jesus (and known only to Him), and will lead there where Jesus wills, in light or in darkness. Only in His heart do such beings wish to have their shelter; and by the same token they also wish their own hearts to be a shelter for the neighbor.

☆

Raïssa said a few words on the subject she wanted to treat, in a short chapter in *Liturgy and Contemplation*, several passages of which I will reproduce here.

"Indeed contemplation is not given only to the Carthusians, the Poor Clares, the Carmelites. . . . It is frequently the treasure of persons hidden to the world—known only to some few—to their directors, to a few friends. Sometimes, in a certain manner, this treasure is hidden from the souls themselves that possess it—souls who live by it in all simplicity, without visions, without miracles, but with such a flame of love for God and neighbor that good spreads all around them without noise and without agitation.

"It is of this that our age has to become aware, and of the ways through which contemplation communicates itself through the world, under one form or the other, to the great multitude of souls who thirst for it (often without knowing it) and who are called to it at least in a remote manner. The great need of our age, in what concerns the spiritual life, is to put contemplation on the roads.

"It is fitting to note here the importance of the witness and mission of Saint Therese of Lisieux. . . . It is a great way indeed—and a heroic one—this *petite voie* of Therese's, which hides rigorously its greatness under an absolute simplicity, itself heroic. And this absolute simplicity makes of it a way *par excellence* open to all those who aspire to perfection, whatever their condition of life may be. This is the feature here that it is particularly important for us to keep in mind.

"Saint Therese of Lisieux has shown that the soul can tend to the perfection of charity by a way in which the great signs that Saint John of the Cross and Saint Teresa of Avila have described do not appear. . . . By the same token, I believe, Saint Therese in her Carmel prepared in an eminent way that diffusion wider than ever, of the life of union with God which the world requires if it is not to perish.

"Let us add that in this contemplation on the roads whose development the future will doubtless see, it seems that constant attention to the presence of Jesus and fraternal charity are called to play a major role, as regards even the way of infused contemplative prayer." [112]

A *constant attention to the presence of Jesus; and fraternal charity*: it matters especially that we turn our attention to these two main characteristics of contemplation on the roads. On the subject of the first, a note from the *Journal de Raïssa* gives us more detailed information.

[112] *Liturgy and Contemplation*, pp. 74–76.

"Certain spiritual writers think that the highest contemplation, being free of all the images of this world, is that which does without images altogether, even that of Jesus, and into which, consequently, the Humanity of Christ does not enter.

"That is a profound error, and the problem disappears as soon as one has grasped how truly and how deeply the Word has assumed human nature, in such a way that everything which is of this nature, suffering, pity, compassion, hope . . . , all these things have become, so to speak, attributes of God. In contemplating them, it is therefore attributes of God which are contemplated. Since apart and below the divine perfections the Word Incarnate possesses human qualities which are God's—they are the objects of a contemplation that is just as spiritual, although it includes images.

"And the soul must not be afraid of passing through the human states and the human pity of Jesus, and of making requests of Him and of praying for the cure of a sick person, for example—all these things being participations in the desires and the compassion of Christ, which belonged to the divine Person itself." [113]

I find in some lines of Père Marie-Joseph Nicolas a remarkable confirmation of these views. In Jesus, writes Père Nicolas, "man finds God himself." The humanity assumed by the Word has no separate consistency and existence which would make of it a creature between the world and God. *To love the Man Jesus, to unite oneself to the Man Jesus, is to love God.*" [114]

What shall I say on the second characteristic of contemplation on the roads pointed out by Raïssa? If fraternal charity is called to play a major role in this contemplation, it seems to me that it is to the extent that love-prayer can and must be pursued in those very relations with men in which those who live in the world are constantly involved. Then, in looking at our brothers and listening to them, in being attentive to their problems and having compassion for their afflictions, we will not only strive to love them as Jesus loves them; at the same time a more secret grace will be given to us. If we give them all the attention we can from our own hearts, that is not much, to tell the truth; but what counts much more, for us and for our

113 *Journal de Raïssa, op. cit.,* pp. 361–362.
114 *Revue Thomiste,* 1947–I, pp. 41–42.

brothers, is the fact that at the same time Jesus' love for them, which gives them His very heart, is drawing to Him the gaze of our soul and the depths of our heart. Père Voillaume told me once that that was truly *seeing Jesus in them*; and Mère Madeleine, of Crépieux—in a more developed formula, to which I would like to stick—that it came to *penetrate, in looking at our brothers and loving them, a little of the very mystery of Jesus himself and His love for each of us.* "For," she added, "since there is only one commandment, the constant love of our brothers, love to the point of wearing oneself out for them, is the fulfillment in act of the love of God and union with Jesus; and it is love that makes contemplation grow, deepen itself, exult."

To see Jesus in our brothers is an abridged formula, and one which could be misunderstood. Did not, however, Jesus make himself one with them, did he not make all their sorrows his own? "I was hungry and you gave me food, I was thirsty and you gave me to drink, I was a stranger, and you welcomed me, I was naked and you clothed me, I was sick and you visited me; I was in prison and you came to me" (*Matt.* 25:35). That is true, but the fact remains that our brothers are mere creatures, confronting our eyes, and not (to us who have not had the chance to see Him with our eyes) God before the gaze of our soul, as is Jesus when we contemplate him in his very humanity. It is not exactly *in them*, it is rather through them and *behind them* that we see Jesus and his love for them. And by the same token, it is *in arrear* of our attention to others, and of our exchanges with them, in arrear of the noise they make and we make, it is in an inner silence in which the spiritual preconscious much more than the conscious is absorbed, that our soul is attracted to Jesus who is there, and to his love for our brothers, who are his brothers. And this inner silence in us—which the man who speaks to us perceives also in a manner much more unconscious than conscious—is no doubt the best part of what he receives from our so much disarmed fraternal charity.

To contemplate, alone with Him alone, God in the humanity of Jesus; and to contemplate Jesus through our neighbor, whom he loves and whom we love—these are the two most highly desirable paths of contemplation for a man engaged in the labors of the world. But neither is easy for him.

In the first kind of contemplating, which in itself is always required (it is commanded by the Lord), one is constantly exposed to difficulties created by lack of time; notwithstanding, we must do everything possible to persevere in this path.

That is not the problem one has to complain about with the second path; the time available for it would be rather too largely offered. And this path also permits a very pure *oraison*, from which all danger of formulas, notions, routines, even the danger of falling asleep, have been swept away. It is in the poor human clay that we learn then to know Jesus and many of his secrets. But it is an arid love-prayer, almost too pure for our feeble heart, because, being much more unconscious than conscious, it comes about in the tiredness of our members and of our conscious faculties, rather than in the repose where we can taste "how sweet the Lord is."

To rediscover this repose we must return to prayer *clauso ostio*, where we are alone with Jesus.

☆

The lack of time to which I just alluded is the practical problem that makes many laymen attracted to contemplative prayer hesitate, and from which suffer most all those who dedicate themselves to prayer in the world. Without speaking of the "second path" of which I just spoke, there are many particular answers, infinitely variable according to the case of each one. (One can *faire oraison* in the train, in the subway, in the dentist's waiting room. One can also have frequent recourse to those short prayers flung out like a cry, which the ancients recommended so highly.) [115] There is no definitive answer except that which Dom Florent Miège once gave: *You must love your chains.* The material obstacles encountered at each moment by one who lives the life of prayer in the world are an integral

---

[115] Cf. Mrs. Etta Gullik's excellent article, *"Les courtes prières,"* in *La Vie Spirituelle*, February 1966 (original English in *The Clergy Review*). The author recalls that St. Francis of Assisi passed an entire night repeating "My God and my All." "Jesus asked us to pray without ceasing. But how can this be done in the bustle of the modern world, when so many people complain that they lack the time to pray regularly every day? Do ejaculations not offer a solution? They are as valid for the Christian who is educated as for one who is not. . . . The desert Fathers made use of this kind of prayer at every moment . . . Cassian recommended the recitation of the first words of *Psalm* 70(69): 'Oh God, come quickly to my aid, Lord, make haste to help me.' "

part of this life, and make up the unavoidably sorrowful side of it. "I have the feeling that what is asked of us is to live in the storm of life, without keeping back any of our substance, without keeping back anything for ourselves, neither rest nor friendships nor health nor leisure—to pray incessantly and that even without leisure—in fact to let ourselves pitch and toss in the waves of the divine will till the day when it will say: 'It is enough.' " [116]

The fact remains that the Lord told us to pray in the secrecy of our chamber, and that we should be bent on doing so as often as possible. In the present state of our civilization women are reduced to slavery by the absence of human help in domestic life; a mother of a family has to do everything by herself in her house, and the more mechanical gadgets she has at her disposal the more she is a slave. Men, too (a little less enslaved), are enchained to their work and most often worn out by the worries of daily breadwinning. In spite of everything, I do not think that it is impossible, since one still finds quite a bit of time for chit-chat or television, to give every day a little time, *however little it might be*, to praying in private, door closed.

That is the only more or less fixed rule, it seems to me, in a state of life that does not admit of fixed rules. And when one has absolutely no time for contemplative prayer, there always remains the desire of the heart, and that benignity of divine manners of which we spoke earlier: "If it happens that someone cannot weep, a single word from a contrite heart is enough for God. And if someone would lose the use of his tongue, God would be well pleased with the moaning of his heart." [117]

★

On the roads of the world we do not encounter only the afflictions of the world, we know also its beauty; we see it "shining from its numberless stars." At every moment we have to deal with the foolish ways of our nature and of our natural love for creatures; at every moment we also have to deal with the grandeur and dignity of our nature, as well as with the sweetness and nobility of our natural love for creatures.

[116] *Journal de Raïssa, op. cit.*, p. 212.
[117] *Des Moeurs divines*, tract attributed to St. Thomas Aquinas (trans. by Raïssa Maritain, Paris, Libr. de l'Art Catholique, 1921).

One is not more subject to temptation in the world than in the desert. One is there, however, less well-armed against temptation than in the desert or the cloister. This is the misfortune of life in the world. But in compensation, one is in a better position not to slander nature,[118] that nature which God had made, to recognize still its grandeur and its dignity even in the midst of temptation,[119] to understand that it is never evil as such that tempts us, it is always some "ontological" good—often even morally innocent and sometimes noble *in itself*—but one that God's law and his love command us to refuse, because to attain it by such given means or under such given circumstances we would have to violate the order of things.

Moreover, it is of course true that grace perfects nature and does not destroy it, but this means in effect that grace perfects nature by going beyond it, and transforms it (according to the law of all transformation) by making it give up that which, in its own order, and not without reason, it holds most dear.

> *Let us go*
> *For the sake of God, beauty itself must be forsaken*
> *He holds in His hand the starry universe.*[120]

"Sacrifice is an absolutely universal law for the perfecting of the creature. Everything which passes from a lower nature to a higher nature has to pass through self-sacrifice, mortification and death.

---

[118] I should have put this sentence in the past tense. Who slanders nature today? Certainly not study gatherings held by members of religious orders. Everyone venerates it; but they do so foolishly, I mean insofar only as nature is mirrored in man's science and the uses he puts it to. Nature is more chaste and more mysterious than we think. When it comes to looking at it and respecting it truly, there are only the poet, the contemplative, and painters like the Chinese, or Breughel or Jean Hugo. If we venerate it so stupidly today, it is undoubtedly because our ancestors slandered it stupidly over too long a period of time, in misreading great ascetic writers. The fact remains that, when a conceited naturalism spreads in consecrated circles, it is there that it shows itself the funniest and the most foolish.

[119] "Nature laments, she pleads her cause with prodigious eloquence, with a terrible power of seduction. She is not rebellious, she is not perverse. She is herself. And being able to desire only life, she has to consent to death. . . ." *Journal de Raïssa, op. cit.*, p. 51.

[120] Raïssa, *Douceur du monde* (in *Lettre de Nuit*). From the translation of Raïssa's thirty Poems by a Benedictine of Stanbrook, Worcester, Stanbrook Abbey Press, 1965.

The mineral assimilated by the plant becomes living matter. The vegetable which is consumed is transformed in the animal into sensible living matter. The man who yields up his whole soul to God through the obedience of faith, finds it again in glory. The angel who has renounced the natural light of his intelligence to plunge himself in the darkness of faith, has found the splendor of divine light. . . ." [121]

A soul given to love-prayer in the world, and within its beauty, is thus in a better position to acquire some understanding—at great price—of the very mystery of temptation (which can stir up in us a great deal of human filth, but does not in itself involve any sin, as long as we do not yield to it). I mean that the contemplative in the world is in a better position to have a presentiment that what temptation aims at operating in us is not so much a destruction as a transfiguration, less an annihilation of something in us than a transference —through death—to a higher life, where it becomes worthy to be offered to God and to unite with him.

> When I have vanquished you, O my life, O my death,
> When I am free of the hard pull of joy
> And have gained my heavenly liberty,
>   When I have chosen the hardest way,
>   My heart will rest in the balance of grace,
> But I shall retain you, love,
> Retain from you not death, but life,
> And I shall discover you, happiness,
> Having given my Lord the whole of myself.
> Like a prosperous ship, her cargo intact,
> Which safe into harbour comes again,
> I shall sail to heaven with transfigured heart,
> Bearing human gifts made free from stain. [122]

I would like to quote here some passages from the *Journal de Raïssa* which express what I would like to say better than I could do: "In the heart of the strong man temptation can acquire a degree of acuteness all the greater because God, who assists at the conflict in

121 *Journal de Raïssa, op. cit.*, p. 55.
122 "Transfiguration," in R. M., *Lettre de Nuit, op. cit.*, p. 80–81.

the soul of the just (or of whoever desires to become so), knows that he will triumph in it by His grace. The human heart is then probed in all its depth. . . . The richness, the complexity of nature is somewhat dazzling. And yet the man tempted to this point, who resists, strong in faith, marvels at a still greater wonder. He soars above all this magnificent and shattered nature by the impetus of his spirit." [123]

"God wants us to offer him, from every thing and every affection, whatever there is in them of being and of beauty.

"He does not want dead offerings. He wants offerings that are pure and full of life. But, of course, where purification has taken place, something has had to die. And what remains is transformed, transfigured. Affection has entered into the order of charity.

"What must be removed from human love—to render it pure, beneficent, universal and divine—is not love itself. No, what must be suppressed or rather surpassed, are the limits of the heart. Hence the suffering—in this effort to go beyond our narrow limits. For in these limits, in *our* limits, is *our* human joy.

"But we have to go beyond these limits of the heart; we have, under the action of grace and through the travail of the soul, to leave our bounded heart for the boundless heart of God. This is truly dying to ourselves. It is only when one has accepted this death that one enters, resurrected, into the boundless heart of God, with all that one loves, all the spoils of love, giving oneself up as prey to the infinite love.

"Death to ourselves makes free room for the love of God. But at the same time it makes free room for the love of creatures according to the order of divine charity.

"Tread one's heart oneself in the winepress. Lay one's heart on the Cross." [124]

"All love must be transformed into Love as grapes are transformed into wine—under the press." [125]

God does not want dead offerings. We must bring him offerings human and without stain. We must go beyond the limits of the heart.

---

[123] *Journal de Raïssa, op. cit.,* p. 61.
[124] *Ibid.,* p. 221.
[125] *Ibid.,* p. 220.

We must transform all love into Love. All that, the one who prays in the world is, I believe, in a better position to understand a little than the one who prays cut off from the world.

☆

"The Church is all mingled with sin"; we were told that earlier.[126] In another way that is true also for those who devote themselves to love-prayer on the roads of this world, no doubt truer for them than for the cloistered. And it is a privilege for their life of prayer. For sin is indeed a great mystery, and it is fitting that those who pray draw a little closer to this mystery "In the very sin of the creature subsists a mystery which is sacred to us; this wound, at least, belongs to him; it is a pitiable good for which he pawns his eternal life, and in whose folds are hidden the justice and compassion of God. To heal this wound Christ willed to die. In order to see as deeply as he does into the sinful soul, one would have to love it with as much tenderness and purity." [127]

When we meet a sinner we should be seized with great respect, as in the presence of one condemned to death—who can live again, and have in paradise, close to Jesus, a higher place than we.

As I write these lines I have before me the memento of Jacques Fesch, "born on Passion Sunday, April 6, 1930, condemned to death April 6, 1957, on the eve of Passion Sunday, executed at dawn, October 1, 1957." He had come back to God in his prison. In his last letters we find the following: "The nails in my hands are real, and the nails *accepted*. I understand better all the purity of Christ contrasted with my abjection. Since I accept wholeheartedly the will of the Father, I am receiving joy after joy" (August 16). "The execution will take place tomorrow morning, about four o'clock in the morning; may the will of God be done in all things . . . Jesus is very near to me. He draws me closer and closer to him, and I can only adore him in silence, wishing to die of love. . . . I await love! In five hours I will see Jesus! He draws me gently to him, giving me that peace which is not of this world. . . ." A little later he observes: "Peace has left me and given place to anguish, my heart is bursting in my breast.

---

126 Charles Journet, *Théologie de l'Eglise.* Cf. p 186.
127 *Frontières de la Poésie,* "Dialogues," p. 115.

Holy Virgin, have pity on me! . . ." And then: "I am calmer now than a moment ago, because Jesus promised me he will take me straight to Paradise, and that I will die as a Christian. . . . I am happy, farewell." (Night of September 30 to October 1, the sixtieth anniversary of the death of St. Therese of Lisieux.)

The enigma of sin raises many questions in our minds, and first of all questions on the enigma of the human being in his relationship with God. "One can also say that there are two categories of men: those who—what mystery!—are capable of assimilating sin, and those who are not capable of doing so (by virtue of some mystery of predestination . . .).

"Those who are capable of assimilating sin, of living with sin, almost of living on it; of drawing from it a useful experience, a certain human enrichment, a development, even a perfecting, in the order of mercy and humility—of arriving, finally, at the knowledge of God, at a certain theodicy, through extreme experience of the misery of the sinner. The Russians are like this, as typified in Dostoievsky's characters. What is rare about them is that they are conscious of this capacity to profit in the end from sin. The majority of sinners have this capacity too, without knowing it.

"Those who are incapable of assimilating sin, because the smallest deliberate sin is like a fishbone stuck in their throat, cannot rest till they have got rid of it by contrition and confession. These are called to be assimilated to Christ. They can accept or refuse. It is a redoubtable moment when they hear this call—it is the voice of Jesus himself." [128]

Why should the smallest deliberate sin be to such souls like a fishbone in the throat? Because they fear hell? Certainly not. Fear of damnation may invade them at certain moments of trial and extreme affliction, but it is certainly not the substance of their lives. The holy fear of God is a fear of offending him, always present because of his infinite transcendence; it is not a fear of him. Fear is a poor regime for the human soul. It is because so many men are still far from God that they have a fear entirely different from the holy fear of God, and which ravages them, a fear of the sanctions of his law—and of God himself.

[128] *Journal de Raïssa, op. cit.,* pp. 226–227.

"If your right eye is an occasion of sin to you, pluck it out" (*Matt.* 5:29). We were told this out of love, not out of a fear of being disobeyed which is proper to the rulers of the earth. And it is love that echoes the precept in us. The closer man comes to God, the more he understands his love and his mercy—did Jesus not come "for sinners, rather than for the just" (*Matt.* 9:13), did he not tell Peter to forgive seventy-seven times seven times? And the parable of the prodigal son, and Jesus at the table of Levi, son of Alphaeus, and at the table of Zacchaeus, and Jesus at Jacob's well confiding unheard secrets to the Samaritan woman, and Jesus before the adultress, and Jesus while Mary Magdalene kisses his feet and covers them with perfume? Has not God a passion to pardon? To such a point that he cannot help himself, as soon as anybody recognizes himself as a sinner? "If someone speaks a word against the Son of Man, it shall be forgiven him; but to him who blasphemes against the Holy Spirit, it will not be forgiven" (*Luke* 12:10). Sin against the Holy Spirit is sin against Love and Mercy, which prevents us from asking God's pardon. "Her sins, many as they are, shall be forgiven her, because she has loved much. The one to whom less is forgiven has a less great love." (*Luke* 7:47)

When they think of such words, are not the saints tempted to envy sinners, and that sort of truly mad trust, enormous to the point of breaking any norm, by which, in wounding God and in breaking his law, they still (without knowing it—though Dostoievsky's sinners have some suspicion of this) render homage to the infinity of his mercy? Does the obedient trust of the saints seem less abandoned (less "mad")? In reality it *is* more abandoned, because there is no fear in it except the fear of offending God; the fear of punishment for themselves, fear for their own skin, has been eclipsed; and their trust demands nothing less than the Infinite One, the Inaccessible One, the divine Life, the kiss of God; their trust is mad with love. Let them not be afraid of having a less great love because less has been forgiven them (they have asked pardon for all human weakness and all the sins of men, they have opened themselves more widely to the supreme gift and pardon that is grace). Whether they have known sin like Magdalene or Augustine, or always preserved the innocence of baptism like Thomas Aquinas or St. Louis de Gonzaga, is all the same—theirs is the greatest love.

What is it, then, that is like a fishbone in the throat to men who are "incapable of assimilating sin"? It is not fear, it is love. They know what love is, and what sin is—it has crucified the God they love. They are drunk with love for God and for Jesus. Through this love they are riveted to Jesus, and to the desire to enter into his heart and into his work, and to carry with him that cross which saves the world.

As to the sinners of Dostoievsky, what they have in their own right, it seems to me, is that, unlike others, they are, in sin—and even with I know not what complacency—attentive to the misery of sin, and have also within them, rooted in the irrational depths of the soul, an obscure awareness of that *enormous and reckless trust* of which I have just spoken, and on which they play their game—as long as despair and suicide do not come along. And they do not know what love is, because they are afraid of it.

☆

One cannot love Jesus without wanting to enter into his work. All those who are dedicated to contemplative prayer, whether in religious communities or on the roads of the world, know this equally well. I readily believe that in religious communities, because, there, one has left everything for God, there are more who put this knowledge into practice, sometimes heroically. But those who walk along the roads of the world, deprived of the help that consecrated people find in their rule and in their vows, are at least offered by their secular life, I think, a kind of compensation: that thing—the call to enter into Christ's work—which it matters essentially to know, they are constantly reminded of it, because they live in the midst of sinners.

To enter into the work of Jesus is to participate in the work of redemption that he accomplished fully by himself; it is to pursue with him and through him, as being one with him, a work of coredemption that will be fully accomplished only at the end of the world, and to which all Christians are called in one degree or another, and under one form or another.

It was not by some gesture of royal amnesty, as He could so easily have done (a single cry of pity before the Father, coming from him, could have saved mankind), that Christ carried out the mission for which he was a man like us. He made atonement in strict justice,[129]

---

[129] He only merited and could merit *for others* in strict justice and *by a right* acquired in this way.

and for all the sins of all men, because he willed to take all men in himself, and "all human suffering." [130] And he also willed, because of his love for them and because of the superabundance "beyond any measure of reason" which is proper to God, that they themselves consummate this work of redemption with him and through him present in them—each for his own sake at first, freely receiving grace, along with the merits communicated by it and by the infinite merits of Jesus—and each *for the others*, paying also for them, not in strict justice (only Christ could do that), but through an effect of the superabundance of the love in which he unites them to himself, and by virtue of those "rights" of another nature, gratuitous rights freely granted by the Loved One to the loving one, which the union of love creates.[131]

Here is that coredemption, the notion of which has such capital importance, and is called upon, I think, to enlighten and help Christian consciousness more and more. Through coredemption—following in the footsteps of the Virgin, who is Coredemptrix in a unique and absolutely super-eminent sense proper to her alone—all the redeemed (to infinitely different degrees, the indigence of some being compensated for by the abundance of others) pursue with Christ, and through him, and in him, his work of redemption, being raised by his love and his generosity from being simply redeemed to being redeemers as well.

" 'Jesus will be in agony till the end of the world.' There must be souls in which he continues to agonize." [132]

The "sensible Christians" who do not understand these things would do well, it seems to me, to ask themselves why the self-subsisting Being, who consummates in himself and in his infinite transcendence all the plenitude and perfection of being, wanted nonetheless *to create* other beings, who add absolutely nothing to divine Being, but into whom are poured out, infinitely remote from his infinite Perfection, finite participations in him. The same sensible

---

[130] *Sum. theol.*, III, q.46, a.5.

[131] It is this that the theologians—in a traditional jargon the specialists are fond of, but which is rather incongruous when applied to what is most precious in the world—call merit *de congruo*, in opposition to merit *de condigno*, of which only the Incarnate Word was capable. They seem to take pleasure in being understood only among themselves, to the exclusion of other mortals. . . .

[132] *Journal de Raïssa, op. cit.*, pp. 233–234.

Christians would do equally well, it seems to me, to ask themselves why Christ, who saved all, in one single moment of time, by the sacrifice of Calvary, has willed to have that sacrifice perpetuated all the days of our time through the Mass, which renders it sacramentally present on the altar.

There is a remarkable study on coredemption by Father Marie-Joseph Nicolas,[133] who, with a theologian's authority I am far from pretending to, gives us basic insight into the subject. Father Nicolas is careful to establish the essential distinction we must make between the unique coredemption of Mary mediatrix, participant in the work of the Redeemer Jesus—in her inferior status as creature receiving all from her Son (but immaculate creature)—*in the very act* of redemption, and, on the other hand, the common coredemption to which all Christians are called, and which makes them participate in the work of Jesus the Redeemer only as to *the application* of the fruits of redemption. I am sorry I cannot reproduce here this entire study. Still I would like to quote a few passages that I found particularly significant.

"It is a greater thing for man *to redeem himself, to make atonement himself for the evil he did, to rehabilitate himself,* than to be saved without doing anything himself. Hence it follows that the economy of Redemption is dominated entirely and down to its last detail by the idea that *man must save himself.* It is because man is incapable of doing so that God becomes man. But in making himself man he did not destroy the part that man has to play in Redemption. On the contrary, he made it fully possible." [134]

"Christ did not want to take advantage of being God in order to suffer less. He bore upon himself all the weight that one who would have been purely a man would have had to bear, he redeemed us *as man,* his divinity diminishing nothing of the human burden, but taking it upon itself and endowing his actions as man with the supreme value of infinite sanctity and the universal range of action that the most painful purely human sufferings could never have attained. God did not make himself man in order to dispense man from satisfying and atoning, but on the contrary in order to permit him to do so. From this it follows, as far as we are able to understand

133 M.-J. Nicolas, "La Co-rédemption," *Revue Thomiste,* 1947, I.
134 *Ibid.,* p. 30.

the profound mystery of the Cross, that the Divine Will linked our salvation to an act [a *human* act of a Person who was *God*] that by its nature comprises all that mankind would have had to suffer in order to purify itself of its faults. *Christus sustinuit omnem passionem humanam.*" [135]

Consequently, "Christ, far from dispensing us from suffering and death by his sacrifice, invites us to follow him and to reenact in ourselves, for us and for our brothers, that Passion which superabundantly merits for us all grace and all beatitude. . . . If the Passion of Christ were not continued in humanity, it would not be a sufficiently human work. . . ." Commenting on the celebrated text of St. Paul to the Colossians already quoted in this book, St. Thomas states: "What was lacking in Christ's own sufferings was that they had not suffered by him in the bodies of St. Paul and of other Christians."[136] Consequently, we must say that "the entire Church is Coredemptrix [137] since she cooperates in the redemption of men, not only as an instrument of the grace of Christ but by the offering of her own sacrifice." [138] And by the same token we must say that "all Christians are coredeemers." [139]

"Of course, many men will be saved without having contributed their full share. Others, on the contrary, will have given in super-

135 *Ibid.*, p. 31. The text quoted is taken from the *Sum. theol.*, III, 46, 5.

136 *Ibid.*, p. 32. Cf. p 184; also farther, p. 252.

137 The entire Church is coredemptrix; the saints above all, but also all the "good people" of whom Tauler speaks, or in brief, all the baptized, as Cardinal Journet says, in the pages of v. II of *L'Eglise du Verbe Incarné* in which he treated of coredemption (pp. 221–227 and 323–340).

" 'And from his fullness have we all received, grace upon grace.' (*John* 1:16). In passing from the head to the members, from Christ to the Church, grace does not lose its properties; and as it impelled Christ to satisfy, it will impel Christians following in his footsteps to join in the great movement of reparation to God for the sins of the world. What Christ did, Christians will strive to do, following his example: 'Christ also suffered for you, leaving you an example, that you should follow in his steps' (I *Peter*, 2:21). How would there be, between the Head and the Body, symbiosis and synergy if the action begun in the Head did not spread in the rest of the Body, if the suffering endured by Christ were not completed in his disciples? 'Now I rejoice in my sufferings for your sake, and in my flesh I complete what is lacking in Christ's afflictions for the sake of his Body, that is, the Church' (*Col.* 1:24). The difficulty does not lie in explaining so simple a truth; it lies rather in explaining how Protestantism came to reject it" (*op. cit.*, p. 221). The question of coredemption has already been touched on p. 184.

138 *Ibid.*, p. 44.

139 *Ibid.*, p. 33.

abundant measure. As charity grows, there is a proportionate increase
in the desire and power of cooperating in the salvation of many
souls. Some, by *special function* and by their *state of life*, are thus
dedicated to the work of salvation, and the charity that they dispense
in the service of the Church inspires not only apostolic action but
self-sacrifice on their part whose bearing goes well beyond the efficacy
of their words. To others it is charity alone, without external works,
that gives this destination. Such a one was St. Therese of Lisieux,
who, in the Body of the holy Church, felt herself to be *the heart*." [140]

"This absolute conformity of the will of the saint to that of God,
which merits for him, St. Thomas said, that God in return accomplish
his will by listening to his prayers for his brothers, is the basis both of
the additional merit due to love, and of the power of intercession.
The greater the charity of a saint, the more powerful is his prayer.
And the more close and personal his ties with the members of the
mystical Body, the more his right to be heard applies to
them. . . ." [141]

"Let us not be afraid to see too many creatures associated with this
unique Creature that is the humanity of Christ. Because strictly speaking, the humanity of Christ is created, but it is not a creature; it belongs substantially and personally to the Creator. Because of that it
is an instrument of God in a unique and incommunicable sense. It
receives in turn the power of associating with itself the rest of the
created world as a sort of extension of itself, and of communicating
to others from its plenitude without ceasing to be the source and the
first principle. When we have understood that the profound meaning
of the Incarnation is the widest possible diffusion of the divine among
creatures, the whole mystery, not only of the divinization of man,
but of the cooperation of man in his own divinization, becomes
clearer." [142]

I have felt it important to recall the foundation of the doctrine of
coredemption as it has been submitted to our reflection by an eminent theologian. The notion of coredemption, indeed, is as old as
Christianity and the Mass. It is because it is simply but one with the
Christian faith in redemption that this notion took a lot of time to

---

[140] *Ibid.*, p. 33.
[141] *Ibid.*, p. 40.
[142] *Ibid.*, p. 43.

emerge explicitly (in the last centuries of the Middle Ages and in the following centuries), and finally to find itself denoted by a special word (about half a century ago, I think), and conceptualized in an articulated theological doctrine (with the element of controversy that is never lacking in such cases). The word now has complete freedom of the city in the Church (it appears in two decrees of the Holy Office,[143] and equivalent terms have been employed in solemn documents of the Sovereign Pontiffs). And it is in the perspective pointed out by Père Nicolas, I have no doubt, that doctrinal agreement will be achieved among Catholic theologians. It would be an accomplished fact today except for the fear, felt by some of our scholars, of annoying that good man Luther, a fear that has nothing to do with a genuinely ecumenical spirit. But this type of easy-going zeal quickly wears off, and if the common agreement in question is not for today, it is for tomorrow, I firmly hope so.

In any case, in order to live in their prayers and agonies the reality of coredemption, with and through Jesus present in us by his grace, contemplative souls did not wait for the speculative intellect gradually to disengage the doctrine and explanations which deal with it. They knew this truth by experience, they knew that, like the truth (of which it is but an essential aspect) of the redemption by the "Son of Man," Head of the mystical Body, it is dear above all to Christian faith and life. St. Catherine of Sienna, St. Catherine de Ricci and St. Angela of Foligno, Tauler, St. Paul of the Cross, Marie of the Incarnation, St. John of the Cross, and St. Therese of Lisieux, and many others—it is not my task to recall all the great testimony that contemplatives since the Apostle Paul have given to this truth.

But since this not-too conventional book (or this sort of testament), written in haste in the evening of my life, is in my mind entirely dedicated to the one who instructed my poor philosopher's head in the things of God; and since this last chapter, in particular, could not have been written without the help I have always received from her, I will certainly be permitted to quote her still further, and to present here some of her thoughts on the subject that occupies our attention.

To a mother tortured by the loss of her child, Raïssa wrote: "That Pasch of which the Lord said, 'With desire I have desired to eat this

[143] Denzinger, ed. 21–23, 1937, no. 1978 a, n. 2.

Pasch with you'—you are eating it now with our Saviour: the Pasch of the Passion and of the Crucifixion, through which salvation comes to men. Through your sorrow and your patience you are coredeemers with Christ.

"It is the sublime yet ordinary truth of Christianity, that suffering united with love works salvation . . .

"God has suddenly plunged you both into the very heart of this ultimate reality: redeeming suffering. And when one knows by faith (that is to say, with all possible certitude) the marvels he works with our suffering, with the substance of our crushed hearts—can one coldly refuse him?" [144]

I am still reading from Raïssa's notes: "In some manner, I am having personal experience of that great mystery St. Paul speaks of, making up *what is lacking* in the Passion of Christ.

"Being the Passion of God, it is forever gathered up into the eternal. What is lacking to it is *development in time.*

"Jesus suffered only during a certain time. He cannot himself develop his Passion and death in time. Those who consent to let themselves to be penetrated by him to the point of being perfectly assimilated to him, accomplish, throughout the whole length of time, what is lacking in his Passion. They have consented to become *flesh of his flesh.* Terrible marriage, in which love is not only strong as death but begins by being a death, and a thousand deaths.

" 'I will espouse thee in blood.'

" 'I am a bridegroom of blood.'

" 'It is a terrible thing to fall into the hands of the living God.'

"And Jesus's words to St. Angela of Foligno: 'It is not in jesting that I have loved you.' " [145]

All Christians, as Raïssa wrote in the letter quoted just before this text, and as Père M.-J. Nicolas reminded us earlier, are called to the

---

[144] *Journal de Raïssa, op. cit.,* p. 105. Further on, apropos of those who by the grace of Christ belong invisibly to the Church in non-Christian lands: "Can we not say that the souls which are saved in this way do not collaborate actively in the salvation of the world? They are saved, but they do not save. . . ." (At least, we thought, they collaborate actively in the salvation of the world only by the fervor of their individual intercession, not by virtue of the great common work of coredemption accomplished by the Body of which Christ is the Head, and into which the baptized are incorporated perfectly enough for the part to act *through the whole,* the member *through the whole body.) Ibid.,* pp. 191–192.

[145] *Ibid.,* p. 228.

work of coredemption, some "without contributing their full share," others "giving in superabundant measure." [146] That superabundant share is the share of the contemplatives, and it is of that share that Raïssa is speaking here.

"There is also," she adds, "a *fulfillment* of the Passion which can be given only by fallible creatures, and that is the struggle against the fall, against the attraction of *this world* as such, against the attraction of so many sins which represent human happiness. That gift Jesus could not make to the Father; only we can do it. It involves a manner of redeeming the world, and of suffering, which is accessible only to sinners. By renouncing the good things of this world, which, in certain cases more numerous than one might think, sin would have procured us—by giving to God our human and temporal happiness, we give him, proportionately, as much as he gives us, because we give him *our all*, the widow's mite of the Gospel." [147]

Why have I, in a section entitled *Contemplation on the roads*, treated of things that concern all contemplatives, and primarily, no doubt, those who have left everything to consecrate themselves to God?

At first, because it seemed to me opportune to recall that they concern *also* those who seek to unite themselves to God on the roads of the world. Then because, in spite of all the difficulties and the obstacles that they encounter on this path—and that oblige them to adopt a rule of "profound and universal humility," perpetual thanksgiving for all the gratuitous blessings they have received, and completely surrendered trust in the mercy of God—they still have a certain advantage, with respect to the *prise de conscience* of the things in question: I mean, as I have already pointed out, that they, more than the others, live in constant contact with sinners and with sin, and therefore with the great mystery into which "so many sinners in the world" force anyone to enter who says to himself: it is for them that Christ came and that he died on the cross, and he does not cease to love them and to will their salvation, and his work of redemption continued by the Church cannot be in vain.

[146] Cf. p. 249.
[147] *Journal de Raïssa, op. cit.*, pp. 228–299.

THE DISCIPLES—JAMES AND JOHN

In the life of every contemplative—depending on Christ's choice, or, in other words, on the requests (sometimes unconscious, perhaps) of the soul and the reply which is made—in the life of every contemplative there may come a moment when it is necessary to answer a great and redoubtable question—even if while not daring to say yes, out of fear (and there is good reason to be afraid), but knowing that that point must certainly be passed and relying on the grace of God, and, in fact, accepting by not saying no—the great and redoubtable question that the Lord asked James and John—the question of the Chalice: "*Potestis bibere calicem, quem ego bibiturus sum,*" are you able to drink the cup that I am to drink? (*Matt.* 20:22). This moment is indeed a crucial one.

Père Lallemant, in *La Doctrine Spirituelle*, told us on the other hand: "It is necessary only to renounce for once and for all, all our advantages and all our satisfactions, all our designs and all our desires, in order to depend no longer on anything but God's good pleasure." And the moment in which the soul makes this renunciation he calls the moment of *passing over the step*. This also depends on the free choice of Jesus, in other words on the desires of the soul and the response that they receive.

I think that the *moment of the Chalice* and the *moment of passing over the step* are but one and the same; [148] and that it presents itself to such and such among us in a different fashion, by reason of the fact that among the souls that have passed under the regime of the gifts of the Holy Spirit, some find themselves above all under the regime of

[148] The moment of which I am speaking here must not be confused with another, which precedes it (cf. p. 231) in which the soul passes *under the regime of the gifts*, or enters into the life of the spirit. In the moment when it entered under the regime of the gifts of the Holy Spirit, the soul, in a manner completely hidden in the spiritual supra-conscious, crossed a threshold, the end of a transitional phase which also is too profound to be perceived by consciousness. From that point on the soul will live under the habitual motion of the gifts of the Holy Spirit.

In the moment of which I am speaking here the soul is already under the regime of these gifts, and it is to a consciously perceived call, to a *question* that it must answer.

those (Wisdom, Understanding and Knowledge) which are concerned more with contemplative life, and others find themselves
under the regime of the gifts which are more concerned with active
life (the first three gifts are always there, of course, in this seven-
stringed lyre on which God plays at will in the soul, but vibrating
then under less frequent and lighter touches, like a muted accompani-
ment of the stronger sound of the other strings).

Among the souls who have entered into the life of the spirit, therefore, there are those who are engaged in the active life (they also have
the contemplation of love, but atypical or *masked*)—let us say that
they follow the lead of Martha, or of the Apostle James; and there are
some who are engaged above all, or exclusively, in the contemplative
life—let us say that they follow the lead of Mary, the sister of Martha,
or that of John, whose head rested on the heart of Jesus at the Last
Supper. For the latter, the moment of which we are speaking now, if
and when it comes, presents itself, no doubt, with particular clarity
and sharpness.

In any case, for both groups it is one and the same moment: the
moment when they are called to become *disciples*, and when they accept or reject the call. (In my opinion refusal is probably quite rare,
yet there is the case of the rich young man who would certainly have
wanted to be perfect, and who went away sorrowful . . .) (*Matt.*
19:22).

There I am touching on something that seems to me terribly mysterious, but of which we must try to be somewhat aware, since its role
is of primary importance in the general economy of Christianity: the
distinction we must recognize, among the members of the People of
God, between the disciples and the great mass of—let us not say "the
ordinary Christians," which would be a rather inept expression, for a
Christian is never *ordinary*—let us say the always beloved of Jesus, for
whom he gave his Blood, whom he thirsts to save, and for whom his
Mother weeps in beatitude. What are we to think, then? It is the disciples that he entrusts in particular with doing the job with him and
through him.

We must admit that they are probably not numerous. Here I quote
Raïssa:

" 'If any man come to me and hate not his father, and mother, and wife, and children, and brethren, and sisters, yea and his own life also, *he cannot be my disciple.'* (*Luke* 14:26)

"The demands of Christ as regards his *disciples* are absolutely inhuman, they are divine. There is no doubt about it, he who wishes to be Christ's disciple—*must hate his own life*. The image of Jesus Crucified is *for the disciple*.

"But such demands are *only* for the disciples. As regards the common body of men, Christianity is *human* in the sense that it accepts men in their weakness and inconstancy, and also in their nature attached to natural goods (father, mother, etc.). They will never feel an inward call as severe as the one that St. Luke records.

"All that is demanded of them is to believe, to love, and to continue to hope after they have gone astray, however wildly.

"Thus it is not the sinners, the 'worldly,' who have the greatest fear of God—rather it is those who, having been chosen as disciples, know that they are, and will be, more severely treated. From these, *all* is demanded." [149]

And Raïssa said further: "I am coming now to take humanity quietly—for what it is. Without exclamations—regrets—sighs—and groans. In a way quite different from that of Leibnizian optimism—all is for the best. *God knows what he permits.*

"He is not like a man who regretfully permits what he cannot prevent. He has let men go their own way armed with their freedom—and they go it. They go, gamble and work, risk everything—win more or less, and perhaps will end by winning everything. God has simply reserved for himself one Man who is his Son. And this Man-God calls to himself, for his own work (which he also has to do with human freedom), calls a small number of men—a handful in every century —to work in his own way. 'He who would be my disciple, let him take up *his* cross and follow me'—and that is sufficient.

"To all is given the precept of charity—the duty of hope—and this word which is the foundation of hope: 'Much will be forgiven her for she has loved much.' " [150]

I have just said that this book, written by the old Jacques with the liberty of those who have seen too much, is all dedicated to Raïssa. It

149 *Journal de Raïssa, op. cit.*, p. 345.
150 *Ibid.*, p. 341.

is fitting, therefore, that it should close with a text of hers, in which one feels the urgency of certain things "that must be said to men," and of which I think our times stand in particular need.

The True Face of God
or
Love and the Law
(Text of Raïssa[151])

Tried and tempted souls feel vaguely that the law, which is so hard for them to observe, cannot be identified with God who is love.

But this feeling either remains vague, or else leads to a certain contempt for the law, or else turns the soul against God who is then seen as a hard and exacting master—which is to deny God—or would be to deny God, if the soul pushed such thoughts to their final conclusion, to their logical consequences.

Well, it is salutary to *distinguish* (to speak in legal terms) *the case of God from the case of the Law.*

Only by grasping that distinction, can the soul behave as it should toward God—and toward the law.

When Jesus felt himself abandoned by God on the Cross, it was because the face of Love was then hidden from him, and the whole of his humanity was subjected to the law, without any mitigation—something which no man except the Man-God would have been able to endure without dying.

Jesus on the Cross, and very particularly at that moment of total dereliction, suffered the full rigor of the law of the transmutation of one nature into another—*as if* he had not been God; it was his humanity as such, taken from the Virgin, which had to feel the full weight of this law. For the head must experience the law that he imposes on his members. Because, having assumed human nature, he had to experience this supreme law to which human nature, called to participate in the divine nature, is subject.

And if he had not suffered from the rigor of this law, it would not

151 *Ibid.*, p. 341.

have been possible to say that the Word took a heart like our own in order to feel for our sufferings.

This law of the transformation of natures—which comprises in it all moral and divine laws—is something necessary, physical, ontological if you like—God himself cannot abolish it, just as he cannot produce the absurd.

But this law—the Law—is not He—He is Love.

So when a soul suffers, and suffers from this inexorable Law of transmutation of a nature into a higher nature (and this is the meaning of all human history)—God is with this nature which he has made and which is suffering—he is not against it. If he could transform that nature into his own by abolishing the law of suffering and death, he would abolish it—because he takes no pleasure in the spectacle of pain and death. But he cannot abolish any law inscribed in being.

The face of the law and its rigor, the face of suffering and death is not the face of God; God is love.

And his love has made him behave toward men in a way that may seem capricious.

To the Ancients, like Abraham and the other Patriarchs, he did not reveal the whole law; in that state of nature he did not even reveal to men all the moral laws inscribed in nature. Because the observation of the whole body of these laws would have supposed the perfection of human nature to be already realized—and this was not so—or else would have demanded the help of Christic graces [152] which were not yet acquired. Hence that strange liberty left to men in the state of nature—even when these men are Abram,[153] Isaac and Jacob—and then Moses and the Jews, up to the coming of Christ. And yet it was in this state that God chose Abram to be the Father of Believers.

Abram, this simple man, with a heart which never resists the voice of God. *He believes God* who speaks to him. He does what God tells him to do. He goes from sacrifice to sacrifice: first he leaves his country

---

[152] All graces received by men since the fall of Adam are Christic graces. But Raïssa is speaking here of the graces of Christ *come*, or of *sacramentally Christic* graces. [J.]

[153] Abraham was first called Abram; that is why Raïssa, in this passage, freely used the two names. Cf. her *Histoire d'Abraham ou les premiers âges de la conscience morale.* English translation in v. I of *The Bridge*, published by Msgr. John Oesterreicher. [Trans.]

and his father—the hearths of Ur of the Chaldees—he accepts the nomadic life. And then he quits easy faith; it is relatively easy to believe God when he promises abundant blessings—and an immense posterity—but when the only son, the still sterile boy, has to be sacrificed, how painful it is to believe! And it would even be impossible to obey—since obedience here requires the commission of what appears to be a crime—if faith did not lead Abram as if by the hand.

Never was greater grace of faith in God given to any man. And never was any man greater in his fidelity—if we except Joseph and Mary.

Thus Abraham, too, knew the hard law of the transformation of the natural man into the spiritual and divine man—but with a wide zone of human liberty in which many laws, left in shadow by God, were put in parenthesis.

And, as for us, he has revealed to us all the terrible demands of the divinization of man.

But in order to reveal them to us, he came himself—not with the blood of goats and bulls—but with the Blood of Christ through which his Love for us is made visible.

Thus the new Law is harsher than the old Law.

But at the same time the love of God (which softens everything) is more widespread.

It is in the blood of Jesus Crucified that the Sacraments are born,
    whether they purify—Baptism
    whether they vivify—Penance
    whether they bring growth—the Eucharist . . .

The law—all the laws—having become so clearly, and so terribly visible,
    the face of the love of God thus risks being obscured.

This is why it is more necessary than ever to distinguish between Love and the Law.

When nature, called upon to obey, groans and suffers, she is not hateful to God, for quitting its own shape is a loss for all nature—a suffering for natures endowed with sensibility.

When human nature shrinks back and fails in this labor, it is not hateful to God; he loves it, he wants to save it—he does save it, provided it does not want to be separated from him, provided it recognizes the need of purification for salvation: if a sinner recognizes this only at the hour of his death, he is saved and goes to Purgatory to be purified.

So what one must first and foremost tell men, and go on telling them, is to love God—to know that he is Love and to trust to the end in his Love.

The law is just. The law is necessary—with the very necessity of transformation for salvation, that is to say, for eternal life with God.

But the law is not God.

And God is not the law. He is Love.

If God has the face of the law for men—men draw back because they feel that love is more than the law—in this they are wrong only because they do not recognize the salutary necessity of the law.

But the observation of the Law without love would be of no avail for salvation.

And love can save a man even at the last second of a bad life—if, in that second, the man has found the light of love—perhaps if he has always believed that God is Love.

Souls must be delivered from that feeling of enmity they experience (passively and actively) toward God when they see him in the apparatus of laws which to them is an image hostile to love—and which masks God's true face.

The Cross—it was the Law that imposed it on Jesus—so Jesus took it in order to share the harshness of the law with us.

These things must be said to men. If these things were not said, men would draw away from God when they suffer, because the law is a thing which seems to separate us from God, and then it presents itself—if we do not think of love—as our *enemy*, and God can never present himself as an enemy.

Law is, in a certain manner, opposed to love. God has made it insofar as he is the Creator of being. But insofar as he is our end and our beatitude, he calls us beyond it.

The law is proposed externally, it implies a subjection—in itself it seems to have nothing to do with mercy—nor with the equality of friendship—nor with familiarity.

It is truly a necessity; only a necessity.

Love *gives over the head of* the Law.

It forgives.

Love creates trust—freedom of spirit—equality—familiarity.

APPENDICES

I ON A TEXT OF ST. PAUL

(CF. CHAPTER 5, P. 119)

In an attempt to give support to his idea of a cosmic Christ, Teilhard invokes the thought of St. Paul, but in doing so he teilhardizes Paul in a way which cannot be accepted.

Let us reread the great text of the Epistle to the Romans (8: 12-22): "I consider that the sufferings of the present time are out of all proportion to the glory that will be revealed in us. For the creation in expectancy is longing for the revelation of the sons of God" [in glorified mankind]. "Indeed the creation has been subjected to vanity [τῇ ματαιότητι] (not of its own will, but because of [διὰ] him who subjected it) in hope, because the creation itself will be set free from the servitude to corruption so as to enter into the liberty of the children of God. For we know that the whole creation is groaning and in pains of childbirth up to that day." [1]

Christian thought did not wait for Père Teilhard to understand the words of St. Paul as it should be, that is, in a cosmic sense. The Greek Fathers already understood them in this sense, as did St. Thomas when he spoke in this connection (*Comm. on the Epistle to the Romans*, Ch. IV) of the *elementa hujus mundi*. But it would be senseless to look on the final end in question—the liberation awaited by creation—as the end result of the Evolution of created things in their ascent toward God and toward the Omega Point—an Evolution that can be conceived only as being of a *natural order* (even assuming that a cosmic Christ is the Prime Mover and the *Noyau collecteur*, the Nucleus in whom everything is gathered. Because if St. Paul's text gives the exegetes a great deal of trouble, one thing is still perfectly clear: that creation awaits a certain fulfillment of a *supernatural order*, since it is tied to the *revelation of the sons of God* and to *the glory that is to be revealed in us*, and to *entering into the glorious liberty of*

[1] The author's translation.

the children of God; that is, in the new world that will be inaugurated
by the Resurrection of the dead.

"Creation was *subjected* to *vanity* not of its own will" (that is to
say, against a consubstantial desire—it is a question of what philosophers and theologians call *un Désir de nature*, a "nature-desire," inscribed in the very being of things—or an ontological desire, even in
man, in whom this "nature-desire" gives rise to a conscious desire),
creation "will be set free from the *servitude to corruption*." What
greater vanity and what worse servitude than that of beings subject to
corruption, and of living beings subject to death? ("Who will free me
of this body of death?" asks St. Paul.) The "nature-desire" we are
speaking of is the desire to escape corruption and death. It is inscribed
in every being here on earth. But it is man who brings it out into the
light of consciousness and gives it a voice—a voice that is not simply
man's voice but that of the entire (material) creation, which man
epitomizes in himself: in such a way that when man bemoans corruption and death, he expresses not only the desire of man but the desire,
carried to its highest point, of all of creation. And yet what is more
impossible, for all creatures in this world, than escaping (through the
sole forces of nature) corruption and death?

It is through the *supernatural* transfiguration of man, head of all
creation (bound to matter, let it be understood—man himself is a
being of flesh) and by virtue of this transfiguration, it is through *the
glory that will be revealed in us,* it is through the *revelation of the
sons of God,* it is through *entering into the liberty* proper to their
glory, that the creation will find itself *supernaturally* transfigured,
transferred to a new world, or (in a perfectly unimaginable way,
moreover) will no longer be subject to corruption and death, and will
be set free.

Until that day it will groan, and will continue to suffer the pains of
childbirth ("in hope," that is, while hoping for liberation). That does
not mean that the coming of the world of glory will be the fruit of
cosmic Evolution! The great rupture caused by the thunderlightning
of the Resurrection, which will change everything, will have put an
end to the Evolution of the world in order to inaugurate the eternal
age of glorified matter and glorified man. The new world will be born
of the pains and groans of the creature, but as the fruit of its transfiguration by an act of God above the entire natural order and the
evolution of the world.

There is no reason to be astonished that a "nature-desire" might
long for something that goes beyond nature, and which nature is unable to satisfy; it is rather the contrary that would be surprising. An-

other example, a classic one in theology, of a "nature-desire" whose fulfillment cannot but be supernatural, is the desire to see God's essence. This desire is natural to man; he desires, precisely because of his intellectual nature, to see the Cause of being in its essence; and there is nothing in the equipment of his intellect (nor in that of the angel) that gives him the power to do so. To see God (to see God in so far as he is God, not in so far as he is the Cause of what is not God), the human intellect must be supernaturally transfigured, and it must see God not through any of the intelligible forms the reception of which can "actuate" it naturally, but through God himself, through the *divine essence itself* filling the created intellect with its infinite intelligibility, and taking within it the place of any intelligible form of which this intellect can make use as a natural means of knowing.

Since the text of St. Paul with which this note is dealing has been subjected all through the history of the Church to the most varied interpretations (those of the Teilhardians not included), and since this text is considered, it would seem, "the exegete's cross," I have deemed it permissible for a philosopher to suggest the interpretation that seems correct to him, after a meditation sufficiently free of intimidating preconceptions.

As to the clause *because of him who subjected it* (the creation has been "subjected to vanity, not of its own will, but because of him who subjected it . . ."), that clause refers, I think, to the pain suffered by all of creation from the fact of original sin, original sin having not only caused man to lose the immortality proper to the preternatural gifts of the state of innocence, but having also obliged the cosmos to remain [2] in that servitude from which it aspires to be set free. (I am assuming that in what St. Paul says is implied the idea that if Man had not sinned, he and the cosmos would have been transferred after a relatively short delay to a final state, "glorious" also, though incomparably less exalted than that which they will enjoy in fact through the merits of Christ crucified and risen. In such a glorious state men would have had the vision of God, but not as members of the Incarnate Son; and the cosmos would have been freed from the servitude to corruption, but without participating through Man in the glory of Christ.)

[2] Obviously the non-satisfaction of the trans-natural aspirations of nature could not, for the cosmos, have been of a *penal* character before the sin of man. If it acquired a *penal* character for the cosmos, it is only inasmuch as the sin of Man has a repercussion on the cosmos by *delaying* excessively (with respect to the original design of the *opus creativum*) the satisfaction of the trans-natural aspirations of the whole (material) creation.

2 ON TWO STUDIES DEALING WITH THE THEOLOGY OF PÈRE TEILHARD

(CF. CHAPTER 5, P. 122)

I am sorry that I did not, until it was too late to mention it in my text, know of the remarkable study of Claude Tresmontant on "Le Père Teilhard de Chardin et la Théologie" (in the periodical *Lettre*, nos. 49-50, September-October, 1962), and that I could refer to it only in this Appendix added after the proofs were ready.

Père Teilhard was neither a metaphysician nor a theologian; but Claude Tresmontant rightly lays stress on the fact that an intense metaphysical and theological preoccupation—entirely dominated, unfortunately, by a visionary scientist's cult for the World and for Cosmogenesis—was constantly at work in his thought, and constantly animated it.

It has always been hard for Teilhard to adjust to the Christian idea of creation. For him, "to create is to unite," [1] which is true only in the order of things effectuated or "created" by nature and by man. To create, he says further, is to "unify," [2] to unify the "pure multiple" —"the scattered shadow of his Unity" that "from all eternity, God saw beneath his feet," [3] and a "kind of positive Nothingness," [4] "a plea for being which it looks as if God had not been able to resist." [5] So that "God consummates himself only by uniting himself" [with the Else], [6] which is a view of Hegelian theogony rather than of Christian theology. [7] In 1953, Teilhard wrote: "What infuses Christianity with life is not a sense of the contingence of the created, but rather a sense of the *mutual Completion of the World and of God* [8]—"pleromization" he says further, [9] improperly invoking St. Paul: another Hegelian theme that can perhaps vitalize Teilhardian meta-Christianity, but is adverse to Christianity.

[1] *Comment je vois*, 1948, Par. 29; Tresmontant, p. 30.
[2] *La Lutte contre la Multitude*, February 26, 1917; Tr., p. 14.
[3] *Ibid.*, Tr., p. 13.
[4] *L'Union créatrice*, November, 1917; Tr. p. 16.
[5] *Comment je vois*, Par. 28, Tr., p. 28.
[6] *Ibid.*, Par. 27; Tr., p. 24.
[7] Cf. Tr., p. 27.
[8] *Contingence de l'Univers et goût humain de survivre*; Tr. p. 32.
[9] *Lettre à C. Tresmontant*, April 7, 1954; Tr. p. 33.

Apropos of another text of Teilhard: [10] "We become aware that in order to create (since, once again, to create is to unite), God is inevitably induced to immerse himself in the Multitude, in order to 'incorporate it' into himself," Claude Tresmontant notes (p. 40) that here Teilhard is alluding to the Incarnation, and that Christian thought will never accept "to link creation and the Incarnation by a bond of necessity, nor to call the Incarnation an 'immersion' in the Multiple": which is in keeping with the remarks that I made in Chapter 5.[11]

Another point on which the metaphysical and theological views of Teilhard clearly depart from Christian thought is the problem of Evil, a problem that, according to him, "in our modern perspective of a Universe in a process of *cosmogenesis . . . no longer exists:* [12] because the Multiple, "since it is multiple, that is to say essentially subject to the play of probabilities of chance in its arrangements," "is absolutely unable to progress toward unity without engendering Evil here or there—by statistical necessity." [13]

"Evil," Claude Tresmontant rightly observes, "is not simply a temporary defect in a progressive arrangement. The death of six million Jews in concentration camps, the resurgence of torture in colonial wars, are not the result of a wrong arrangement of the Multiple—but of the perverse freedom of man, of what is properly wickedness, contempt for man, the taste for destruction, falsehood, the will to power, the passions, the pride of the flesh and of the spirit." [14] "Evil is the work of man, and not of matter. Man is fully responsible for the evil that he does to man, for the crimes against man committed in the whole of mankind and in all places." [15] That is what Teilhard has always been reluctant to see. (He did not cry out in protest against the extermination of the Jews by the Nazis; while, in spite of the nobility of his heart, his passion for cosmogenesis led him to write intolerable lines on the "profound intuitions" of totalitarian systems, on the Abyssinian War, on the myths of fascism and communism.[16])

Claude Tresmontant is right to conclude: "No, sin, demoniacal deeds, cannot be explained by a 'statistical disorder.' This would come

[10] *Comment je vois*, Par. 29; Tr., p. 39.
[11] See p. 122.
[12] *Comment je vois*, Par. 29–30; Tr. p. 41.
[13] *Ibid.*
[14] Tr., pp. 42–43.
[15] Tr., p. 43.
[16] Cf. *Charles Journet, Nova et Vetera*, April–June, 1966, pp. 148, 149.

down to transposing to another order, the spiritual one, processes of thought that are valid in the study of Brownian movements." [17]

As for original sin, it is explained "for Teilhard, like evil, of which it is only a particular instance, by the Multiple. In summary, it is materiality that is responsible for evil, for sin, and more particularly for original sin:—a Platonic, not a Christian explanation." [18] "For Teilhard, original sin is coextensive with all of creation, physical as well, and biological." [19] On this subject we must read the letter of June 19, 1953, too long for me to quote it in its entirety, in which Teilhard declared that "fundamentally, our Universe has always been (and any conceivable Universe could not be otherwise) in its totality and from its origins, mingled with good and bad turns of luck; that is to say, it is impregnated with evil; that is to say, in a state of original sin; that is to say, baptizable." [20] Here, too, Claude Tresmontant is right to conclude (p. 52): "Sin is not such a thing, it is an act of freedom, and original sin is the deprivation of divine life. Neither matter nor the multiple has anything to do with it."

After a lengthy study on *"Pierre Teilhard de Chardin penseur religieux"* (*Nova et Vetera*, October-December 1962), Cardinal Journet published recently—too late for me to make use of it in my text —a briefer but illuminating article,[21] where we find further important remarks on the theological effort of Teilhard, as well as other distressing quotations from him. I ill quote only one here: "In sudden, clear and vivid impressions, I perceive that my strength and my joy all stem from the fact that I see realized for me, in some manner, the fusion of God and the World, the latter giving *Immediacy* to the Divine, the former spiritualizing the tangible." [22]

Such a text almost makes me regret having suggested in Chapter 5 [23] that there were probably touches of supernatural mystique in the religious experience of Teilhard. For anyone who reflects on this passage, weighing the meaning of the words, it is in any case a text of singular significance. In the sudden, clear and vivid impressions of Père Teilhard, it is through the World, *through the created*, that the Divine was made "immediate" to him! Père de Lubac assures us that

[17] Tr., p. 45.
[18] Tr. p. 51.
[19] *Ibid.*
[20] Tr. p. 51.
[21] *"La synthèse du Père Teilhard de Chardin est-elle dissociable?"* *Nova et Vetera*, April–June, 1966.
[22] Journet, 1918; p. 147. (The word *Immediacy* is underlined by Teilhard.)
[23] See pp. 118–119.

"Père Teilhard was a mystic. A genuine one." It all depends on what one means by "*a mystic, a genuine one.*" If we mean in the manner of Ibn 'Arabī and the masters of natural mystique, which can certainly coexist with the state of grace, then yes, Teilhard was a true mystic *of that mystique.* But in the manner of the disciple "whom Jesus loved," and of all the masters of that mystique in which the soul is supernaturally raised to the experience of things divine by the grace of the theological virtues and the gifts of the Holy Spirit—in other words, in the sense in which a Catholic theologian's readers would understand, as self-explanatory, the words "a mystic, a genuine one." The more I think about it, the more doubtful it seems to me.

I will now quote some passages from Cardinal Journet's conclusion: "Coming paradoxically to the defense of Teilhard," he writes (pp. 180-181), "we hold that his doctrine is logical, that his vision of the world is coherent, that one must either accept it as a whole, or reject it as a whole. But the dilemma is a serious one.

"If we reject it, we are being faithful to all of traditional Christianity, we are accepting Christian revelation as it has been preserved and developed in the course of centuries by the divinely assisted magisterium. And of course, in this perspective, it will be the duty of Christian thought to be constantly open and attentive to the prodigious progress of the sciences in our times, and, in particular, to *assume,* in its proper perspective, all the true and even probably true elements that are to be found in the idea of the evolution of the whole universe of matter, and especially of living organisms . . .

"If, on the contrary, we accept Teilhard's vision of the world, we know from the start—we have been duly warned—which notions of traditional Christianity will have to be *transposed,* and which we must bid farewell: 'Creation, Spirit, Evil, God (and, more particularly, original Sin, Cross, Resurrection, Parousia, Charity. . . .' " [24]

The list is that of Père Teilhard himself in a text of January 1, 1951,[25] in which he declares that "from the mere transposition" of the traditional [26] vision into "*dimensions of Cosmogenesis,*" "all these

[24] Journet, p. 150.
[25] Journet, p. 146.
[26] He describes this vision as "traditionally expressed in terms of *Cosmos.*" A singularly meaningful misjudgment of a pseudo-theology obsessed by Physics: as if traditionally Christian thought had ever, at any time at all since the days of evangelical preaching, expressed the concepts of Spirit of Evil, of original Sin, of the Cross, of the Resurrection, of Parousia, of Charity, of God himself, *in terms of Cosmos!* The Christian faith tells us that God is the creator of heaven and

notions, transported into dimensions of 'genesis,' become clarified
and cohere in an astounding way." Cardinal Journet is right in observing that in that case we will have to bid them farewell. Because thus
transported "into dimensions of Cosmogenesis," there remains in
them nothing Christian but the name; they make sense only in a
Gnostic cosmo-theology of a Hegelian variety.

I return to Cardinal Journet's text to quote from it still another
passage. "We hold this inner vision of Teilhard to be powerful and
intrinsically coherent. Consequently, a kind of apologetics that, anxious to be timely, founds upon the evolutionist synthesis of Teilhard,
must, under penalty of lapsing into a 'Religion of Evolution' constantly intervene *from outside that synthesis* in order to right it and
turn it in the direction of orthodoxy.[27] Such a kind of apologetics will
perhaps have partially happy results in the short run, but not without
laying the groundwork for serious disappointments in the future.
The question that presents itself here is that of the very nature of
apologetics." [28]

"Must apologetics" asks Cardinal Journet, "be primarily preoccu-
pied with timeliness, and turn toward doctrines which, at the price of
serious misunderstandings, . . . have the strongest grip on our
times? . . . Or should it turn toward the truest doctrines, whether
they please our contemporaries or not?" [29] I, myself, would ask, with
the bluntness proper to the Peasant of the Garonne: is it the function
of apologetics to lead minds to the Truth by using the seductions
and approaches of any error whatever, as long as with such tricks the
takings are good, since the only thing which matters is efficacy, and
a maximum output in the manufacturing of baptized souls? Is it its
function to produce shock Christians with respect to whom any kind
of stimulant is enough, as soon as they help to make a crowd and are
organized? Or do apologetics have to lead us to Truth *via* truth,
frankly showing the way to those who have a desire for the Truth
that makes us free, be it in paying the price of curing ourselves of a
lot of illusions? *Deus non eget meo mendacio,* St. Augustine said:
God does not need my lie.

---

earth, of all things visible and invisible—Creator of the Cosmos, yes! But it would
be nonsensical to claim that because of that he is conceived *in terms of Cosmos.*
Whether or not the cosmos is in genesis, God is its Creator *by the same right,*
and changing absolutely *nothing* in the notion of the First Transcendant Cause;
Creation remains, *by the same right,* creation *ex nihilo.*

[27] A futile job, in my opinion. [J.M.]
[28] Journet, p. 151.
[29] *Ibid.*

But to conclude this Appendix, let us leave Teilhardism and come back to Père Teilhard himself. If some readers of the preceding pages, who perhaps have good reasons to be grateful to him, feel outraged by my frankness, I beg them simply to turn to the texts from him that I have quoted, and, leaving my comments aside, to think over these texts with unbiased attention.

As a matter of fact, Teilhard's ardent metaphysical and theological concern played a central role in his thought. It is the themes engendered by this constant concern (noble in itself, but misled) that are cosmological synthesis. About the evolution of the world and life, taken *in its reality discernible to reason*, it has taught us nothing that all men of science today did not already know. If we remove the element of myth from Teilhard, there remains of his personal contribution little more than a powerful lyrical impulse, which he himself has taken for a sort of prophetic anticipation. He was not afraid to see, in his own case modestly attributed to the favorable workings of "pure chance (temperament, education, environment)," a "new proof that it is enough that Truth appear a single time, in a single mind, then nothing can prevent it from invading and inflaming all." [30] He was without a doubt a man of great imagination.

[30] *Le Christique*, March, 1955; Journet, p. 147.

3 A SHORT EPISTEMOLOGICAL DIGRESSION

(CF. CHAPTER 6, P. 141)

In the text I insisted on the irreducible distinction that must be recognized between the approach, the mode of conceptualization, the kind of relation to the real (in other words, the kind of truth) which are proper to the sciences of nature [1] and those proper to the philosophy of nature.[2] To come back to that in a slightly more detailed way, I would like to point out first why it has also been said in the text that the natural sciences of nature themselves are far from making up a company of the same tenor from the epistemological point of view.

From the fact that they resort to mathematical intelligibility as their elected mode of interpreting phenomena, the *completely mathematized* sciences, like nuclear physics, or the *more mathematized*, like physics in general, find themselves, with respect to interpretation or explanation, transferred, by participation, to the type of intelligibility proper to mathematics, which depends on the "second degree of abstraction" and which deals, indifferently, with objects of thought either detached from the real by abstraction, but still corresponding to some determinate ingredient of the real, or subsequently constructed as mere *entia rationis* or merely ideal entities. In resorting to mathematical intelligibility as their elected means of interpreting phenomena, the completely mathematized sciences and the more mathematized sciences translate, therefore, or transpose the (observed reality) into signs or symbols (whether they be particular systems of equations or general theories like relativity) which are proper to the mathematical type of intelligibility and are *intelligible only mathematically*. And it is in this way, and in this way only, that they know, "understand," or explain "phenomena," that is to say, the real observed insofar and only insofar as it is observed.[3] From that it fol-

---

[1] By "sciences of nature" I mean all sciences (physics as well as biology, etc.) which deal with things pertaining to the world of matter.

[2] To adopt the vocabulary of the *Degrees of Knowledge*, let us say that the sciences of nature and the philosophy of nature are both related to the *first degree of abstraction*, but the first with a view to an *empiriological* knowledge and the other with a view to an *ontological* knowledge.

[3] "Empirio-metrical" or empirio-mathematical knowledge.

lows that they are, no doubt, *in their various particular results,* pregnant with ontological content, but that this ontological content, being transposed into the symbols and ideal entities of mathematical explanation, remains indiscernible to philosophical intelligence. The philosopher is therefore justified in saying that the sciences in question control matter (and in what a formidable fashion) but as an *unknown* reality on which one acts by means of *signs,* which in a way links these highly modern sciences with ancient magic.

Yet they themselves do not stop there. By very virtue of their congenital aspiration to apprehend the real, an aspiration they share with the other sciences except for mathematics, they strive to retranslate their mathematical translation of phenomena into the ordinary language of men, and for that they resort to hypothetically drawn pictures of the observed real or pictures of the world which appeal to the imagination but are, as such, of no avail for philosophical intelligence (except as mere imagery and frame of reference with no ontological meaning). Of the ontological content with which these sciences are pregnant, there is discernible to philosophical intelligence only the very general existential data, the very general facts that are part of the *first foundations or first coordinates of their whole work.* Philosophical intelligence can avail itself of these general facts only and give ontological value only to them.[4]

Turning now to those sciences of nature which, while of course employing measure, are *not* mathematized (biology, psychology, sociology, etc.), they do not translate the observed (observed reality) into signs or symbols depending on the mathematical type of intelligibility. It is not by mathematics that they know, "understand" or explain "phenomena," that is to say, the real observed insofar and only insofar as it is observed. It is by the observable that they explain the observable,[5] or in other words by "causal" relationships or rather links of conditioning between phenomena. (And this is the reason why the ontological content with which they are pregnant may be discernible to the philosophical intelligence in certain of the *particular results* themselves of the scientific elaboration.)

But whether one considers the mathematized sciences or the nonmathematized sciences, they all have in common this essential character of depending (whether primarily or totally) on that intellection

---

[4] It is just so, it seems to me, that Claude Tresmontant proceeds with respect to astrophysics, in his work on *the problem of the existence of God,* mentioned previously.

[5] "Empirio-schematic," or simply empiriological knowledge.

of an empiriological order [6] which takes hold of the real insofar and only insofar as it is observable. Empirio-mathematical or simply empiriological, it is not their business to use signs grasped in experience in order to attain, through them, the real in its ontological structure or in its being, by a type of intellection [7] that penetrates to the very essence (not apprehended in itself, certainly, but through those of its properties that fall under experience, outward or inward). That is why, as I insisted in Chapter 6, there is an absolutely typical, essential, difference between *philosophical* knowledge and *scientific* (in the modern sense of the word) knowledge, and in particular between the *philosophy of nature* and the *sciences of nature* taken in general.

The ancients were not aware of this distinction because their science was still in homogeneous continuity with their philosophy of nature and still used the same conceptual vocabulary as the latter. If the Thomist philosophy of nature needs to be reshaped, it is not only because the science with which it was connected no longer has any value, it is also (and primarily) because this connection itself was of a kind that is now worthless. In the course of the last three centuries science has in effect won complete autonomy with respect to philosophy, and this only intensifies the urgency of the reshaping in question.

Such a reshaping must take into account, first of all the fundamental epistemological datum that I am trying to emphasize here: there is continuity, no doubt, between the sciences of nature and the philosophy of nature, but not the *homogeneous* continuity the ancients believed there to be (from the very fact that their science was not yet autonomous). It is a continuity *of connection* between areas of knowledge of specifically different types. The philosophy of nature does not have to reinterpret in its (ontological) fashion the various pictures of the macroscopic or microscopic world drawn by science (this would be a pretty mess, especially in dealing with mathematized sciences); it has to judge of the epistemological value of these pictures, and above all it has to disengage—wherever possible—from the researches and discoveries of science the ontological content with which they are pregnant—a job in which science is not interested. This content may be of great philosophical value without, for that matter, being furnished in great abundance by science. As examples of such content I might mention, on one hand, the simple, very general fact, of basic value to astrophysics and nuclear physics, that the cosmos itself and all that is contained within it, down to the ele-

6 "Perinoetic" intellection.
7 "Dianoetic" intellection.

mentary structures of matter, is in a state of evolutionary becoming; and on the other hand I would mention the fact, woven into the particular results of scientific elaboration (but already known by the ancients), that between the chemical and the biological (the simplest living cell) there is an uncrossable threshold that has been crossed. It is the business of philosophy to interpret these facts in its own perspective.

In brief, we are confronted here with two knowing entities which are working according to two fundamentally different operational systems. Let us think of two typewriters equipped with different keyboards—or, to use another comparison, of two singers whose ear and voice would supposedly be naturally attuned to two different musical keys: the scientist singing only songs composed in G, and the philosopher only songs composed in E. If they are to sing together, it will be necessary for the scientist to learn how to sing (more or less well) in E, and, similarly, for the philosopher to learn how to sing (more or less well) in G. These more or less felicitous comparisons lead us back to the two different keyboards of which I spoke earlier.[8]

We might add that the experimental data of which intellection of an ontological order makes use, and on which the philosophy of nature has to be constructed, are not only those that the sciences of nature furnish and from which an ontological content can sometimes be extracted. There is a vast field of experience and observation open to the natural intelligence of man where the philosopher, if he has enough discernment, can find, without needing to resort to the sciences of nature, a whole available stock of simpler, and more obvious, data offered by sensible experience. That is why a duly reshaped Thomist philosophy of nature will, in this very reshaping, have to take into account many principles and fundamental notions already used by St. Thomas (amid the exemplifications of an unfortunate scientific context).

[8] Chapter 6, pp. 140–141.

4 ON THE UNITY AND VISIBILITY OF THE CHURCH

(CF. CHAPTER 7, P. 181)

I take the liberty, in this Appendix, to submit to the judgment of the theologians some ideas that I believe to be true, but that I express in my own manner as a philosopher.

One must say, it seems to me, that—precisely because the *Una Sancta* is the *one and only* Church of Christ—her *intrinsic organic unity*, which is perfect in the Catholic Church and is perfect only there, deteriorates to the degree that it extends beyond this great city perfectly one, and beyond the personality whose seal she bears, to embrace all those men (whether they belong to non-Catholic or to non-Christian religious families, or profess unbelief or atheism) who live in the grace of Christ and charity: so that all those are, in an imperfect way, no doubt, but in act, members, invisibly, of the only fully formed and fully visible Church, which is the Catholic Church.

One must also say, it seems to me, that the visibility of the Church is a dependent variable of the unity that binds together the members of her body, animated as it is by charity, which is her soul: full and complete visibility when the unity of the body is full and complete (that is to say, in the Catholic Church)—diminished, and further and further and diminished, to the extent that the unity of the body decreases more and more as it extends beyond the perfectly one structure which is that of the Catholic Church.

Here we are confronted with the question of the body of the Church and of her visibility. When we speak of the "body" of the Church as contradistinguished from her soul, the word "body" does not mean the mystical Body, because the mystical Body obviously comprises the soul as well as the "body" of the Church (it includes even the angels, St. Thomas says). The body of the Church is first of all the human beings who (belonging to her openly and normally if they are baptized) are living in grace and charity (which is the created soul of the Church)—human beings, at once carnal and spiritual, and visible insofar as carnal. But it is not exactly by reason of the visibility of these men that the Church is visible; it is by reason *of the visibility of the things that she herself accomplishes when she possesses her full and complete unity:* her profession of faith, her form of worship, her sacraments, her teaching and judicial authority—and likewise her fecundity, visible through all centuries, in engendering saints—are things that are apparent to the senses and outwardly manifested. The men who are her members are naturally visible *as men*, but they are visible *insofar as members of the Church*—in other words they are *visibly* members of the visible Church—*because they participate in what the Church herself accomplishes in a visible or outwardly manifest way.*

It must not be forgotten, moreover, that this notion of the body of the Church, as contradistinguished from her soul, is a metaphorical notion, an image drawn from the human being, which cannot be applied rigidly to an infinitely more mysterious reality. We understand that better if we observe that, on one hand, the soul of the Church is spiritual, as is the human soul (and more so), while on the other hand, the body of the Church is no more separable (and even less so) from her soul than the body of an animal not endowed with reason is separable from its soul. But even more, the body of the Church defies comparison with the human body in this respect, that the body of the Church, completely and perfectly *formed* in the Church—who is herself fully formed, and whose organic unity is perfect and completed by personality (in other words in the Only Church, the Catholic Church)—nevertheless oversteps beyond this perfectly formed organism to extend, just as the soul of the Church does—on one hand to religious families that are still organized but not integrated into her perfect unity (the non-Catholic Christian confessions), and on the other hand to the great diaspora of those human beings who, in the non-Christian religious families or in the areligious spiritual families, open themselves to the grace of Christ and to charity.

How can we imagine this? We would have to resort to a fictitious poetic image: let us say a large firebird of an extraordinary kind, which would trail behind itself a living fire that is still its body animated by its soul, but lacking the perfect organic unity proper to the bird itself. This fire, as long as it still has some organic unity, is still visible to men (less and less, the more distant it is from the perfect organic unity that it enjoys in the bird); but it can also lose all organic unity, in a vast galaxy of stars, in each of which it shines in a way that is visible to the angels but invisible to men, for the only unity which still binds these stars to the other members of the body of the Church is that of charity (which no doubt manifests itself in each one through a certain behavior, but which, in this case, bears the mark of the Church only in the eyes of the angels).[1]

[1] Cf. Ch. 7, p. 181, n. 17.

In other terms, the Church is essentially visible, but this visibility is full and complete only in the Catholic Church, and that is her glory: only she bears the torch of God in its fullness, as only she is the Church of the Incarnate Word. The body of the Church becomes less and less visible the further those who belong to her in the other spiritual families escape from her perfect unity. All these men are part of the perfectly visible Church, but without being integrated into her perfect unity and therefore into her perfect visibility.

Is it possible to elaborate this truth in greater detail? In my opinion the answer is to be found in the communion of saints [2]—I mean in the communion of saints understood *not in reference to God*, or insofar as charity unites us to God (in this aspect the communion of saints is but one with the soul of the Church), *but in reference to men*, or in another of its aspects (too often neglected, except by some men of great intuition like Léon Bloy), where charity unites together the *human members* of the Church through a mysterious interdependence. From this point of view, is not the communion of saints but one with the *body* of the Church? I believe it is. The communion of saints is the Church herself. It is fitting, therefore, to distinguish in it an aspect that corresponds to the soul of the Church and an aspect that corresponds to her body.

Let us consider the multitude of those "saints" living in grace and charity—let us say those "just" or "righteous" ones—who are visible members of the Church. Is not the supernatural solidarity that unites together these visible members of the body of the Church—in a vast human family "whose goods are marvelously reversible," [3] a human family that is much more than a "society" (it is a "communion") —is not this solidarity part of the body of the Church, just as are those whom it binds one to the other? In the case in question this supernatural solidarity is made manifest, because these visible members of the body of the Church are integrated into her perfect unity. But it is not made manifest to the eyes of men there where the righteous ones, the men who live in grace, are not integrated into the perfect unity of the fully formed and fully visible Church; for these righteous men have charity within them but charity lacking the three notes ("cultual, sacramental, and oriented") [4] which it has in the fully formed Church and which enables it to receive the seal of the Church's personality. And they belong to the body of the Church, but in a state of

[2] Cf. *L'Eglise du Verbe Incarné*, v. II, pp. 662–667.
[3] *Op. cit.*, p. 662.
[4] Cf. p. 178, note 14, line 6.

dispersion in the individual persons of a vast galaxy without organic unity. The only unity that subsists among them and the other members of the body of the Church is that of charity, that of the supernatural solidarity which unites all the just together in the communion of saints, but the latter, this time, is not made outwardly manifest and remains hidden in its mystery.

As a result, we understand better that a righteous man who is a non-Christian is *invisibly* part of the visible Church, by reason of the communion of saints, in which he participates, and which, when there is no integration into the perfect unity of the fully formed Church, is still—in the aspect I have indicated—the body of the Church, but this time the body of the Church *in a state that is invisible or not manifest to the eyes of men.*

The body of the Church is as mysterious as the Church herself. Fully visible in the human multitude integrated into the perfect organic unity of the Catholic Church, it is, in the diaspora of righteous men who live in the grace of Christ while remaining attached to non-Christian spiritual families, invisible to the eyes of men and to the eyes of these righteous men themselves. Which is not to say that the body of the Church is ever, even there, absolutely invisible, or invisible "of itself." Because even there it remains visible "of itself," and visible to the angels; but it is not visible to the eyes of men (except perhaps, I should add, to the eyes of those among Christians who, fully familiar with the spiritual families I am alluding to, and having a sufficiently thorough knowledge of the righteous men in question, would be able to discern in them the signs which make perceivable the fact—unknown to themselves—that they invisibly belong to Christ and to his visible Church. In general such a discernment could only be more or less probable, but why could it not, in a given instance, appear as certain to the Christians of whom I am speaking? Massignon, who knew the mystics of Islam perfectly well, wished that some day the Church would canonize Hallāj).